Understanding Teaching and Learning in Primary Education

Understanding
Teaching and Learning
in Primary Education

Edited by
Mike Carroll and **Margaret McCulloch**

SAGE

Los Angeles | London | New Delhi
Singapore | Washington DC

Los Angeles | London | New Delhi
Singapore | Washington DC

SAGE Publications Ltd
1 Oliver's Yard
55 City Road
London EC1Y 1SP

SAGE Publications Inc.
2455 Teller Road
Thousand Oaks, California 91320

SAGE Publications India Pvt Ltd
B 1/I 1 Mohan Cooperative Industrial Area
Mathura Road
New Delhi 110 044

SAGE Publications Asia-Pacific Pte Ltd
3 Church Street
#10-04 Samsung Hub
Singapore 049483

Editor: James Clark
Assistant editor: Rachael Plant
Project manager: Bill Antrobus
Production editor: Thea Watson
Proofreader: Caroline Stock
Indexer: Anne Solamito
Marketing manager: Catherine Slinn
Cover design: Naomi Robinson
Typeset by: C&M Digitals (P) Ltd, Chennai, India
Printed and bound in Great Britain by Ashford
Colour Press Ltd.

Editorial arrangement, Preface and Chapter 1 © Mike Carroll and Margaret McCulloch 2014 Chapter 2 © Julie McAdam and Evelyn Arizpe 2014 Chapter 3 © Mary Wingrave 2014 Chapters 4, 9 and 18 © Mike Carroll 2014 Chapter 5 © Maureen Farrell and A. Graeme Pate 2014 Chapter 6 © Margaret McCulloch 2014 Chapter 7 © George Head 2014 Chapter 8 © Vivienne Baumfield 2014 Chapter 10 © Mike Carroll and Fiona McGregor 2014 Chapter 11 © Margaret Sutherland and Niamh Stack 2014 Chapter 12 © Louise Hayward and Ernest Spencer 2014 Chapter 13 © Alan Britton 2014 Chapter 14 © Leonardo Franchi and Leon Robinson 2014 Chapter 15 © Moyra Boland, Margaret Jago and Jan MacDonald 2014 Chapter 16 © Stephen Boyle and David McKinstry 2014 Chapter 17 © George MacBride and Margaret McCulloch 2014 Chapter 19 © Beth Dickson and Irene McQueen 2014 Chapter 20 © Christine Forde and Margery McMahon 2014

First edition published 2014

Library of Congress Control Number: 2013948469

British Library Cataloguing in Publication data

A catalogue record for this book is available from the British Library

MIX
Paper from
responsible sources
FSC® C011748

ISBN 978-1-4462-5482-0
ISBN 978-1-4462-7062-2 (pbk)

TABLE OF CONTENTS

LIST OF FIGURES AND TABLES

Figures

Tables

LIST OF ABBREVIATIONS

The following abbreviations will appear in the text, particularly in citations:

BERA	British Educational Research Association
CPAG	Child Poverty Action Group
CWDC	Children's Workforce Development Council
CfE	Curriculum for Excellence
DfCSF	Department for Children, Schools and Families
DfCELLS	Department for Children, Education, Lifelong Learning and Skills
DfE	Department for Education
DfE(NI)	Department of Education (Northern Ireland)
DfEE	Department for Education and Employment
DES	Department of Education and Science
DfES	Department for Education and Skills
DHSSPS	Department of Health, Social Services and Public Safety (Northern Ireland)
EYFS	Early Years Foundation Stage

GTCNI	General Teaching Council for Northern Ireland
GTCS	General Teaching Council of Scotland
GTCW	General Teaching Council for Wales
LTS	Learning and Teaching Scotland
NCCCE	National Advisory Committee on Creative and Cultural Education
NCE	National Commission on Education
NIA	Northern Ireland Assembly
OECD	Organization for Economic and Co-operative Development
Ofsted	Office for Standards in Education
QAAS	Quality Assurance Agency Scotland
QCA	Qualifications and Curriculum Authority
QCDA	Qualifications and Curriculum Development Agency
SED	Scottish Education Department
SE	Scottish Executive
SG	Scottish Government
SOED	Scottish Office Education Department
UNICEF	United Nations Children's Fund
WAG	Welsh Assembly Government

ACKNOWLEDGEMENTS

We would like to thank our editors at SAGE, particularly James Clark who was involved in the production of this text from the very start. Throughout the period of writing James was a constant source of intellectual and emotional support, providing invaluable guidance to help shape the UK-wide focus of the book.

We are very grateful to our colleagues in the School of Education at the University of Glasgow who contributed to the book despite the competing demands they face in their personal and professional lives.

We would also like to thank our students and the teachers we work alongside in schools. It is this network of professional connections that is the source of observation and dialogue, giving rise to numerous interesting questions that have challenged our thinking and helped to refine our ideas.

Finally we would like to acknowledge the contribution of our families in providing us with the time and space to make this book possible. We are deeply grateful for their forbearance; in them we take great pride.

Publisher's Acknowledgments

SAGE and the editors would like to thank the following reviewers whose feedback on the proposal and draft chapters has helped to shape this book:

Sandra Eady – University of Stirling

Nadia Edmond – University of Brighton

Victoria Foster – Bath Spa University

Julia Holden – Leeds Trinity University

Vini Lander – University of Chichester

Fi McGarry – University of Dundee

ABOUT THE EDITORS

Dr Mike Carroll

Mike Carroll is the PGDE (Primary and Secondary) Programme Leader as well as being the Director of the MEd Professional Learning and Enquiry programme in the School of Education, University of Glasgow. Mike contributes to a range of Initial Teacher Education programmes. He has also been involved in programmes for serving teachers, with a particular interest in the development of leadership at all levels in the school; this work has included contributions to courses for teacher leaders and middle leaders as well as the Scottish Qualification for Headship. Mike has published a number of articles on his research interests including the development of collaborative enquiry, professional learning communities, accomplished teaching and science education. He contributed to the Literature Review on Teacher Education in the 21st Century in support of the Donaldson Review of Teacher Education (Scottish Government, 2010). Mike is a Fellow of the Higher Education Academy and the College of Teachers.

Dr Margaret McCulloch

Margaret McCulloch is a University Teacher within the School of Education, University of Glasgow. She worked for many years as a primary teacher, specialising in Support for Learning, before becoming an Inclusion Development Officer, and she has extensive experience of working collaboratively with parents, teachers and colleagues from other professions. She is a year co-ordinator on the BEd programme and teaches on the Masters in Inclusive Education programme; she is also the School of Education's disability co-ordinator. Her research interests include professional identity in teacher education, inclusive education and dyslexia. She has written on inter-professional approaches to practice (Forde et al., 2011); she contributed to the Literature Review on Teacher Education in the 21st Century (Scottish Government, 2010) and to the Assessment at Transition report (Scottish Government, 2012).

ABOUT THE CONTRIBUTORS

Dr Evelyn Arizpe

Evelyn Arizpe is a Senior Lecturer at the School of Education, University of Glasgow. She has taught and published widely, both in the UK and internationally, in the areas of literacies, reader-response to picturebooks and children's literature. She is co-author, with Morag Styles, of *Children Reading Pictures: Interpreting Visual Texts* (Routledge, 2003), *Reading Lessons from the Eighteenth Century: Mothers, Children and Texts* (Pied Piper Press, 2006). She has recently co-edited *Picturebooks: Beyond the Borders of Art, Narrative and Culture* (Routledge, 2013). Her forthcoming book is an account of the international project, Visual Journeys, which investigated immigrant children's responses to wordless picturebooks (Bloomsbury Academic, 2014).

Professor Vivienne Baumfield

Vivienne Baumfield is Professor of Pedagogy, Policy and Innovation in the School of Education, University of Glasgow, and works with practitioners and policy makers in education both in the UK and overseas. She has led research projects aimed at furthering our understanding of the benefits of collaborative school–university research partnerships in the development of teaching as evidence-informed practice. Professor Baumfield has published research on pedagogy in primary schools and has worked with government agencies and professional organisations in the UK and internationally on the development of inquiry-based approaches to promoting professional learning. She is a Lead Editor of the *British Educational Research Journal*. Professor Baumfield is also the University of Glasgow's International Dean for South Asia and Eurasia.

Moyra Boland

Moyra Boland is a Senior University Teacher in the Creativity, Culture and Faith knowledge transfer group based in the School of Education, University of Glasgow. Moyra is the Director of Learning and Teaching. Moyra has worked in children's theatre and theatre in education, as well as teaching drama in primary and secondary schools. She teaches on a wide variety of undergraduate and postgraduate courses within the School of Education including practitioner inquiry, drama in education and interdisciplinary learning in the primary school. Her main scholarship interests centre on learning in classrooms through drama, creative contexts for learning and Initial Teacher Education. She is a Fellow of the Higher Education Academy.

Stephen Boyle

Stephen has wide-ranging experience of using technology to enhance teaching and learning. He was the first to design and implement a Masters-level course on the use of interactive ICT devices for teachers. He created an innovative E-learning and Communications Development course that progresses the professionalisation of childhood practice leaders through an e-portfolio system enhancing self-regulated communities of inquiry. Stephen is involved in using MIE (moving image education) to develop the social and thinking skills of school pupils and university students. One recent project commissioned by the Scottish Government is FAST (Film and Science Teaching), designed to re-invigorate science teaching in the primary school, whilst a work in progress is a website to share university students' uses of ICT via online video thereby developing social entrepreneurship.

Dr Alan Britton

Alan began his career in education as an English Language Assistant in the South of France, and after graduating with Honours in Politics from the University of

Glasgow, he worked as an outdoor instructor before becoming a teacher of French and Modern Studies. In 1999 he was appointed head of the Scottish Parliament Education Service. From 2001 to 2005 he was Stevenson Lecturer in Citizenship at the University of Glasgow and he is currently the Director of the Education for Global Citizenship Unit in the School of Education, University of Glasgow. He has published and edited a number of books, journal articles and chapters around themes related to global citizenship. Alan has recently completed his Doctorate in Education.

Dr Beth Dickson

Beth Dickson is Deputy Head of School in the School of Education, University of Glasgow. She led the team which developed the PGDE into an M-level qualification, the first Scottish Masters-level route into teaching. She is now leading curriculum change on the 4-year programme for Initial Teacher Education. She has been involved in radical moves to improve the quality of teaching placements for student teachers. Her research interests are in curriculum development in Initial Teacher Education. She is a member of the Scottish Qualification Authority's Curriculum Area Review Group for national qualifications in literacy and numeracy.

Dr Maureen Farrell

Maureen Farrell is a Senior Lecturer in the Creativity, Culture and Faith knowledge transfer group based in the School of Education, University of Glasgow. She was formerly the Programme Leader of the B.Ed. degree programme and served as the Associate Dean for Initial Teacher Education for several years. She has worked in Initial Teacher Education for many years and has research interests and publications in the field of children's literature, Scottish children's literature in particular. Maureen teaches across a range of undergraduate and postgraduate programmes. She has wide experience in delivering continuing professional development for teachers, particularly in the field of literacy across learning. She is involved with a number of research projects focused on children's literature and on picturebooks funded by the United Kingdom Literacy Association (UKLA) and the Esmée Fairbairn Foundation.

Professor Christine Forde

Christine Forde is Professor of Leadership and Professional Learning in the School of Education, University of Glasgow. She mainly works in the area of leadership and teacher professional development including the Scottish Qualification for Headship and a range of early and middle leadership programmes. She has published a number of books and articles with colleagues including *Professional Development Reflection and Enquiry* (Paul Chapman, 2006), *Putting Together Professional Portfolios* (Sage, 2009) and *Contemporary Issues in Teaching and Learning* (Sage, 2010). Currently, she is working with colleagues on a project looking at the development of accomplished and expert teaching. In addition, she has published books in the area of gender and feminist perspectives in education including *Feminist Utopianism and Education* (Sense, 2008).

Leonardo Franchi

Leonardo Franchi teaches Religious Education in the School of Education, University of Glasgow, where he is Course Convener for Theology in Education. Leonardo is currently the Head of the St Andrew's Foundation for Catholic Teacher Education. He has an MA in Modern Languages (University of Glasgow) and a M.Ed. in Religious Education and Catechetics (Maryvale Institute). He has wide experience of teaching in schools and higher education. His principal research interests are the relationship between catechesis and Religious Education and early Christian education. He has a particular interest in St Augustine of Hippo's contribution to educational thought. He is the editor of *An Anthology of Catholic Teaching on Education* (Scepter, 2007) and co-editor (with Stephen McKinney) of *A Companion to Catholic Education* (Gracewing, 2011). Leonard has recently completed his Doctorate of Philosophy degree.

Professor Louise Hayward

Louise Hayward is Professor of Educational Assessment and Innovation in the School of Education, University of Glasgow. For more than 20 years Louise has worked with researchers, policy makers and practitioners to attempt to offer children and young people in Scotland better life chances by bringing research, policy and practice in assessment into closer alignment. She has researched and published extensively in the fields of assessment, social justice and transformational change. Louise was a member of the Management Committee for the Scottish Government's National 'Assessment is for Learning' Programme and chaired its Research and Development Group. She was a member of the UK Assessment Reform Group and has contributed to an extensive world-wide network of research collaborations related to assessment.

Dr George Head

George Head is a Senior Lecturer in the School of Education, University of Glasgow. George teaches on Initial Teacher Education, taught postgraduate programmes as well as supervising postgraduate research. George researches and publishes in areas of support for learning and inclusive education. He has a special interest in the learning of children and young people with social, emotional and behavioural difficulties (SEBD). He is the author of several journal articles and book chapters on behaviour and relationships in schools, including his book *Better Learning, Better Behaviour* (Dunedin Academic Press, 2007), which is widely used in teacher education courses in Scotland and beyond. He is co-editor of *Children's Services: Working Together* (Pearson, 2012) on interdisciplinary working to support young people in schools.

Margaret Jago

Maggie Jago is Programme Leader for the Bachelor of Education Programme. Maggie also has responsibility for coordinating art and design for those students who are undertaking the B.Ed. and the PGDE Primary programmes. Maggie qualified from Glasgow University in 1995 with specialisms in art and design and English language. Maggie has used her specialist knowledge and skills to develop whole-school art policies and to encourage children's involvement in art projects that allowed them to share their works with their local communities. Maggie has extensive experience of working with children, student educators and qualified teachers, through delivering continuing professional development courses, to explore skills and knowledge relating to creativity. Maggie's scholarship interests centre on nurturing creativity in learners and on the role that museum collections play in encouraging young people to access and use their imaginations. Maggie is currently undertaking her Doctorate in Education with a focus on museum education.

George MacBride

George MacBride is an Honorary Senior Research Fellow in the School of Education, University of Glasgow. George taught for 37 years in Glasgow secondary schools. He was a council member of government educational bodies, most recently of the Advisory Council of Learning and Teaching Scotland, and participated in national working groups on assessment, curriculum, National Qualifications and teacher education. He was a member of the Curriculum Review Group which produced

Curriculum for Excellence, the CfE Programme Board and the CfE Validation Group. He has carried out commissions for the Scottish Government and LTS in assessment and curriculum development. In the University of Glasgow he has contributed to research projects on school curriculum and assessment, as well as assessment at transition.

Jan Macdonald

Jan Macdonald is an Associate Tutor in the School of Education, University of Glasgow. Jan contributes to a range of Initial Teacher Education programmes including PGDE and B.Ed. She has also supervised and taught on a wide range of Masters programmes. Her interests include drama and the arts in education and more generally creativity. Jan has contributed to a wide variety of academic journals, has been the Editor of the *Journal for Drama in Education* and Chair of National Drama.

Julie McAdam

Julie McAdam is a University Teacher within the School of Education, University of Glasgow. She has developed and worked on undergraduate and postgraduate courses on Initial Teacher Education in Scotland and the Middle East. She has been involved in projects associated with the use of picurebooks to promote learning in diverse classrooms funded by UKLA and the Esmée Fairbairn Foundation. Julie is currently working on two Comenius funded projects that are looking at how to support teachers working with New Arrival Children across Europe. She has published in the area of troublesome knowledge and threshold concepts in literacy teaching, learning communities, the use of culturally responsive pedagogy and the use of children's literature in the classroom. She is committed to promoting the need for diverse teachers for diverse learners.

Fiona McGregor

Fiona McGregor is a University Teacher in Art and Design Education within the School of Education, University of Glasgow. She is Course Leader for the PGDE art and design programme and contributes widely to a diverse range of taught undergraduate and postgraduate programmes. She is an experienced musician who has initiated many highly successful creative arts projects for national and international arts, and disability organisations. Formerly she was a Principal Teacher of Art and Design at a secondary school. She is a national subject assessor for art and design national qualification courses. Fiona's research interests include: the philosophy of art and design education; interdisciplinary learning and teaching; music, art and emotional literacy; inclusive education; education and human values; and global citizenship. Fiona is currently undertaking her Doctorate in Education.

Dr David McKinstry

David McKinstry is a Social Studies teacher at Inverclyde Academy, Greenock. He is also an Associate Tutor in Education at the University of Glasgow where he contributes on a range of courses for student teachers. David is a frequent contributor to the *Scottish History Yearbook* and has written articles on the American civil rights movement and the First World War. He is the author of *We Shall Overcome* (VDM Publishing Group, 2008), and is currently working on his latest book on the civil rights policies of the Kennedy Administration. As well as teaching and research David is a marker for the Scottish Qualifications Authority and works with the BBC designing resources for Curriculum for Excellence.

Dr Margery McMahon

Margery A. McMahon is Senior Lecturer in Professional Learning and Leadership at the University of Glasgow and Director of the University of Glasgow International Educational Consultancy. She was previously Head of the Department of Educational Studies. In 2013 she was seconded by the Scottish Government to become Lead National Coordinator for the proposed new Scottish College for Educational Leadership. She is author of a number of publications focusing on professional learning including *Educating for a Global Future – International Education* (Dunedin, 2011); and co-editor with Christine Forde and Margaret Martin of *Contemporary Issues in Learning and Teaching* (Sage, 2010). She teaches on a number of courses relating to professional practice including an Ed.D. programme on 'Critical Reflection in Professional Learning and Practice' She is a member of the Board of the International Council for Education for Teaching (ICET) and the Universities Council on Education of Teachers (UCET).

Irene McQueen

Irene McQueen is a Lecturer, Adviser of Study and Ethics Officer for the School of Education, University of Glasgow. She is Course Leader for Evaluating Learning and Teaching, a core course on the PGDE programme. This course focuses on the critical and evaluative skills needed by teachers in order to undertake classroom-based practitioner inquiry. She is a member of the School of Education's Pedagogy, Policy and Practice research and knowledge transfer group whose key themes include teacher learning and school–university–local authority partnerships. She has contributed to and published papers related to funded research such as Schools of Ambition (Scottish Government, 2009), Evaluating Accomplished Teaching (GTC Scotland, 2010), and the Literature Review on Teacher Education in the 21st Century in support of the Donaldson Review of Teacher Education (Scottish Government, 2010).

A. Graeme Pate

Graeme has been the Director for the Bachelor of Education and the MA Primary Education Programmes at the University of Glasgow. He is currently the Director of the School Experience and Child Development courses in the School of Interdisciplinary Studies at the University's campus in Dumfries. Graeme has a particular research interest in the effective use of technology to enhance learning and teaching, focusing on the use of tablets, social media and online learning programmes. He also has a keen interest in modern languages in the primary school, and co-authored the popular MLPS Glasgow Primary French materials.

Leon Robinson

Leon Robinson gained a joint Honours degree in Philosophy and Theology from Oxford University before embarking on a series of adventures in theatre, music, writing and art. He has taught widely, in schools, colleges, universities and adult education. He is currently Programme Leader for the MA in Religious and Philosophical Education in the School of Education, University of Glasgow. He teaches at undergraduate and postgraduate levels for Initial Teacher Education, and lectures on Hinduism in Theology and Religious Studies. He is currently working with colleagues from Philosophy on the questions, challenges and opportunities connected with sacred and magical objects in museum collections.

Ernest Spencer

Ernest Spencer is an Honorary Senior Research Fellow in the School of Education, University of Glasgow. He has extensive expertise in all aspects of assessment. He led major assessment research projects at the Scottish Council for Research in

Education and policy and CPD as the HMIE (Scotland) National Specialist for Assessment during the development over some 20 years of assessment for learning, national monitoring and national qualifications. He has participated in and published material on international assessment developments, including the planning and implementation of IEA and IAEA monitoring surveys, an ESRC-funded series of seminars on new assessment paradigms and the OECD study of formative assessment in secondary schools. Current research interests include the interactions among curriculum, learning/teaching activities and assessment. He has in recent years conducted or participated in assessment-related research in the context of curriculum change for the Scottish Government, Education Scotland and the Scottish Qualifications Authority.

Dr Niamh Stack

Niamh Stack is a Senior University Teacher in Developmental Psychology in the School of Psychology, University of Glasgow. She is Development Officer for the Scottish Network for Able Pupils (SNAP) supporting professional knowledge exchange partnerships with the Scottish Government and local education authorities through providing CPD activities to teachers focused on gifted development. She is actively engaged in research activities related to gifted and talented education. She has presented papers at national and international conferences on gifted and talented education and other areas of atypical development. She is a member of the British Psychological Society Developmental Psychology Section, the World Council for Gifted and Talented Children and the European Council for High Ability.

Dr Margaret Sutherland

Margaret Sutherland is director of the Scottish Network for Able Pupils (SNAP) and is the programme leader of the M.Ed. in Inclusive Education at the University of Glasgow. She has extensive experience in primary schools, behaviour support and in higher education. She has published a number of articles and books in the field of gifted education including *Gifted and Talented in the Early Years* (Sage, 2012), nominated for The Texas Legacy Book Award 2013. She serves on the general committee for the European Council for High Ability and is on the editorial board of the Korean Educational Development Institute *Journal of Educational Policy*. She regularly gives keynote addresses at national and international conferences and has led courses, workshops and seminars on gifted education. She has worked with teachers, researchers and students in Tanzania, Malawi, Korea, Denmark, Slovenia and the USA on the theme of gifted education.

Mary Wingrave

Mary is the programme leader for the undergraduate and postgraduate programmes in Childhood Practice. Mary worked for many years as teacher and is an experienced senior manager in the primary sector; she also develops and delivers continuing professional development courses to practitioners relating to nurture groups. She teaches across a suite of postgraduate leadership programmes offered by the School of Education as well as contributing several inputs to the Initial Teacher Education programme. Much of the focus of her research is on leadership and early years with a particular interest in the development of nurture groups and the professionalisation of the pre-5 sector. She is currently undertaking her Doctorate in Education and is a Fellow of the Higher Education Academy.

PREFACE

The authors of this text contribute to supporting the professional learning of students engaged in initial and continuing teacher education. We often find ourselves writing material in order to provide students with an overview of a particular area of practice. Therefore the initial idea was to produce a text that would support the diverse range of students that we teach across a range of programmes.

More importantly, we are keen to develop a critical awareness of the contested nature of education. Education in the United Kingdom, as in many other countries, is a key element of social and economic policy and arguably these policy statements and guidelines are designed to direct and constrain teachers' practice. Consequently we are keen to establish connections between the processes of teaching and learning and the wider theoretical, research and policy contexts, and to set this within our evolving understanding of professionalism focused on the role of the primary teacher.

Rather than focus on 'top tips' for teachers, which may be of limited help, we aim to help readers develop their teaching identity and skills, based on evidence gathered from a range of sources: theory, research, policy and practice. We aim to encourage readers to develop the skills and knowledge to become reflective, evidence-based practitioners who can adopt a flexible enquiry approach to meeting the needs of children and their colleagues.

The text will provide insights as to the professional knowledge and understanding (the 'what'), and professional skills and abilities (the 'how') necessary to construct classroom environments which are conducive to positive learning. It will also provide insights as to the professional values and commitments (the 'why') necessary for teachers to become 'leaders of learning' both within and beyond their classrooms.

The text will engage readers in reflection about what it means to be a primary teacher through an exploration of values, beliefs and assumptions relating to learning and teaching in the primary school. Our aim is to support readers in building their confidence as teachers by focusing on a range of contemporary issues relevant to classrooms the length and breadth of the United Kingdom, and beyond. The book has been structured to allow for group discussion as well as individual reflection. Each chapter will provide an overview of the key issues, supported by illustrative views from practice, along with key questions for reflection and some suggestions for further reading.

WALKTHROUGH TOUR

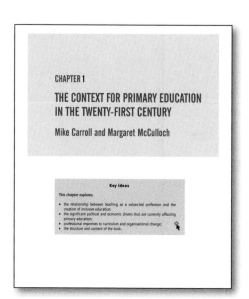

Key ideas set out the main topics covered, and what you will learn by reading the chapter.

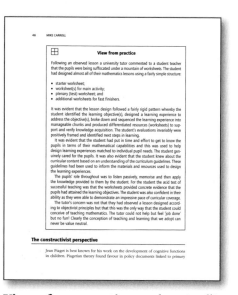

Views from practice explore intelligent and engaging teaching in primary classrooms.

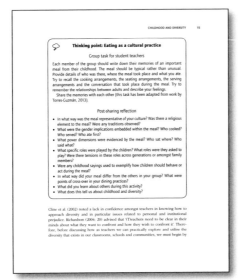

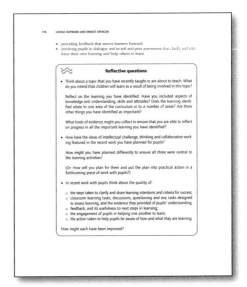

Thinking points invite you to engage critically with what you have read and apply it to your own teaching.

Reflective questions ask you to think back on the chapter as a whole and relate it to your experiences in the classroom.

Further reading suggestions direct you to more specialist literature.

CHAPTER 1

THE CONTEXT FOR PRIMARY EDUCATION IN THE TWENTY-FIRST CENTURY

Mike Carroll and Margaret McCulloch

Key ideas

This chapter explores:

- the relationship between teaching as a values-led profession and the creation of inclusive education;
- the significant political and economic drivers that are currently affecting primary education;
- professional responses to curriculum and organisational change;
- the structure and content of the book.

Introduction

Research suggests that, based on their own positive and negative experiences as pupils, pre-service teachers commonly aspire to be 'academic and pedagogically skilled and caring teacher(s)' (Lyngsnes, 2012: 6), focusing on the relationship between teacher and learner, and taking a strong view on the teacher's responsibility to make 'a positive and principled contribution to society' (Younger et al., 2004: 258). However, students are, understandably, generally unaware of the teacher's role within the larger systems of which the individual classroom is only a part; nor are student teachers always aware of the many external constraints which there may be on their initial expectations of how they will teach. These understandings develop over the period of teacher education and beyond.

While a crucial component of teacher preparation is the time spent in schools, we believe strongly that school experience alone is not sufficient to allow you to develop a robust professional identity as a teacher which will enable you to cope with the pressures which you will face during a career in teaching in the twenty-first century. This book will support you as a student or novice primary teacher to recognise that learning and teaching are complex concepts about which many conflicting views are held. It should encourage you to gather and reflect on expert knowledge which will allow you to justify your practice not simply on the basis of experience and instinct, but on the basis of evidence from theory and research and through having considered different perspectives on key aspects of practice. At a time when teachers are under constant pressure to increase pupil attainment and to respond to different local, national and international initiatives around curriculum and practice, it is vital that we are able to articulate our knowledge and understanding of the body of knowledge which we possess about learning and teaching processes from an 'expert' position, as opposed to those whose understandings may be based simply on their own experiences of having been at school. And crucially, we must be sure that our practice aligns with our professional values.

Linking values and practice – an example of challenge: inclusive education

Teachers across the United Kingdom are required to meet the appropriate professional standards (DfE, 2013a; GTCNI, 2007; GTCS, 2012; GTCW, 2010); each refers to values understood by the different professional bodies to be fundamental to a teacher's professional identity. One key element of teaching standards is a commitment to social justice and inclusion and this should be seen as underpinning this book as a whole. There is no separate chapter on 'inclusive education', which might have suggested that we see this as a 'stand-alone' aspect of practice. We make the assumption that we will organise learning and teaching in our classrooms in ways which allow us to provide equitable opportunities for all young people to learn; that is, we understand that some will require additional support at some times for a range of different reasons but that, as far as possible, our pedagogy should allow us to include all learners without having to make significant separate provision for individuals (Florian and Black-Hawkins, 2011).

However, the concept of inclusive education is by no means a simple one. 'Inclusion', as well as being centred on issues of 'human rights, equity, social justice and the struggle for a non-discriminatory society' (Armstrong and Barton, 2007: 6), also has at its heart the right of individuals to be recognised and accepted for themselves. Inclusion is not something that can be 'done to' someone. It is not in our gift to 'include' anyone in our classrooms. Inclusion implies a state of 'being' where individuals can participate in and feel part of a larger group *as themselves*. But while policies and overarching legislation may support and encourage the development of inclusive education, we often find conflicting policies in other areas which might lead to *exclusive* practices. We need then to be able to articulate clearly the reasons for our decisions around our classroom organisation and pedagogy and our response to policy directives.

As we consider some of the other key issues currently impacting on primary education in the twenty-first century we will highlight questions which arise for us which underline our need to be secure in our knowledge and understanding of learning and teaching processes.

Some further key issues impacting on primary education

Alongside the human rights movement which has led to the development of inclusive education, and causing some tensions with issues arising from that, the two main political and economic drivers which have impacted on the education system since the late twentieth century are individualisation and globalisation. It is not the aim of this chapter, or indeed this book, to discuss these in detail, but it is important that as student teachers you are aware of these concepts, briefly outlined below, as they will affect your life as a teacher by having an impact on the pedagogical strategies that you deploy in the classroom.

Individualisation

Since the late 1970s, there has been a move in most of the wealthy countries of the world towards much greater individualisation; that is, the extent to which individuals have to take responsibility for their own lives and identities has increased. This is largely as a result of successive governments which have taken a neo-liberal stance. Simply put, neo-liberal philosophy is based on a belief in the market economy, holding that improvement emerges from competition; individuals are seen as entrepreneurs who manage their own lives, free from government interference as far as possible.

Practical examples of this in education can be seen in ongoing changes in legislation since the 1980s which have widened parental choice when selecting a state school. Parents may choose to send children to a different school from their own local one, or to a different type of school altogether such as a 'free' school (this last choice is only available in England; in other parts of the UK, schools remain under the control of the local authority). This puts schools in direct competition with each other to attract 'clients'. One of the results of this legislation has been a hugely increased emphasis on recording and publishing statistics about pupils' progress. It would appear that what is of 'value' is not learning itself but something which is measurable.

The increasing pressures which parents may feel to make the 'right' choices and to be responsible for their children getting the best possible education are significant, although there is debate about the extent to which real choice is available to those who are less able to make use of the system. For many young people the educational landscape is a bleak one in which 'societal inequalities are played out and reproduced rather than places where they can be overcome' (Gillies, 2008: 88). The Scottish Curriculum for Excellence (CfE) is seen as a vehicle to overcome this, with the aspiration of creating a 'Scotland in which every child matters, where every child, regardless of his or her family background, has the best possible start in life' (SE, 2004: 6). However, the evidence suggests that despite education leading to social mobility for many it nevertheless, at the same time, causes social inequalities to widen such that many poor working-class families find themselves 'stuck at the bottom of the social ladder' (Waks, 2006: 848).

Thinking point

- What might be the impact of applying a market system, which operates on an understanding that there will be winners and losers, on the development of an inclusive education system?
- How can teachers respond effectively to parental concerns about the progress of all children in their class, using their knowledge of learning and teaching?

Globalisation

Due to the increasing speed of communications, both 'virtually' via the internet, and physically through significantly increased access to relatively cheap air travel, we live in a shrinking world, one in which there seems to be a 'compression of time and space across the planet' (Lauder et al., 2006: 31). 'Globalisation' is a blanket term which covers a range of factors which have impacted particularly on the wealthier countries of the world including: the blurring of national and cultural boundaries; a decrease in trading restrictions; increasing mobility for workers in multi-national companies, or for those who are able to move to a higher-income country to look for more lucrative employment; job insecurities for those whose jobs are moved to lower-income countries; almost immediate transmission of news, knowledge and ideas through information technologies across the world. Increased migration is evident in the new diversities (ethnic origins, languages, faiths and attitudes) of the increasingly multicultural classroom.

In order to help countries to compete successfully in a rapidly changing global economy, in which the 'knowledge economy' plays an important part, governments are concerned that the education system should provide children and young people with necessary skills and knowledge. Tensions arise, reflected through the curriculum, around what these skills are, what kinds of knowledge are most useful, and how both should be addressed in schools. This has led some to comment that 'schooling, in all its phases, has become subordinated to the perceived requirements of the labour market' (Brehony, 2005: 31). Gillies (2008: 88) makes a similar point, describing 'the education system as a servant to the economy'. This suggests that at the heart of the curriculum the economic imperative is more important than learning.

Thinking point

- What sorts of pressures might teachers face as a result of discussions around what sorts of skills, knowledge and learning are 'necessary' in the future?

Technological change

In the first decades of the twenty-first century we realise that information about any topic can be accessed instantaneously from online sources by those who have the appropriate hardware and software. You may be reading this text as an e-book yourself. Information can then be used and transformed by the finders, if they have the skills to identify, sort through and select relevant material and to synthesise this with other knowledge they may have, leading to the creation of new understandings. Education is the way in which we transform information, through learning, to knowledge.

Thinking point

- How might the teacher's role change over the course of the twenty-first century as technological advances continue?
- What might be key elements of learning and teaching in a digital age?

Curriculum change

The curriculum is a reflection of knowledge valued by society; consequently it is a site of contestation. Whose curriculum? In the UK, part of the educational policy debate over the past decade has centred on whether the curriculum should comprise of either discrete or integrated subjects for more effective learning to take place. The National Curriculum has often been criticised for being too prescriptive and content-laden (Hayes, 2010) with a heavy emphasis on raising standards in literacy and numeracy at the expense of some other subjects. This leads to the suggestion that only teaching discrete subjects tends to result in knowledge becoming fragmented. The inherent problem here is that life is not fragmented into subject areas so it has been argued that a curriculum burdened with excessive content does not adequately prepare children to deal with real-life problems. In the search for a solution to real-life problems we tend to call upon knowledge and skills from any and all sources that might be helpful, rather than seeking the parts of discrete subjects that can help us arrive at a solution; consequently a curriculum organised around discrete subjects is 'an artifice of life, and in that sense, an obstacle to education that has unity and meaning' (Beane, 1991: 9).

Curriculum change is frequently seen as necessary to meet challenges facing any country, and UK governments have taken this route in response to the impacts of globalisation. For example, the Scottish Government (SG) has reinforced this view stating that a 'Curriculum for Excellence' (CfE) (SE, 2004) will support its aspiration to create a more successful Scotland, with opportunities for all, by tackling strategic objectives: to make Scotland smarter, safer and stronger, wealthier and fairer, greener and healthier (SG, 2008a: 3). The Curriculum for Excellence has moved away from a content-based approach, offering teachers some autonomy in their choice of content and teaching methodologies. At the same time, the new National

Curriculum in England for 2014 is taking a different approach to addressing the perceived needs of the education system. It confirms the statutory status of 'core' subjects by identifying specific content, closely related to age and stage, for these curricular areas, while suggesting that other non-statutory curricular areas, or 'foundation' subjects, will be less tightly prescribed to allow teachers 'greater professional freedom over how they organise and teach the curriculum' (DfE, 2011a). The curricular choices that are made by policy makers are not value neutral.

Thinking point

- What do you see as the teacher's role in curriculum development?
- What might be your professional responsibilities in this area?

Changing notions of teachers as professionals

Over the past few decades, neo-liberal approaches have led to education policy being based on notions of productivity and performance, with managerialist policies encouraging 'compliance and conformity' amongst teachers. It is suggested that very specific guidelines around practice have led to teachers' professional identities being challenged and eroded through loss of professional autonomy (Forde et al., 2006). Professional identity is also affected by external factors such as the expectations of society, public perceptions and how schooling is valued. Being seen by others and by oneself as having expert knowledge, both about specific subjects and about learning, is also an important element.

It could be argued that, currently, the public perception of schooling is that it is not as highly valued as it was in the past. Furthermore, everyone who has been to school feels he or she is an 'expert' in education and many consider that their views and opinions are of equal importance with those who have studied the discipline of education and have developed their practice as educators. Indeed, the views of parents as to how or where their child should be educated and the views of the politicians responsible for the overall system *are* of equal importance to those of the teachers working with the young people. The question is whether or not teachers can speak with real authority on matters of learning and teaching and have their voice heard.

It seems clear that in a situation where teachers are under constant scrutiny in relation to children's progress and achievement from parents, media and government, we need to be confident in our professional and practical knowledge and understanding of how learning and teaching processes work. We need to know why we are making particular decisions around classroom organisation and practice, and we must be able to articulate this authoritatively in discussion with others. We are regularly called upon to justify our actions and these justifications must be based on more than experience and feelings. Rather, they must be grounded in a thorough knowledge and critical understanding of relevant theory and research.

Structure and content of the book

Understanding Learning and Teaching in the Primary Classroom is made up of 20 chapters, each of which address key issues with which you as student teachers should engage critically as you develop your own professional identity.

We recognise that all of you as student teachers will have your own unique experiences of learning and of being taught, which will naturally influence your practice as teachers. You will also have a set of key values and beliefs about learning and teaching, and about human relationships, which will underpin this practice. However, we firmly believe that it is vital that as students you should interrogate these experiences and identify the assumptions which underlie the beliefs you hold, consciously or unconsciously about how learning 'works' – your epistemology – and, therefore, about how teaching 'works'. As you read this book, you will be asked to respond to 'thinking points' which often suggest that you reflect on whether what you have read has challenged what you think or believe.

In the next chapter, Julie McAdam and Evelyn Arizpe explain the importance of reflecting critically on how our beliefs and attitudes to diversity are shaped by our own experiences in the context of the increasingly diverse cultural nature of primary classrooms in the United Kingdom. They make clear suggestions for ways that teachers can develop culturally responsive pedagogies for the children in their classrooms including through the use of children's literature.

Chapter 3, by Mary Wingrave, outlines the principles and philosophy underpinning Early Childhood Education and Care, on which there is growing emphasis. The key issues of play and assessment are discussed; the roles of adults and children in constructing the learning environment are considered. Readers are invited to consider implications for effective practice in the early years of primary school and beyond.

In Chapter 4, Mike Carroll presents alternative models of understanding learning and teaching and discusses the theories relating to these models. The implications for practice arising from taking these different views of how learning and teaching 'work' are considered.

Chapter 5, by Maureen Farrell and A. Graeme Pate, investigates some of the theoretical and practical issues related to effective planning for learning. Readers are encouraged to think critically about the planning process and practical examples of developing learning intentions and success criteria are offered.

Chapter 6, by Margaret McCulloch, addresses social and emotional contexts for learning. Some theories of social and emotional development are discussed and important issues relating to the development of positive relationships in the classroom are identified. The importance of teachers' own emotions and feelings is highlighted.

In Chapter 7, George Head explores some of the different issues around the concept of social, emotional and behavioural difficulties, and highlights the danger of taking a deficit view. He suggests a move towards 'complementary pedagogies' which are based on building relationships of mutual trust and respect amongst learners and teachers.

In Chapter 8, Vivienne Baumfield discusses some of the approaches which have been taken to developing children's capacity to learn, giving practical examples from major projects in schools. She also highlights the implications that these approaches have for teachers' practice and professional identity.

Chapter 9, by Mike Carroll, outlines the theoretical background to collaborative learning, and identifies the key features of planning effective group working. A range of useful classroom strategies are described and explained.

Chapter 10, by Mike Carroll and Fiona McGregor, provides an overview of the shifting policy landscape with respect to interdisciplinary learning. They argue that planning for interdisciplinary learning should be a collaborative endeavour as it requires teachers to connect ideas conceptually across subjects, based on a sound understanding of subject-specific knowledge.

In Chapter 11, Margaret Sutherland and Niamh Stack consider the contested nature of 'ability' and the ways in which our expectations of children may be limited. They make a strong argument for providing challenge for all students, including highly able pupils.

In Chapter 12, Louise Hayward and Ernie Spencer outline some important issues in the area of assessment for learning. They argue that assessment for learning is integral to all effective learning and, when implemented thoughtfully, can contribute to the development of independent learning.

Chapter 13, by Alan Britton, addresses the area of education for global citizenship and sustainable development, looking at the skills, knowledge and values involved in this area. The central notions of pupil voice and participation are highlighted along with the role played by the individual teacher in encouraging pupils' engagement with an important area of learning.

Chapter 14, by Leonard Franchi and Leon Robinson, looks at spiritual development and considers how teachers can promote this amongst young people. Issues of human flourishing and the 'good life' are discussed, and some of the challenges arising from linking 'spirituality' and 'religion' are highlighted, with examples of good practice being offered.

In Chapter 15, by Moyra Boland, Margaret Jago and Jan Macdonald, the concepts of creativity and creative teaching are explored. The rationale behind the current emphasis on creativity in education is discussed and they give suggestions as to how teachers may encourage creativity in their classrooms.

In Chapter 16, Stephen Boyle and David McKinstry look at ways in which information and communications technology can be used not simply as a means of collecting information but as a vital pedagogical strategy to enhance all areas of teaching, and to support a holistic approach to pupil learning, encouraging interdisciplinarity and motivating young people to learn.

In Chapter 17, George MacBride and Margaret McCulloch outline some of the issues around transition experiences, both into and out of primary schools. They argue that planning around transition should take account of learning as much as of pastoral issues, and that the learner has a vital role to play in effective sharing of information.

Chapter 18, by Mike Carroll, addresses the issues arising from working with other adults in the classroom, with a focus on the role of School Support Assistants, and the teacher's responsibility to supervise and encourage them. Suggestions are made for developing positive working relationships and for ensuring that additional personnel in the class do not in fact have a negative effect on pupil learning.

Chapter 19, by Beth Dickson and Irene McQueen, explores aspects of practitioner inquiry, looking at the development of this as a stance expected of all professional educators. They consider the progressive nature of practitioner inquiry and identify ways in which both pupil learning and attainment can be impacted by the teacher's engagement with professional inquiry in the classroom.

In the concluding chapter, Christine Forde and Margery McMahon explore the meaning of 'leadership for learning' particularly in relation to what this means for the primary teacher becoming a leader of learning. The authors address the dimensions of the teacher as a leader both having influence over learning in the classroom as well as exerting influence over the practice of their colleagues. Fundamental to their analysis is the notion of the school as a professional learning community. In common with other chapters in this book the educational arena is seen as a contested place. The changing expectations of primary teachers within today's policy environment require teachers to develop a notion of professional practice that requires them to become leaders *for* learning, leaders *of* learning and leaders *by* learning. This is the challenge that they present to you for your professional practice.

Summary

Increasingly the policy discourse is one that seeks to focus on 'practice' and 'practical knowledge' whilst devaluing the teacher's sense of professionalism. The primary teacher for the twenty-first century should be wary of attempts to position them solely as technicians with a responsibility to bring about measurable improvement in a narrowly-defined range of performance indicators. This is not to say that pupil achievement, pupil behaviour and the quality of teaching are not important, they are! However, it is important that primary teachers make informed professional judgements in order to develop a pedagogy that places matters of social justice and care at the heart of the educational endeavour. We hope that you will find this book helpful on your professional journey.

Reflective questions

- What forms of inequality have you observed or experienced both as a learner and as a teacher?
- How might you demonstrate a commitment to social justice and inclusion?

Further reading

Brady, L. (2011) 'Teacher values and relationship: Factors in values education', *Australian Journal of Teacher Education*, 36(2), 56-66. http://ro.ecu.edu.au/ajte/vol36/iss2/5 (accessed 9 August 2013).

Laurie Brady provides a thought-provoking exploration of teacher values. Although set within the context of Australia and particularly orientated towards teaching values in schools, the values discussed are nevertheless applicable to all areas of the curriculum and to all primary teachers in UK and elsewhere.

Patrick, F. and McPhee, A. (2011) 'Professional identity', in M. McMahon, C. Forde and M. Martin (eds) *Contemporary Issues in Learning and Teaching*. London: SAGE. pp. 130-41.

This chapter highlights a range of factors that exert an influence over the construction of a teacher's professional identity. The authors argue that an understanding of how your professional identity is shaped will provide insights with respect to teaching practice.

CHAPTER 2

CHILDHOOD AND DIVERSITY

Julie McAdam and Evelyn Arizpe

Key ideas

This chapter explores:

- childhood, as a contested and complex concept;
- the notion that diverse childhoods are the norm;
- how our beliefs and attitudes towards diversity are shaped by our own childhood experiences;
- the ways in which schools operate as complex social systems, so that planning for diversity needs to take place across the entire system;
- children's literature as one practical way of exploring our understanding of diversity.

Introduction

The past decade has brought with it global population change on an unprecedented scale; these changes are most apparent within the population of primary school-aged children (Dunnell, 2008). In England, 27.6 per cent of this age group are from minority ethnic backgrounds (DfE, 2012a), while in Scotland over 147 languages have been recorded as the home languages of children in schools (SG, 2009a). In sharp contrast to the diverse school populations, teachers in these countries are predominantly white, female and monolingual (SG, 2009b; Smyth et al., 2011). This means that for many teachers, their own childhood landscapes and perspectives on childhood may be very different from those of the children they teach. This chapter will begin with an exploration of the historical forces that have shaped our current views of childhood, showing that childhood as a concept has been in constant flux.

This chapter will also focus on the impact of global migration on school communities and classrooms, taking the view that teachers who work in these classrooms can meet the needs of all children through the use of culturally relevant pedagogy (McAdam and Arizpe, 2011; Nieto, 2010). It is important that we are mindful of 'deficit thinking that pathologises minority ethnic, working class or disabled pupils' (Mitchell, 2012: 4) and work towards creating a discourse that presents diversity as a celebration of humanity (Education Scotland, online-a) rather than as a challenge to be overcome on a Monday morning. In order to be able to reflect on and address these changes and issues, we have based the ideas presented in this chapter on two core concepts:

- There is no fixed notion of childhood; instead there are diverse childhoods.
- Children bring their experiences from these diverse childhoods to our school communities as valuable 'funds of knowledge' (Gonzalez et al., 2005) that form the basis for learning and interaction with planned curricula.

The complexity of childhood

Concepts of childhood reveal themselves through art, literature, religious texts and archaeological records. Childhood as a concept has been contested over time and has been heavily influenced by Western frameworks. From a teacher's perspective there are three broad themes emerging from the literature which are worth considering. These are:

1. Current definitions of childhood from the UN and UNICEF are based on biological life stages. The UN Convention on the Rights of the Child (1989) has been approved by all member states except for the US and Somalia and came into force in the UK in January 1992. The convention classifies a child as any person under the age of 18, but we need to remember that anthropological studies of childhood evidence variations on this perspective through time, space and culture (Lancy, 2008). Teachers are required as part of their professional practice to '(d)emonstrate respect for the rights of all children and young people without discrimination as defined in the United Nations Convention on the Rights of the Child' (GTCS, 2006: 15).

2. Concepts of children are often presented as binaries based on good and evil. On one hand, Christianity and concepts of original sin led teachers and parents to become concerned with strict moral guidance and punishment. On the other, children were also seen as innocent angels of the type portrayed in religious works of art. Childhood was a period of time where children had to be protected and separated from the evils of adulthood.

   These opposing binaries influenced the work of scholars, and the concept of childhood kept evolving until the eighteenth century, when philosophers such as Locke and Rousseau valued childhood 'as a stage of life in its own right' (Cunningham, 1995: 61). As teachers we need to be cautious of the ways in which these constructs of childhood have woven themselves into the very fabric of our lives, leading us to make unexamined assumptions about who children are and what they are capable of.

3. Childhood is a social construction. Sociologists argue that it is not a natural or a universal feature of human groups, but appears as a specific structural and cultural component of society. Childhood can never be divorced from other variables such as class, gender or ethnicity. Comparative and cross-cultural analysis reveals a variety of childhoods rather than a single childhood. Consequently, children must be seen as active agents in the construction and determination of their own lives (Jenks, 2005).

It is this final point about the plurality of childhoods that is important to us as educators, and provides us with a reason for analysing our own childhood biographies. To do this in detail would involve an enormous amount of work, but the following group task can be used to explore diverse childhoods through focusing on a daily cultural routine that is practised by all in different ways. Embedded within dining practices are different layers of meaning that tell us about our values and beliefs towards children and diversity and allow us to witness diverse childhoods as a norm.

Thinking point: Eating as a cultural practice

Group task for student teachers

Each member of the group should write down their memories of an important meal from their childhood. The meal should be typical rather than unusual. Provide details of who was there, where the meal took place and what you ate. Try to recall the cooking arrangements, the seating arrangements, the serving arrangements and the conversation that took place during the meal. Try to remember the relationships between adults and describe your feelings.

Share the memories with each other (this task has been adapted from work by Torres-Guzmán, 2013).

Post-sharing reflection

- In what way was the meal representative of your culture? Was there a religious element to the meal? Were any traditions observed?
- What were the gender implications embedded within the meal? Who cooked? Who served? Who ate first?
- What power dimensions were evidenced by the meal? Who sat where? Who said what?
- What specific roles were played by the children? What roles were they asked to play? Were there tensions in these roles across generations or amongst family members?
- Were any childhood sayings used to exemplify how children should behave or act during the meal?
- In what way did your meal differ from the others in your group? What were points of cross-over in your dining practices?
- What did you learn about others during this activity?
- What does this tell us about childhood and diversity?

Cline et al. (2002) noted a lack in confidence amongst teachers in knowing how to approach diversity and in particular issues related to personal and institutional prejudice. Richardson (2004: 20) advised that '(T)eachers need to be clear in their minds about what they want to confront and how they wish to confront it'. Therefore, before discussing how as teachers we can practically explore and utilise the diversity that exists in our classrooms, schools and communities, we must begin by exploring our own attitudes and experiences of diversity in our lives and the contexts within which we work. By reflecting and theorizing on the ways in which we experience diversity personally and professionally we can begin to build a framework for understanding how to harness the powerful learning experiences that a diverse classroom affords.

Using autobiography to explore your own attitudes and beliefs

Biographical studies of teachers' personal and professional beliefs (Day et al., 2006) show that prior experience shapes identity and that these experiences play a huge part in creating a set of values and attitudes through which teachers screen all subsequent experience. Clandinin and Connelly (2000) carried out further work in this field and advocated for the use of narrative as a means of helping teachers to become more aware of their own 'personal practical knowledge'. A recurring theme emerging from teacher biography studies was the importance of childhood experiences in shaping a teaching identity (Arshad, 2012a; Maylor and Read, 2007; Sugrue, 1997). This is one reason why all teachers should examine their past, reflect on and question how this might have shaped and contributed towards their current views and beliefs about children and diversity.

 Thinking point: Narratives of diversity

Sugrue (1997) described several influences on a teacher's identity. These can be used to organise your biography. How have each of the following influences shaped your attitudes and beliefs about diversity?

- Your immediate family.
- Significant others or extended family. (This is similar to the above, but can include work colleagues, friends, partners or teachers encountered in your own past.)
- Atypical teaching episodes. (These could include volunteer work, or general work situations where students were involved in work with children.)
- Policy contexts. (For examples, see Tables 2.1 and 2.2.)
- Tacitly required understandings. (These are sometimes known as folk pedagogy or myth; something taken to be fact, but which after further examination is not a fact. The media play a huge part in creating tacitly required understandings of teaching.)

Through writing your own biography and reading the biographies of others you can begin to build a mental picture of the qualities required of teachers to work with diverse children. Richardson's (2004: 32) research found that teachers who were clear on the stance they were taking towards Islamophobia showed empathy, listened, treated children fairly, used procedural neutrality, saw their own classrooms as sites of enquiry in which to develop a critical understanding of issues, and were prepared to 'muddle through' and admit they did not have all the answers.

School as social system

Having explored our attitudes and beliefs surrounding diversity and childhood, we also need to examine the contexts where we work with children. The work of Banks (2008: 37) is helpful in offering a structure for understanding the complex nature of a school system. The diagram below has been adapted from his work on the school as a social system and shows the connections across the system.

The diagram can be read from the outside in, starting with policy and the way it impacts on schools, teachers and their communities, or it can be read from the inside out with children placed at the centre of all we do. Banks (2008) points out that while many educators begin individual initiatives within any of the named

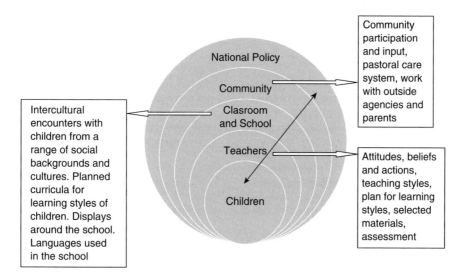

Figure 2.1   Diagram of school social structure (drawing on work of Banks, 2008; DfES, 2004a; Maylor and Read, 2007)

contexts for learning, transformation needs to take place across all areas of the social system for a school truly to meet the needs of diverse learners.

View from practice: Two schools

To embed principles of diversity across a school social system requires action at a number of levels. The two schools in the table below have vastly different pupil profiles and geographical locations, but what is similar is their commitment to meeting the needs of their diverse pupils and embedding diversity at the heart of their school systems. Both schools have effective leadership teams, who have high expectations of their pupils, and encourage staff to take forward transformative projects. Over the past year both schools have been involved in international work through Comenius projects and both schools have been recognised by their respective inspectorates for the quality of their work.

Table 2.1   How different schools meet diverse needs

	John Donne Primary School	**John Ogilvie Secondary School**
Location	Southwark, London	South Lanarkshire
Statistics	Southwark has largest stock of social housing in western Europe.	Situated in Blantyre.
	174 languages recorded in the borough.	963 pupils using 50 additional languages. Main languages are English, Punjabi, Polish and Urdu.
	Outstanding school in Ofsted report.	Recent HMIe report awarded very good in all five categories.
Leadership	Clear leadership with an emphasis on building esteem and expectations amongst staff.	Effective leadership with an emphasis on encouraging innovative practice amongst staff.
Home–school Links	Assemblies, community choir, cultural awareness of managing children's anger. Dedicated member of staff to liaise with parents (empower rather than involve).	Family learning project, takes referrals from EAL team. Children and families learning English together.
Staff Development	Mobility for staff on international projects, focus on teacher transformation. Working with Goldsmiths, University of London.	Involved in a European Comenius Project: Portfolio of Integration. Working with the University of Glasgow, School of Education.
Transition	Challenging, 60 children from 22 schools.	Deputy head using Shaun Tan's *The Arrival* to look at the idea of journeys. Linking this to the journey to secondary school.
EAL support	Dedicated team member working with teachers across school.	Polish speaking EAL teacher working across local authority.

This desire for transformation exists within the policy documentation of Scotland, Wales, Northern Ireland and England. To conclude this chapter we will provide an overview of the main policy documents that inform our thinking about diversity and expand on how this can translate into practice within a school curriculum and individual classrooms.

From research to policy: A guide

The origins of education for diversity grew out of the civil rights movement in the US and encapsulated a desire for a vision of democracy and social justice (Banks, 2008). Within the US it was known as multicultural education. In the UK, multicultural education developed as 'a pragmatic response' to children from former British colonies (Tomlinson, 2009: 125) and as a way to bring about assimilation. Arshad's (2012b) coverage of the UK response looks at how the language used to discuss diversity education has changed with each decade. The 1980s saw intense debate as to whether multicultural education was tokenistic and assimilationist (Troyna and Williams, 1986), or a necessary means of tackling racism. School curricula responded in two ways, by adopting either a 'contribution approach' (Banks, 2008: 48) where schools would take the stance of tourists visiting another country or celebrating festivals from around the world, or an 'additive approach' where diverse texts and literature would be used throughout the school. These approaches introduce children to the concept of otherness and cultural difference, perhaps challenging inequalities at a personal or cultural level, but they do not challenge the structural and institutional forces that bring about inequality and prejudice in the first place (Bartolo and Smyth, 2009: 128).

The death of Stephen Lawrence in 1993 triggered a long public inquiry that acknowledged that racism was institutionalised. One of the key recommendations in moving forward was for curricula throughout the UK to be 'aimed at valuing cultural diversity and preventing racism, in order better to reflect the needs of a diverse society' (Macpherson, 1999, para 67). Banks (2008: 48) also argues for a shift in thinking so that curricula embed transformative or social action approaches, allowing inequality to be questioned and students to take social action to address identified issues of inequality. These approaches encourage students to participate as citizens and use critical pedagogies (Cho, 2013) to publicise inequality or motivate the wider community to take action. This type of approach links to recent work on citizenship; a review of curriculum documentation from Scotland, England, Ireland and Wales shows that at a policy level these ideas have been embedded in documents.

A review of research and policy over the past ten years reveals three key areas of advice. In chronological order these are: *Minority Ethnic Pupils (MEP)* (2002–4),

Table 2.2   Overview of main policy documents related to working with Minority Ethnic Pupils, 2002–4

Document	Purpose/Main Ideas	Ideas to follow up
Minority Ethnic Pupils (2002–2004)		
Cline, T., de Abreu, G., Fihosy, C., Gray, H., Lambert, H. and Neale, J. (2002) *Minority Ethnic Pupils in White Schools, Research Report RR365*, DfES.	Research carried out in schools which had MEP populations of 4–6%. Schools not do not 'adequately prepare their pupils for adult life in a society that is culturally and ethnically diverse'. Cautions against 'one-size-fits-all' approaches. Report contains extracts from interviews with children, teachers and parents.	Report advises more work with children and families (encourage bilingualism, ethnic identity and complementary schooling); implement reporting systems for bullying and name calling; develop curriculum input beyond RE departments and encompass citizenship; provide support for teachers to build confidence; strengthen provision within ITE.
DfES (2003) *Aiming High: Raising the Achievement of Minority Ethnic Pupils: Consultation Document*, London, DfES/0183. Based on Race Relations Amendment Act 2000 which was a response to the Stephen Lawrence Inquiry.	Sets out the characteristics of a successful school: strong leadership, high expectations, effective teaching and learning, ethos of respect, parental involvement. Presents case studies that exemplify good practice in each of the above areas.	Reports on Ethnic Minority Achievement Gap and identifies three main areas for further work: parental expectations, fluency in English and tackling institutional racism. Acknowledges the need for a diverse teaching workforce and further support at ITE level.
DfES (2004a) *Aiming High: Understanding the Educational Needs of Minority Ethnic Pupils in Mainly White Schools: A Guide to Good Practice*, Nottingham: DfES. Drafted and Edited by Robin Richardson and Angela Wood.	Draws on three philosophical principles: equality, diversity, and belonging and cohesion. Provides case studies of practice. Provides practical advice on English as an Additional Language, prejudice and racism and Education for All.	Highlights six themes that can permeate a school (20–30). Provides an appendix of useful websites covering policy, EAL, culture and identity, race and racism and Internationalism. Detailed bibliography provided.

Meeting the Needs of New Arrivals (2005–9) and, more recently, *Citizenship and Diversity* (2007–present). These three areas illuminate shifts in language use which reflect our evolving knowledge of children, childhood and diversity. Table 2.2 shows three key documents published between 2002–4, which engage with the question of how we meet the needs of minority ethnic pupils.

Emerging from this work was the need for a closer look at how newly-arrived children use English as an Additional Language and develop their home languages as a means of embracing their ethnic identity. The next phase of policy developed across the UK centred on meeting the needs of new arrival children. An analysis of three policy documents (DfCSF, 2007; DfES, 2005a; HMIe, 2009) written to provide guidance on meeting the needs of new arrival children identify the following themes for schools to develop: welcoming children and parents to the school learning community; carrying out an initial assessment of the children's needs;

Table 2.3 Key features of current policy documents

Maylor, U. and Read, B. (2007) *Diversity and Citizenship in the Curriculum: Research Review*, Research Report RP819: DfES.	This research report examines identities and how they are constructed; reaching the conclusion we need to challenge ideologies that construct national identities in a way that excludes minority ethnic groups. Diversity should be seen as a curriculum opportunity not a threat.	Effective provision is provided when there is strong and effective leadership, clear planning and guidance for staff and students, pupils are encouraged to make links with their own experiences and pupil idealism is tapped into. Teachers need to understand their own prejudices and attitudes towards diversity.
IILT and SELB (2007) *Together Towards Inclusion: Toolkit for Diversity in the Primary School*, Dublin and Armagh: Integrate Ireland Language and Training and Southern Education and Library Board.	The toolkit is written in four sections, Getting Started, Early Days, Moving On, and What Next? The emphasis is on what a school needs to do to be welcoming and inclusive and the term integration is used in this context. The toolkit contains practical advice, visual examples, checklists and step by step guides.	A CD companion exists. Toolkits also exist for the post-primary phase, with a section on transition. The Early Days section focuses on Buddying, intercultural awareness, sense of place and the silent period. The Moving On section offers detailed advice on the Common European framework for Language Competence and developing language for use across the curriculum.
Welsh Assembly Government (2010) *Unity and Diversity*, Cardiff: Welsh Assembly Government.	Provides guidance on where schools should begin, drawing on policy and case studies of practice, ideas of equity and excellence and community engagement. There are sections on developing curriculum, supporting teachers and evaluating school performance in the area of promoting race equality and diversity.	Includes useful appendices. Appendix five is helpful for assessing the texts used in schools. Appendix two provides mindmaps for each area of the curriculum in order to provide a starting point for teachers to promote race equality and diversity.
Education Scotland (no date) *Promoting Diversity and Equality: Developing Responsible Citizens for 21st Century Scotland.* Based on the Equality Act 2010	This policy was written after the Equality Act 2010 and promotes diversity and equality beyond the requirements of the Act through models of citizenship. The policy challenges schools to develop children as responsible citizens who show respect for each other. Children need to know that discrimination is unacceptable and know how to challenge it.	Provides reflective questions. Links to Curriculum for Excellence Experiences and Outcomes to exemplify how these can feature across many areas of the curriculum. Provides links to key bodies and resources. Contains a specific section on sectarianism.

developing classroom practice; promoting children's participation and making connections between the home and the school. If we return to the two key ideas stated at the start of the chapter then we can see that across the UK the need to work in close partnership with children, parents and communities, making clear connections across the sites of learning, becomes a focus for moving forward. The last round of policy has moved away from language of separation and embraces the idea that diverse childhoods are the norm. Table 2.3 demonstrates how current documents from across the UK highlight the themes of inclusion, unity and citizenship.

Articulating diversity through the curriculum

The findings of the Stephen Lawrence Inquiry and of research in the field (Banks, 2008; Maylor and Read, 2007), and the policies detailed in Table 2.3 all point towards the need for educators to address diversity through the curriculum. Scotland, England, Northern Ireland and Wales are all at various stages of curriculum reform and implementation, so we offer the following advice adapted from *Aiming High: Understanding the Educational needs of minority ethnic pupils in mainly white schools* (DfES, 2004a: 20–1). By initiating discussions around key principles, teachers can begin to consider how to embed diversity across school curricula at a whole-school level and then move these discussions to thinking about their own classrooms or subjects, regardless of their geographical context. Things to consider:

- Begin from the starting point that we are all part of a 'shared humanity' and that this can be explored across all areas of the curriculum (arts, science, maths, language).
- Difference and diversity can be articulated across all areas of the curriculum in the materials selected and used.
- Cultures are not static and cultural hybridity is an on-going process of borrowing, mingling and mutual influence.
- All cultures carry examples of excellence, and these examples should be included, so that the Western bias that permeates many curricula is challenged.
- There is no one way of expressing identity; multiple identities exist. These points can be explored in citizenship studies.
- Students need to know what they can do to address issues of racism and prejudice.

These principles overlap with the following dimensions of multicultural education set out by Banks (2009: 32): content integration, knowledge construction, prejudice reduction, equity pedagogy and empowering school culture. One way to embrace these principles is through using children's literature that presents examples of diversity, cultural hybridity, non-Western narratives and includes children who are prepared to take social action.

Reflecting the diversity within your own classroom using children's literature

The metaphor of children's literature as a mirror, window and door (Bothelo and Rudman, 2009) is helpful in understanding why it has the potential to support educators who wish to promote diversity within their school communities. Diverse children's literature has the potential to act as a mirror allowing children to see representations of themselves and explore expressions of their own identity (Arizpe et al., 2013). Children can use the literature to make connections with other texts and their own experiences, connecting the present to the past (Gough, 1998). This ultimately allows the children to develop a growing awareness and sense of their own cultural experiences (Kornfeld and Prothro, 2005).

Children's literature also allows the reader to see alternative and possible worlds (Kornfeld and Prothro, 2005) and form new understandings of others (Ee Loh, 2009) as the text poses options and alternatives (Gough, 1998) and the idea of living in a complex culturally diverse world (Gopalkrishnan and Ulanoff, 2003). Children can begin to compare what they see out of the window with what they see in the mirror, contrasting their own value systems with those portrayed in the literature (Meek, 1988) as a means of developing and questioning their own belief systems. Sleeter and Grant (2002) would argue that this ability to see beyond themselves is the beginning of practising citizenship.

View from practice: Journeys from images to words

The Journeys from Images to Words Project took place in two upper primary classrooms in Glasgow with a high multi-ethnic population, including asylum seekers and refugees. Three books were selected which reflected the theme of migration and journeys and had different combinations of words and images: from a picturebook to a chapter book with no images.

Overview of visual strategies and multimodal responses:

1. Creating an inclusive classroom ethos by building a visual collage, 'Rivers of Reading', of the children's literacy practices and using the metaphor of a river to represent their reading outside of school at home and in their local communities.
2. Entering the world of the book with 'Walk- and talk-throughs' by setting the context, and allowing time and space for looking closely at the images and their relationship with the text as well as co-constructing meaning, making personal links and testing hypotheses about the plot and characters.
3. Applying critical reading strategies through:

   a) annotations of visuals: a more comprehensive observation of one particular image that slows reading down and allows a deeper 'excavation' of meaning through pictures by the addition of speech or thought bubbles, questions or speculations;

(Continued)

(Continued)

b) annotations of text: a closer textual analysis that encourages a focus on figurative language and other structural aspects of the text also by the addition of speech or thought bubbles, questions or speculations;

c) photo journals: an invitation to photograph elements of home life and organise them into collages in order to share events and stories in the classroom;

d) other creative visual responses: illustrating the text, drawing narrative graphic strips and other flexible and reflective tasks relevant to particular text or images.

Cummins (2001: 667) wrote of the need for educators to engage in genuine dialogue and collaboration in diverse classrooms and argued for the use of 'pedagogical approaches that empower students', allowing them to 'assume greater control over setting their own learning goals and to collaborate actively with one another in achieving these goals'. This project used pedagogical approaches that embraced the principles of diversity.

This metaphor of mirrors, windows and doors can be expanded so that teachers can easily audit the texts and cultural artefacts that surround children at school and ensure that stories and narratives draw on a range of media (art, dance, music, picturebooks) and represent a range of languages and cultures. By looking at the walls, the visitors and even the fieldtrips (DfES, 2004a), we can begin to think more realistically about reflecting the diversity of the children and the communities in which we work and surround our children with mirrors, windows and doors.

Summary

Within this chapter we have looked at the complex nature of childhood, the way our own childhood influences our attitudes and beliefs, the way in which a school is comprised of social structures, the way policy has changed over time to reflect the diverse identities that make up the citizens of the UK and the way this policy translates into curriculum and the work within our own classrooms. What we all must keep sight of is that these structures and policies translate into actions that impact on children, teachers and parents. Exploring our own values and attitudes towards diversity means that we have to enter intercultural spaces in our classrooms and communities and transform challenges into opportunities. This chapter should act as a stimulus for this journey.

Reflective questions

- In what ways has the chapter challenged your thinking about childhood?
- How will it have an impact on classroom actions?
- Thinking about the school as a system, what changes will you make within your own classroom?
- On entering a school how will you find out about the work they do to embed diversity across the curriculum?

Further reading

On childhood:

Brooks, L. (2006) *The Story of Childhood: Growing Up in Modern Britain*. London: Bloomsbury.

Teaching biographies:

Clandinin, J., Huber, J., Huber, M., Murphy, M.S., Orr, A.M., Pearce, M. and Steeves, P. (2006) *Composing Diverse Identities: Narrative Inquiries into the Interwoven Lives of Children and Teachers*. London: Routledge.

For further information on Comenius funding in the UK, see http://www.britishcouncil.org/comenius.htm.

For further information on the project *Journeys from Images to Words* visit the website, which contains examples of the texts, the strategies used and the outcomes of the project: http://www.journeys-fromimagestowords.com/.

CHAPTER 3
EARLY YEARS EDUCATION

Mary Wingrave

Key ideas

This chapter explores:

- the expansion of pre-5 education;
- play, its role in developing learning;
- the environment for learning;
- assessment in early years.

Introduction

This chapter will consider the crucial role of Early Childhood Education and Care (ECEC) and the part it has in supporting children's early development and learning. It will look at some of the developments that have taken place in recent times, particularly with respect to expansion of provision and policy. Play as the primary medium of delivery of experiences will be discussed in terms of its benefits to the learning process. The engagement of adults and children in constructing the learning environment and assessment in ECEC will also be explored to highlight their importance and place in the pre-5 setting.

Early years provision

ECEC takes the form of non-compulsory education and care services which provide for children from 0–5. It blends the dual importance of both care and education in the development and learning of young children. Provision of ECEC services in the UK is diverse and in some cases there can be a fragmentation as services are provided by a range of groups including local authority and private, voluntary and partnership sector providers. This chapter discusses ECEC services which provide for children in their pre-school and ante-pre-school year.

The need for ECEC

It is argued that in today's ever-changing society there is a need to prepare our youngest children to enter school ready to learn and succeed (Heckman and Masterov, 2007; OECD, 2006). Consequently ECEC has, in recent times, taken centre stage in many developed countries' educational and political agendas (Gammage, 2008: 10). It is claimed that economically, pre-school education will save money both for the compulsory schooling system and the state, not just in the short term but, as indicated by Heckman and Masterov (2007), as a long-term investment which will shape and develop the economy. From this perspective, providing children with access to the benefits from ECEC will impact positively on both social and economic infrastructures. ECEC services seek to enhance child development and to support parents (Friendly and Beach, 2004) to improve children's wellbeing, development and prospects for life-long learning (OECD, 2006). A longitudinal research project, 'The Effective Provision of Pre-school Education' (EPPE, 1997–2003) (Sylva et al., 2004), examined the impact of pre-school provision for 3–4 year-olds. The study highlights the importance and the positive benefits ECEC has for children and their families in terms of social justice, by including children from disadvantaged backgrounds in education at the earliest opportunity.

Evidence from longitudinal research demonstrates that the early years of children's lives have a profound and lasting impact on their futures and as such adequate provision for learning and development is essential to achieving social justice (Siraj-Blatchford and Woodhead, 2009). ECEC attempts to diminish the detrimental developmental effects of poverty, for example, by providing childcare to low income families, often predominantly lone female parents, thus allowing them to seek work. It also provides early intervention (New and Cochran, 2007) for children, as ECEC supports an inclusive approach for children who may require additional resources to meet their developmental and learning needs (Bennett and Tayler, 2006).

The OECD recommends that governments support and regulate ECEC programmes (OECD, 2006: 39). Successive governments in the UK have, since the 1990s, shown a commitment to improving ECEC services with commissioned reports and a plethora of policies, such as: *Starting with Quality*, the Rumbold Report (DES, 1990); *Learning to Succeed* (NCE, 1993); *Start Right* (Ball, 1994); and the *National Childcare Strategy: Sure Start* (DfEE, 1998), which have helped shape and support 'high quality early childhood education' (Calman and Tarr-Whelan, 2005: 1).

The *National Childcare Strategy, Sure Start* programme was launched in 1998 by the UK Labour government and aimed to give children the best start through a cross-departmental strategy to improve social and educational experiences. The programme has had a long-term impact on the provision of childcare availability across the UK. Statistics from the Department for Education (2012b) indicate that the number of 3 and 4 year olds benefitting from 'some free early education' in England is 96 per cent, and in Scotland free nursery education for all 3 and 4 year olds has been increased from 475 hours a year to 600 hours (SG, 2012a).

The National Child Care strategy also precipitated policies such as: *Every Child Matters: Children's Workforce Strategy* (DfES, 2005b), *The Early Years Framework I and II* (SG, 2008b), and the *Review of Pre-School Education in Northern Ireland* (DfE(NI), 2004) which have helped change the provision of ECEC and the position of its workforce across the four countries which make up the UK. In addition, delivery of curricula has been reviewed and this has resulted in comprehensive, progressive documents being developed to guide practice.

 Thinking point

There are two main drivers for policy developments in the UK for ECEC:

1. The long lasting positive impact on child development.
2. The desire to reduce child poverty by providing opportunities for parents (primarily mothers) to return to employment.

Why do you think both drivers are important to the long-term prospects for children?
    Can you identify any other reasons for developing ECEC provision?

Curriculum

The commitment shown by the UK towards ECEC has resulted in not only a reconsideration of the availability of services but also of their content. This has resulted in each country in the UK creating its own distinct curriculum.

Whilst there are many common areas of focus for children's development and learning, each curriculum has distinctive features. For example, in the *Curriculum for Excellence* (SE, 2004) the early stage includes religious and moral education and the *Foundation Phase; Framework for Children's Learning for 3 to 7-year-olds in*

Table 3.1 Curriculum organisers for early childhood education, UK

Country	What is covered
England: *Statutory Framework for the Early Years Foundation Stage* (DfES, 2012b)	Personal, social and emotional development
	Communication, language and literacy
	Problem solving, reasoning and literacy
	Knowledge and understanding of the world
	Physical development
	Creative development
Scotland: *Curriculum for Excellence* (Scottish Executive, 2004)	Health and wellbeing
	Languages
	Mathematics
	Sciences
	Social studies
	Expressive arts
	Technologies
	Religious and moral education
Northern Ireland: *Curriculum Guidance For Pre-School Education* (Dept for Education (NI), 2006)	The arts
	Language development
	Early mathematical experiences
	Personal, social and emotional development
	Physical development and movement
	The world around us
Wales: *Foundation Phase: Framework for Children's Learning for 3 to 7-year-olds in Wales* (Dept for Children, Education, Lifelong Learning and Skills, 2008)	Personal and social wellbeing and cultural diversity
	Physical development
	Creative development
	Language, literacy and communication skills
	Welsh language development
	Mathematical development
	Knowledge and understanding of the world

Wales (DfCELLS, 2008) specifically includes the development of the Welsh language. These characteristics reflect the culture and social needs of the country from which they originated. However, play is the common medium for the delivery of these curricula. The use of play supports the development of both intellectual and social skills for children, and also their understanding of what it is to be part of the world. These skills are crucial for the child's independence, self-esteem and wellbeing; this requires those who work in ECEC settings to be skilled and committed to the development and learning of children.

Staff in ECEC

Traditionally, ECEC has been perceived as a separate sector from formal education, in part due to its non-compulsory nature (OECD, 2000) and the differences in staff qualifications. The relocation of ECEC into the education agenda and the introduction of coherent curricular frameworks have resulted in a focus on the qualifications of the workforce. ECEC staff are traditionally women with a wide and varied set of qualifications, from extensive practical experience without formal qualifications to qualified teachers (Menmuir and Hughes, 2004). In Scotland, in 2008, there existed 44 similar job titles for ECEC staff (Adams, 2008: 199) ranging from Early Years Worker to Child Development Officer. The variety of skills, qualifications and job titles in ECEC has not only resulted in staff being traditionally undervalued and seen as only 'looking after the weans' (Mooney and McCafferty, 2005) but has also led to a tension in terms of pay, conditions of service and recognition of professional status. The introduction and consultation for Early Years Professional Status (EYPS) Standards (CWDC, 2012) and the *Standard for Childhood Practice* (QAA Scotland, 2007) aim to establish a professional status at graduate level for those who lead and manage pre-5 centres but who are not qualified teachers. However, the Nutbrown Review (2012: 8) cautions against being too complacent and accepting that these measures will solve the tension in the pre-5 sector as she highlights that there is still a lack of parity with those who hold Qualified Teacher Status (QTS). Nutbrown does, however, acknowledge that EYPS has contributed to the improvements in ECEC and suggests that further work is still required.

The role staff play

The role of all those involved in delivering pre-5 education is to ensure that the physical environment and daily practices of education and care promote the health, safety and wellbeing of children. Staff aim to create a reciprocal partnership with parents to support the children in their care and readily consult them in relation to the experiences, likes/dislikes, cultural and social background which is particular to each child. Staff demonstrate the values of equality, justice and diversity in supporting the learning and development of each individual child, in the context of family and society. Umbrella social policies such as: *Getting it Right for Every Child* (GIRFEC) (SG, 2008c), *Every Child Matters: Change for Children; Multi-agency Working Fact Sheet* (CWDC, 2007) and *Understanding the Needs of Children in Northern Ireland* (DHSSPS, 2011) guide and support those who work in the pre-5 sector by promoting communication with multi-agency partners and other professionals in the community who support children and families.

Through consultation, observations and interactions with the children, staff are able to build and develop supportive, trusting relationships with children. All staff have the responsibility to design and plan learning opportunities in consultation with the children, families and other staff. The activities and routines are stimulating and encourage positive child development and social interactions which are required to promote effective learning. The primary mode of curricular delivery is through play, which is enjoyable, stimulating and motivating to the child.

Play and the learning environment

Play is of paramount importance in ECEC and it is through play that learning and development are fostered and nurtured. Froebel was one of the first advocates of the kindergarten and he promoted play as 'the serious business of childhood' (Dunne, 2008: 263). Play supports social skill building which allows children to derive pleasure and develop their imagination and creativity and influences self-expression when language skills are still developing. Through play children learn 'their capacity to act and to recognise that actions have consequences' (James and James, 2004: 24). Play can enhance children's ability to: role-play, think before acting, develop their capabilities to show empathy and self-regulate their emotional understanding of the society in which they reside. This allows them to develop their understanding and become 'social actors' (James and James, 2004: 27). Children are able to develop some concept of what works and they 'try on' emotions through play (Zahn-Waxler and Radke-Yarrow 1990: 117). Also, 'trying out' situations allows children to develop a concept of the rules of the society in which they exist (Miller, 2009).

However, a tension exists with the use of play in ECEC settings, as many forms of play are 'chosen but not freely, directed but not personally, motivated but not intrinsically' (Brown, 2008: 124). Some play experiences in ECEC can be over planned and used to conform to learning outcomes outlined in curriculum documents, rather than to meet the development needs of the child. In addition, according to Markstrom and Hallden (2009), there is often an over structuring of the day by the timetabling of events and activities and the need for evidence of learning for regulatory bodies such as HMIe, Care Inspectorate (Scotland)[1] and the Office for Standards in Education (Ofsted). This tension can result in the benefits of play for children's development being undermined and restricted. Therefore the role of the adult in children's play is crucial if children are to benefit from the positive opportunities and experiences play can provide.

The adult's role in play

As in all educational settings, the nursery needs to support children by creating an environment which allows them to feel safe, cared for and supported. Play is a fundamental part of children's holistic development and should be guided by children and supported by adults. ECEC encourages children's engagement in meaningful play by providing opportunities which allow children to experience positive interactions with both adults and peers. Ideally a balance is sought so that children benefit from both free play and adult-initiated play in order to develop social and cognitive skills (Sylva et al., 2004). Staff expect children to think critically and act with autonomy (Dunne, 2008) by seeking their opinions and involving the children in decision making, thus supporting and empowering children to develop and shape their world.

To effectively utilise play the child has to be at the centre of the learning experiences offered. If autonomy and choice are to be promoted in ECEC, children should be encouraged to contribute and engage with the planning of adult-led play. Staff can use floorbooks,[2] mind-mapping, picture/photo walls and discussions with children to plan and to identify children's interests. Planning also needs to make effective use of resources, including staff, and space to facilitate the learning experiences. Cohen and Uhry (2007) alert those who plan play to avoid solely using toys with specific purposes as they do not cultivate creative, imaginative, or collaborative learning. Opportunities for both free and adult-led play encourage problem solving, critical thinking, collaboration, negotiation and friendships whilst ensuring that the child's learning and developmental needs are supported.

In the two examples below, you are introduced to Seth and Ayesha who are happy in the nursery environment. The children's personal interests are used as the starting point for the planning of their learning and development. Interventions should not be overly prescriptive or imposed as these are more likely to fail.

View from practice: Seth

Seth is a quiet, happy 4-year-old. He has two older brothers. Mum and dad confirm that Seth is content to come to nursery and that at home he enjoys listening to stories and playing with toy cars and motorbikes.

Seth has been in the pre-school room for 2 months but has been in the nursery environment since the age of 2. He has settled well and enjoys playing on the climbing equipment and riding the bikes outside. He is sociable and has many friends in the nursery. He also enjoys story time, singing and playing with water and sand: However, staff have noticed that Seth's fine motor skills are still relatively immature.

Staff are considering Seth's development needs and wish to explore possible avenues to encourage play which will promote and develop Seth's fine motor skills.

Seth has been identified as requiring the development of his fine motor skills. These are the small fine movements that are made using the fine muscles in the hands which allow the use and control of different equipment, for example, pencils and scissors. The development of fine motor skills also requires the refinement of hand-eye coordination. This involves vision and hand movements working together. In early years there are substantial differences in the development of fine motor development among children; therefore the difficulties Seth is experiencing

Table 3.2 Matching activities to skills development (a)

Interest	Activity	Skill
Sand/water	Hiding objects in the sand/water and asking Seth to retrieve them.	Hand-eye co-ordination. Pincer grasp – finger and thumb working together to pick up small objects.
Stories	Turning pages of books. Finger puppets of the story characters. Placing objects relating to the story in play dough to be retrieved.	Hand-eye co-ordination. Isolation of finger movements, using one finger at a time. Hand-eye co-ordination and development of pincer grasp.
Singing songs	Playing instruments.	Holding instruments correctly and operating them; movements will depend on the instruments.
Playing with others	Pop the bubbles on large or small bubble pack with friends, pinching the bubbles with thumb and index finger.	Hand-eye co-ordination. Pincer grasp.
	Playing with play dough.	Rolling, pressing, cutting, etc. will help develop all muscles in the hands and all of the above skills.
	Collages, encouraging the use of scissors.	Hand-eye co-ordination. Pincer grasp.

are not uncommon. Most children develop their fine motor skills on their own; however, activities and adult support will also help with their development. Table 3.2 suggests a few activities relating to Seth's interests which can be used to develop his skills.

View from practice: Ayesha

Ayesha is 4, and she and her dad were born in the UK. Her mum is from India and does not speak English. The language spoken at home is Urdu and Ayesha, whilst having no developmental problems in her first language, has not had sufficient exposure to English to have developed confidence and proficiency. Dad says Ayesha enjoys singing and playing games at home.

Ayesha is in her pre-school year and has been in nursery for 2 months. She is a happy child who is content to play alongside others and will readily communicate with children who speak Urdu. She is also able to use non-verbal communication with children whose first language is English. However, she is not inclined to use any form of spoken language communication with staff, preferring to point or take staff to whatever she desires. Ayesha enjoys doing jigsaws, playing in the home corner, construction toys, singing songs and playing outside.

Staff are now reviewing Ayesha's development needs and they wish to explore possible avenues and activities to support her development of English.

The nursery staff have already established that the other children know how to pronounce Ayesha's name and whilst they encourage her to be involved in the life of the nursery they know it can be counterproductive to insist on speech too early. Ayesha needs to have time to 'tune in' to English. Key staff who work directly with Ayesha have learned some simple phrases, numbers, colours and greetings in Urdu. This demonstrates to Ayesha that her first language is valued and that she can still use it, which will allow her to feel more secure. Ayesha has already started to make friends with other children although she does not verbally communicate with all of them. The staff therefore wish to help support Ayesha's development of English. Like learning a first language, this needs to be supported and learned in a context, where practical meaningful experiences and interaction occur with others. Ayesha will need to spend time listening before she will start to speak English and it is likely that she will be able to understand much more of what is going on than she can express. Ayesha's English will develop through interaction with others but supporting this development through play opportunities which are planned will help

Table 3.3   Matching activities to skills development (b)

Interest	Activity	Skill
Games	Games which involve taking turns, e.g., picture lotto, picture snap.	Social interaction.
		Introduce new vocabulary.
	Sorting activities, by colour, shape or size.	Social vocabulary, e.g., please, thank you.
		Motivation to communicate.
	Matching activities.	Language is modelled by others.
Stories	Story tag lines which are repeated throughout the narrative.	Repetition helps with word recognition/meaning/context.
		Vocabulary development.
		Vocabulary development – learning to label objects.
	Picture books.	Language is modelled by staff/children.
		Social interaction.
Singing songs	Use repetitive choruses, rhymes and songs.	Repetition helps with word recognition/meaning/context.
		Vocabulary development.
		Social interaction.
Playing with others	Puppets.	Social interaction.
	Soft toys.	Using/experimenting with new vocabulary.
	Dressing up clothes.	Social language – please, thank you, etc.
	Construction toys.	Vocabulary development.
	Garden activities.	Vocabulary modelling.

this process and ensure that Ayesha does not feel isolated. Table 3.3 suggests some activities which can support Ayesha's development of English.

Thinking point

The activities listed in Tables 3.2 and 3.3 are not exhaustive and many more activities can be used to engage and develop the needs of both these children. What other play activities can you think of, using the children's interests and development needs, which will support each of these children?

Effective assessment in ECEC

It is also necessary to assess progress and identify next steps to ensure that the child is developing and learning. Assessment is a shared activity and is part of an ongoing process. Curricula have 'moved away from foregrounding developmental outcomes and deficit-based assessment to much broader-based learning goals and narrative assessment' (Whitty, 2010: 43). As such, assessment information gathered can be used for early intervention and prevention, as well as enrichment and development to support the child. Assessment generally serves four purposes:

- to identify children's needs;
- to discern the next steps in development and learning;
- to evaluate programmes and impact;
- to monitor and evaluate the quality of the setting's service.

Effective assessments should happen in the child's natural learning environment and the tasks should be familiar and appropriate. Assessments are not just the purview of the staff, but rather all those involved with the child, and including the child, should have a part in the process and consideration needs to be given to the family care setting and cultural environment in which the child is developing. Policy recognises the importance of engaging parents and carers in the process:

> Parents are children's first and most enduring educators. When parents and practitioners work together in early years settings, the results have a positive impact on children's development and learning. (EYFS, 2007, comment 2:2)

The process of assessment ensures that the child's progress is supported, and guides any interventions, choices and activities planned. Assessment is critical and includes observing and assessing behaviour and development. Genuine assessment is done when children are in their natural setting and performing real tasks. Observations should take place when the child has chosen the play activity; if the activity is imposed the observer is unlikely to get an accurate picture of the child's engagement or response to the activity. Observations of the child at self-initiated play allow the skills and knowledge developed during planned adult-led sessions or through self-discovery to be assessed. Observations should be kept short and positive and should be of something which the child has had previous experience. Assessments can be made by observing and documenting children's activities and interactions, as observations are in themselves tools for learning (Smidt, 2005). Observations can be:

- spontaneous: things observed about the children during the course of play activities;
- informal: an observation relating to a particular skill/development (observation is over a period of time (for example a week or a term) and is recorded when the focus occurs).

Knowing what and why observations are being done is important; however, it is also necessary to record the information collected. Organised systems to record observations help to ensure that progress or concerns are documented and should be built into the daily routine of the playroom. Recording information does not need to be complicated, for example, it might include the use of:

- a pencil and Post-it notes being readily available to allow short notes to be made; these are easily stored in a poly-pocket or a notebook and can be examined, considered or discussed later;
- a digital camera to record events, interactions, development of skills, such as riding a bike, climbing stairs;
- a video camera to record children in interactive situations, such as role play, co-operative play;
- a success-box, in which children place pictures or other creations that they are pleased with, thus allowing the child to self-assess and providing opportunities for peer assessment;
- floorbooks to record children's choices, ideas and involvement.

Assessments also ensure that the planned programmes are effective and that they are having a positive impact on the children. In addition, assessments may help to identify areas of development for staff, allowing staff to recognise and plan their own engagement with professional development opportunities. This helps to guarantee that the learning and developmental activities offered to the children are appropriately planned and supported by well-trained staff.

Identification and development of children's needs is a benefit of good ECEC provision; however, there is a danger that current policies have 'an increasing emphasis on children's academic outcomes ... and its "schoolification"' (OECD, 2006: 138). This places a focus on assessment which assumes standards about the 'normal' child (see, for example, James et al., 1998: 18–19) and has created an academic agenda for ECEC (Alasuutari and Karila, 2010). The emphasis on outcomes and 'schoolification' could arguably be to justify government investment and a desire to see a return for the financial support to provide places for pre-school children. It is argued that ECEC will improve children's school readiness, resulting in higher achievements in school, and a future increase of skills and employability, thereby generating productive and economically contributing future citizens (Heckman and Masterov, 2007). The danger that the agenda for ECEC becomes too focused on outcomes and school readiness requires that the fundamental principle of ECEC should be preserved, where children benefit from the opportunities to develop in a supportive, creative environment at their own stage and pace without fear of failure. ECEC should not be seen as just a preparation for school, rather it is a distinct and valuable experience, and is a source of enrichment, enjoyment and development for our youngest children.

Thinking point

- What are the benefits of assessment for children?
- Can you identify any drawbacks relating to assessment?
- What can be done to minimise these drawbacks?

Summary

In today's society, engaging children with learning at the earliest possible opportunity will help support the development of social, emotional and cognitive skills. ECEC has more recently been recognised as benefiting children's wellbeing, learning and social inclusion, and has both immediate and long-term economic benefits for children and their families. However, a child's time in ECEC should not be seen simply as a preparation for the next stage, school; it should be valued and appreciated for what it offers each individual child in the here and now.

ECEC is a non-compulsory provision where pre-school children are able to develop both cognitive and social skills. Staff plan learning through play using the child's individual experiences, allowing the child to build on their strengths and interests in order to learn and develop. All children can benefit from ECEC as it provides opportunities for every child to learn and develop in a safe and secure environment. Staff are committed and willing to involve families in the children's development and assessment. Assessments need to take place in relaxed natural situations and should be recorded so that next steps can be planned. Staff need to ensure that assessment does not become perfunctory, to meet regulatory standards, but rather ensure that assessments inform next steps in learning and development.

Reflective questions

- Can you identify the benefits of ECEC?
- What are the benefits of adult-led play and free play?
- What is the role of the adult in an ECEC setting?
- What is the purpose of assessment in ECEC? What can we learn from ECEC assessment strategies in primary school contexts?
- In what ways might we try to keep the child at the centre of the learning process in primary classrooms?

Further reading

Gammage, P. (2008) The social agenda and early childhood care and education: can we really help create a better world? *Online outreach paper 4. The Hague: Bernard van Leer Foundation, at:* http://www.bernardvanleer.org/The_social_agenda_and_early_childhood_care_and_education_Can_we_really_help_create_a_better_world

James, A. and James, A. (2004) *Constructing Childhood. Theory, Policy and Social Practice*. London: Palgrave. (This book examines how society's views about children have changed in terms of their place in society. It shows that children are social actors with a right to be consulted in relation to decisions which affect them.)

Smidt, S. (2005) *Observing, Assessing and Planning for Children in the Early Years*. Abingdon: Routledge. (This book will support practitioners in their daily practice to observe and plan further learning experiences for all children in the setting. It provides a variety of vignettes which demonstrate how children's interests and needs can be used to support children's learning.)

Sylva, K., Melhuish, E., Sammons, P. and Siraj-Blatchford, I. (2004) *Effective pre-school education*. London: DfES http://eprints.ioe.ac.uk/5309/1/sylva2004EPPEfinal.pdf (accessed 24 June 2013).

Nursery World: Online resource for all those working in Nurseries. http://www.nurseryworld.co.uk/

Notes

1. Formally known as Care Commission, which was set up in Scotland in April 2002 under the Regulation of Care (Scotland) Act 2001 to regulate all adult, child and independent healthcare services in Scotland.
2. Floorbooks are a record of children's ideas and thoughts. They are used for planning and recording, through pictures, photographs or adult notation of children's involvement in the process. Adults do not re-frame or re-interpret the children's thinking.

~~CHAP~~TER 4

MODELS OF TEACHING AND LEARNING

Mike Carroll

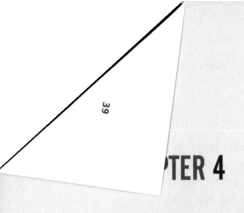

Key ideas

This chapter explores:

- behaviourist-influenced perspectives on teaching and learning;
- constructivist perspectives on teaching and learning;
- socio-constructivist perspectives on teaching and learning.

Introduction

Models of teaching and learning are rarely explicitly stated in official documentation. Despite this, they have influenced as well as determined government policy. Most of the recent reform efforts linked to raising standards within education in the United Kingdom have focused upon teaching rather than learning (MacGilchrist et al., 2004) with little understanding that teaching and learning are in fact interdependent. Arguably, policy makers assume that in getting the teaching right learning will automatically follow.

There are many different models of teaching and learning. This chapter will look at two broad approaches evident in many primary classrooms. The first approach can be termed the objectivist perspective, often referred to as the traditional approach. From an objectivist perspective knowledge is something that exists outside of the pupil. The objectivist perspective on learning has, in its most extreme form, developed a view of the curriculum-as-product, comprising a fixed body of knowledge that the pupil must come to know (Kelly, 2009). Within such a perspective the aim of education is to transmit the knowledge teachers have acquired to the pupil. The role of the teacher-as-expert is to serve as the conduit for the transfer of information, which is broken down into manageable 'chunks', through teacher-talk, worksheets and textbooks.

The converse of this transmissive approach to teaching and learning is the emerging social constructivist perspective which asserts that learning involves pupils making sense of learning experiences through discussion with others, so developing shared understandings. This leads to a view of the curriculum-as-process (Kelly, 2009) whereby the teacher's role is as a facilitator of the pupils' learning; this is often referred to as the progressive approach. These models are not mutually exclusive but rather represent a diversity of approach that lies at the heart of good quality teaching and learning.

Different ways of seeing pupils as learners

Bruner (1999) suggests that there are four models as to how teachers see pupils and the learning process. The adoption of any given model by a teacher is dependent upon the context in which the teacher is working. Bruner (1999) sees these models as being hierarchically arranged with the fourth model being seen as superior to the others. The four models are outlined below:

- *Seeing pupils as imitative learners* (acquisition of 'know how'): The teacher-as-expert transmits skills they have acquired to the pupil, who in turn absorbs the information received through imitation or practice.
- *Seeing pupils as learning from didactic exposure* (acquisition of 'know that'): Learning is something that happens to pupils through the actions of their teachers. The pupil's mind is seen as a *tabula rasa* (empty slate) onto which the teacher writes. Didactic teaching chunks the facts to be learned, remembered and applied. This model views pupils from the 'outside' rather than trying to understand what is happening internally. Learning follows a defined path, which is

linear and sequential in nature, with knowledge being fixed. The first two models are consistent with an objectivist perspective.

- *Seeing pupils as thinkers*: Pupils are seen as constructing their own meaning from experience with the teacher seeking to understand what pupils think and how they arrive at this thinking. The teacher's role is to alter the pupils' conceptions in order that they arrive at a shared understanding. This is achieved through active experience involving discussion. This model is more concerned with interpretation and understanding rather than with the acquisition of factual knowledge or skill performance. This is consistent with a constructivist perspective.
- *Seeing pupils as knowledgeable*: This model seeks to develop an awareness in pupils of the difference between personal knowledge and 'what is taken to be known' by the culture. Discussion is used to facilitate learning taking place in a socio-cultural context. The focus of learning is on understanding knowledge that has withstood scrutiny, having been tested and verified. This is consistent with a socio-cultural constructivist perspective.

The behaviourist-influenced perspective

Burrhus Frederic Skinner was primarily concerned with observable indications of learning and what these observations imply for teaching. Skinner focused on observable 'cause and effect' relationships by examining the relationship between stimulus (S) and response (R) bonds or connections (Jordan et al., 2008). Current-day thinking on the 'behavioural' aspects of teaching and learning through behaviour modification techniques can be linked to Skinner's work.

Within the classroom, appropriate pupil responses are acknowledged through a variety of praise systems (for example, ticks in jotters, verbal praise, smiley faces in jotters, good conduct awards, being given a special task or 'responsibility'). The assumption is that all pupils will strive to work towards achieving these rewards (or reinforcers) given that the instructional events being provided are appropriate to the stage of progression of the pupils. Those pupils who are unwilling to play the 'behaviour game' are classed as disruptive and deviant rather than as learners who are constructing a different and impoverished meaning from the experiences with which they are provided.

The Skinnerian perspective states that pupils learn best by being rewarded for 'right responses', or for responses that show evidence of having the potential eventually to lead to 'right responses'. Skinner's general principle stated that if the response is followed by a reinforcing stimulus the rate of responding will increase (Jordan et al., 2008). Skinner elaborated what he called the 'law of positive reinforcement', which includes the notion that pupils can be trained to replicate certain behaviours if they come to associate such behaviour with the receipt of tangible rewards. A positive reinforcement is any stimulus (reward) that when added, following a desired response, increases the likelihood that the response will occur (Jordan et al., 2008).

A negative reinforcement is any stimulus (punishment) that when removed, following a desired response, increases the likelihood that the response will occur. The converse of this is an aversive stimulus which is an unpleasant or painful stimulus (punishment) which seeks to extinguish an undesirable behaviour. Skinner was opposed to the use of aversive stimuli as they were, in his opinion, not very effective (Jordan et al., 2008). Your role, within such a perspective, would be to facilitate the modification of the pupils' behaviour by introducing situations which reinforce pupils when they exhibit desired responses.

Behaviourist thinking has become muddled with objectivist thinking leading to the notion that learning arises out of a transmissive, instructional approach which is teacher-directed involving whole-class didactic teaching. The pupil's mind is seen as an empty vessel to be filled with pupils having a passive role in the learning process. Knowledge is broken down into small chunks and transmitted in a coherent, ordered and logical way linked to tight control of classroom behaviour (Pollard, 2008).

Implications for practice

Two important insights have been derived from a behaviourist-influenced perspective: learning intentions and chunking. Providing pupils with specific learning intentions (or objectives) supports the pupils' understanding of what you want them to achieve. Feedback can then be used to support progressive movement towards achieving the specific learning intentions (SLIs). It is important that the SLIs describe learning, and not classroom activity, using action verbs drawing on Bloom's Taxonomy. (You may wish to look at Chapter 5 which examines planning in more detail.)

Chunking involves breaking down learning into carefully sequenced incremental steps (Jordan et al., 2008). Breaking learning down in this way has the advantage of achievability and provides the basis for planning instructional events (see below). This approach provides insights as to how it is possible for pupils to work step-by-step towards externally imposed goals through the use of highly structured materials. Initially you would determine what the pupil already knows and can do to establish a start point; thereafter, each time the pupil achieves a step in the learning sequence this would be rewarded with immediate positive feedback followed by moving onto the next step.

> **Thinking point**
>
> - What does this approach say about the nature of the teacher–pupil relationship?
> - How might this approach be useful in day-to-day teaching and learning in the classroom?

Planning instructional events

Robert Mills Gagné argued that the acquisition of knowledge is a process in which every new experience builds on a foundation established by previously learned experiences (Gagné, 1985). Gagné applied this thinking to the sequencing of instruction in the classroom. Your task as the teacher would be to identify learning tasks that will achieve a desired learning outcome. Within an instructional event it will be necessary to break down the learning into a planned sequence of sub-tasks by a process of learning task analysis.

Nine instructional events were identified (Gagné, 1985); the first five events are designed to facilitate the acquisition of knowledge, whilst the last four are designed to determine whether this knowledge has been processed. This would involve you in the following activities:

- *Gaining attention*: Present a problem or a new situation. Try to grab the pupils' attention so that they will watch and listen, while you present the learning point.
- *Inform pupils of the objective*: Allow the pupils time to organise their thoughts around what they are about to see, hear and do. Describe the goal of the lesson, state what the learners will be able to accomplish and how they will be able to use the knowledge.
- *Stimulate recall of prior learning*: Allow pupils to build on their previous knowledge or skills by reminding them of prior knowledge relevant to the current lesson.
- *Present the stimulus*: Chunk (break down and chain) the information to avoid memory overload.
- *Provide learning guidance*: Provide instructions on how to learn. The aim is to reduce time lost or confusion amongst the pupils who may base their performance on incorrect facts or poorly understood concepts.
- *Elicit performance*: Enable the learner to do something with the newly acquired behaviour, skill or knowledge.
- *Provide feedback*: Provide the learner with specific feedback (information) on their performance.
- *Assess performance*: Test to determine if the information has been learned.
- *Enhance retention and transfer*: Review the lesson, provide additional practice or present similar problems and link to future learning.

Implications for practice

In order not to demoralise or demotivate the learner, interfering with their steady progress, the instructional formats should, as far as possible, be 'error free'. Lessons should have a coherent structure, determined by the teacher through the production of a lesson plan which would 'fix' your words, questions to be asked and pupil activities in advance. Lesson planning normally involves you outlining the following:

1. Lesson title.
2. Curricular area(s) to be addressed.
3. Broad aim of the lesson linked to curricular framework.
4. Links to previous learning.
5. Specific learning intentions (using action verbs linked to Bloom's Taxonomy).
6. Success criteria statement(s) (linked to specific learning intentions).
7. Assessment of children's learning (how this will be achieved, for example, discussion, observation, questioning, task completion).
8. New skills, concepts or vocabulary to be introduced.
9. Feedback strategies (including opportunities for self and peer evaluation).
10. Health and safety requirements.
11. Structural elements and time allocations (introduction, main task(s) and plenary).
12. Chunking and sequencing of material:
    a. main concepts and key questions (your role);
    b. pupil activities and differentiation (pupils' role);
    c. resources linked to activities.
13. Evaluating effectiveness of lesson:
    a. children's learning;
    b. your teaching.
14. Next steps and modifications:
    a. children's learning;
    b. your teaching.

Thinking point

- As your career develops, detailed lesson planning should become the exception, not the rule. At your present stage of development how much detail do you feel is needed in writing lesson plans?
- What is the consequence if the intended learning objective is not achieved? How will you know? What will you need to do to ensure attainment?

View from practice

Following an observed lesson a university tutor commented to a student teacher that the pupils were being suffocated under a mountain of worksheets. The student had designed almost all of their mathematics lessons using a fairly simple structure:

- starter worksheet;
- worksheet(s) for main activity;
- plenary (test) worksheet; and
- additional worksheets for fast finishers.

It was evident that the lesson design followed a fairly rigid pattern whereby the student identified the learning objective(s), designed a learning experience to address the objective(s), broke down and sequenced the learning experience into manageable chunks and produced differentiated resources (worksheets) to support and verify knowledge acquisition. The student's evaluations invariably were positively framed and identified next steps in learning.

It was evident that the student had put in time and effort to get to know the pupils in terms of their mathematical capabilities and this was used to help design learning experiences matched to individual pupil needs. The student genuinely cared for the pupils. It was also evident that the student knew about the curricular content based on an understanding of the curriculum guidelines. These guidelines had been used to inform the materials and resources used to design the learning experiences.

The pupils' role throughout was to listen passively, memorise and then apply the knowledge provided to them by the student. For the student the acid test of successful teaching was that the worksheets provided concrete evidence that the pupils had attained the learning objectives. The student was also confident in their ability as they were able to demonstrate an impressive pace of curricular coverage.

The tutor's concern was not that they had observed a lesson designed according to objectivist principles but that this was the only way that the student could conceive of teaching mathematics. The tutor could not help but feel 'job done' but no fun! Clearly the conception of teaching and learning that we adopt can never be value neutral.

The constructivist perspective

Jean Piaget is best known for his work on the development of cognitive functions in children. Piagetian theory found favour in policy documents linked to primary education during the 1960s and 1970s (Moseley et al., 2005), with perhaps the two most influential reports being *Primary Education in Scotland* (SED, 1965, *The Primary Memorandum*) and *Children and their Primary Schools* (DES, 1967, *The Plowden Report*). Towards the end of the twentieth century, in stressing a 'progressive' pupil-centred pedagogy, Piagetian thinking came increasingly under attack from governments wishing to return to an objectivist paradigm (Barrow, 2005).

Cognitive (constructivist) learning theorists argue that an understanding of the internal processes of the pupil is critically important. Constructivism is a metaphor for learning which suggests that knowledge is 'constructed' by pupils. This differentiates it from views of education that presume that it is possible to transfer information directly into a pupil's mind. Constructivism asserts that real learning can only occur when the pupil is actively engaged in operating on or processing learning experiences facilitated by the teacher through play and active experimentation. Furthermore, the interpretation of these learning experiences depends on previous learning. The basic premises of constructivism are that:

• learning is an active and interactive process;
• knowledge is constructed, not transmitted;
• prior knowledge has an impact on the learning process;
• learning is essentially a process of making sense of the world;
• effective learning requires meaningful, open-ended and challenging problems for the learner to solve (adapted from Fox, 2001).

Stages of cognitive development

Piaget asserted that thinking patterns evolve through a series of stages, linked to specific age ranges, in which cognitive structures become progressively more complex. Contemporary thinking on this age-and-stage model suggests that individual pupils go through the stages at different rates. Piaget postulated four stages of cognitive development (Woolfolk, 2007) which have influenced 'age-and-stage' thinking in policy documents linked to primary education:

• The sensorimotor stage (0 to 2 years).

  Towards the end of this period the child, by exploring the world through sensory experiences and movement, begins to represent the world in terms of mental images and symbols through the acquisition of basic language.

• The pre-operational stage (2 to 7 years)

  The pre-operational stage is sub-divided into pre-conceptual and intuitive stages:

  o The pre-conceptual child (2 to 4 years) is unable to abstract and discriminate the attributes of a concept: inductive reasoning. Neither can the child use deductive ways of thinking. Instead they use what Piaget terms transductive reasoning, going from one specific instance to another specific instance, so forming pre-concepts.

o The intuitive child (4 to 7 years) considers only one variable of a situation at a time to the exclusion of all other aspects. In the Piagetian framework this is called centring.

- The concrete-operational stage (7 to 11 years)

  The child begins to think hypothetically where two or more variables can be considered at once. However, there may still be a tendency to adjust the facts to meet the hypothesis: an assumptive reality. The development of logic structures continues to require concrete experience so that logic can be applied.

- The formal-operational stage (11 years onwards)

  During this period the child starts to use abstract reasoning. Abstract hypotheses can be built along with the capability to hold some variables constant while manipulating other variables in order to determine their influence. Analytical and logical thought no longer requires reference to concrete examples.

For Piaget the development of human intellect proceeds through a process of adaptation to the environment. Adaptation becomes necessary when pupils are confronted with new knowledge leading to cognitive conflict. Two complementary processes help to resolve cognitive conflict: assimilation and accommodation. When a new experience is incorporated alongside existing knowledge, assimilation is said to occur. The pupil's thinking does not really change as a result of assimilation. When new experiences require an adjustment to take place in a pupil's thinking then accommodation is said to occur. Assimilation and accommodation act together to bring about cognitive equilibrium or internalisation of new learning.

Implications for practice

The translation of Piaget's ideas into the classroom has proved to be difficult as his theoretical framework does not offer much by way of pedagogy, despite being linked to the notion of pupil-centred education. A key insight is that teachers should design learning activities that are practical and experimental in nature. This has encouraged some teachers to opt out from teaching 'difficult ideas', until the pupils are intellectually ready (Moseley et al., 2005). The notion of 'readiness' has been used to argue that any attempt to 'accelerate learning' across the stages is ultimately futile, or at best will only have a marginal effect, as development can only take place when the pupil has the cognitive structures in place to assimilate new experience.

Teachers influenced by the constructivist perspective provide pupils with opportunities to experience learning as an active, social process of making sense of experience; as opposed to 'instruction' whereby pupils are given facts and theories. This is not to say that facts are not important, but rather it is the context in which they are examined which is important within a constructivist perspective. Teachers engage pupils in their learning (hands-on, minds-on) through creating stimulating classroom environments containing centres of interest such as the 'shop corner' to stimulate a classroom culture of inquiry. Pupils can determine for themselves the focus and pace for their learning through pupil-chosen topics (Pollard, 2008) so promoting high levels of motivation. Such an approach tends to promote concept and skill acquistion at the expense of curricular coverage.

Discovery learning

Jerome Seymour Bruner provides a number of important insights as to how teachers can improve learning experiences. Bruner (1960) suggests that it is possible to identify, break down and sequence the structural components of any body of knowledge in order that it may be passed on and understood by almost any pupil. Bruner (1960) also asserts that schools waste a great deal of the pupil's time by postponing the teaching of important areas because they are deemed to be 'too difficult'.

Bruner's idea of the spiral curriculum involves pupils engaged in learning experiences revisiting previous experiences, through repetition and revision, to allow for gradual progression (Bruner, 1960). Within such a curriculum the pupil constantly revisits 'previous' learning and understandings in order to assist the development of 'new' learning and understandings; consequently learning is not a linear process!

Bruner (1961) also advocates that pupils should be provided with opportunities to develop their understanding through experience with the environment. Rather than being 'given' answers pupils should 'find out for themselves' through discovery learning (Bruner, 1961). However, Bruner does not advance the argument that pupils are involved in 'discovering' solutions to problems which run counter to established thinking. What is being suggested is a problem-solving methodology which is more likely to lead to a deeper level of understanding than would be possible by a transmissive methodology. This approach is more demanding of the teacher as it involves learning with the focus being on ideas and thinking rather than on facts.

Implications for practice

Bruner suggests that instructional events should incorporate 'discovery learning' techniques as they are more likely to promote learning by providing pupils with opportunities to search for solutions and meaning through the exploration of alternatives. Developing problem-solving activities which are challenging but for which solutions are achievable becomes the key task for teachers. These activities should be integrated with the pupil's knowledge base, establishing links with previous learning. Problem-solving activities are more likely to activate the pupil's curiosity and encourage them to explore.

Bruner argues that developing an interest in the material to be learned is the best stimulus to learning. Bruner accepts that reinforcement has a role to play in supporting learning; however, external motivation has a short-lived effect upon learning. The will and drive to learn can only be maintained through intrinsic motivation. This can either be already present in the individual or, more importantly, arise out of an interest in the activity itself.

The significance of intrinsic and extrinsic motivation should not be lost within the classroom where it is essential that teachers present pupils with tasks that will stimulate their interest, as well as ensuring that this interest is sustained. This may well involve the teacher in assisting the pupils in 'seeing' the relevance of the task by projecting beyond the task itself and establishing a link to future learning. Watkins et al. (2001) developed this thinking by distinguishing between 'metacognition' and 'meta-learning'. The former is essentially 'thinking about thinking', suggesting that it is important for learners to have a sense of control over their own learning. Meta-learning is a much broader concept involving an awareness of the goals, feelings, social relations and the context of learning (Watkins et al., 2001).

The socio-constructivist perspective

Lev Vygotsky was interested in understanding the socio-cultural context of cognitive development and, in particular, the role of language in the development of learning. The Vygotskian perspective asserts that pupils' development is affected by the social environment or culture in which they live. In simple terms this culture is responsible for teaching the pupil not only what to think, but how to think. Pupils come to understand through collaborative social engagement. Knowledge is not merely handed-on, nor is it discovered by the pupil, but rather it is part of a process of co-construction.

This co-construction takes place through problem-solving activity that enables pupils progressively to access the world of knowledge that is initially beyond them, but of which they are a part. Learning takes place when internalisation occurs; this is the process whereby the social becomes the psychological: from the interpsychological plane (between you and others) to the intrapsychological plane (inside yourself) (Jarvis, 2005).

Vygotsky also rejected the Piagetian idea that learning must wait for development to take place. Vygotsky asserted that pupils are capable of learning within a zone of proximal development (ZPD). The ZPD is the difference between actual development as determined by independent problem solving and the level of potential development as determined by problem solving under adult, or more able peer guidance (Woolfolk, 2007). This gives rise to the notion of the more knowledgeable other (MKO) as someone who supports pupils towards higher levels of attainment than they would be capable of working alone.

Learning and development therefore is a social and collaborative activity that cannot be 'taught' to anyone. It is up to pupils to construct their own understanding in their own minds, supported through social interaction. The teacher has a crucial role to play in this by designing appropriate activities and experiences which involve discussion.

From a Vygotskian perspective any activity which seeks to do little more than transmit knowledge should be avoided. Discussion is central to this process enabling us to share and co-construct meaning supported by social interaction. For Vygotsky the pupil's ongoing interaction with the social world will lead to the development of an ever more complex view of reality; along with the development of their language skills which become the primary tool of intellectual adaptation.

View from practice

A newly qualified teacher sought to use an understanding of socio-constructivism in the classroom by creating a learning environment in which the pupils were encouraged to participate actively in their learning through dialogue. In designing learning experiences the teacher thought carefully about what was referred to as the interactional matrix by planning and structuring talk linked to the specific learning intentions. This matrix was an integral part of the classroom organisation and was intimately linked to the relational climate the teacher sought to create in the following ways:

- Whole-class teaching – question and answer sessions were planned to be supportive with pupils being encouraged to contribute ideas without fear of embarrassment over giving a 'wrong' answer. The teacher used a variety of no-hands techniques, such as names on lollipop sticks. Question and answer sessions were also cumulative in nature as the teacher used a variety of bounce techniques (moving from child to child), such as phone-a-friend, so allowing pupils to build upon each other's responses.

(Continued)

(Continued)

- One-to-one – teacher and pupil interactions during which individual pupils were encouraged to contribute and extend their answers by being challenged to think in different ways. The teacher provided feedforward by giving the pupil specific information focused on helping to inform and project the pupil's thinking forward. The teacher had a poster on the wall which stated 'We thrive on information!'
- One-to-one – the pupils had a designated shoulder partner whom they regularly consulted using techniques such as Think-Pair-Share (described in the chapter on collaborative learning). The pupils were encouraged to listen to each other, share and link their ideas, so leading to much fuller answers rather than partial and fragmented understandings.
- Group work – used periodically to provide opportunities for collective learning. The pupils 'replicated' many of the techniques modelled by the teacher in pupil–pupil exchanges enabling them to consider alternative viewpoints and link together their understandings in order to devlop a much fuller response to the task set.

Implications for practice

According to Vygotsky, learning is possible only when the teacher presents the pupil with a problem to be solved. In working towards a solution it is necessary to provide substantial opportunities for discussion, stressing the importance of language in the classroom situation. Discussion is used as a tool to enable pupils, working collectively, to negotiate a change in their thinking. As discussion is a key feature the classroom can often appear to be 'noisy'.

Pupils learn through problem-solving activity, supported by more knowledgeable others, including their teacher. The support provided is called scaffolding, a term developed by Wood et al. (1976). Scaffolds can include focused questioning, prompts, hints, think-aloud time and direct instruction (Hartman, 2002). This support should only be provided when the pupil requires assistance to bridge the gap between actual and potential development (ZPD). This support does not alter the nature of the task but rather enables pupil participation through graduated assistance (Hodson and Hodson, 1998). Crucially, this support is temporary and should be gradually removed as the pupil achieves success. Consequently teacher–pupil interaction becomes a dynamic process with the teacher constantly gauging when support is needed, the nature of support required, how much support is needed as well as considering when and how to progressively remove the scaffolding. Scaffolding suggests that learners, with assistance, are capable of performing tasks that they would not be capable of without support.

Thinking point

- Consider ways in which the learning environment can be constructed to incorporate the notion of the ZPD.
- Personalisation of the curriculum implies that teachers should also individualise scaffolds in their classroom. What do you see as the implications of such an approach?

Cognitive acceleration

Adey and Shayer's (1994) work utilised the Piagetian framework as well as drawing upon Vygotsky's work to develop cognitive acceleration teaching strategies. Adey and Shayer (1994) demonstrated that it was possible to 'accelerate' or support learning by providing pupils with general thinking strategies. Shayer and Adey (2002) outlined 'six pillars' of cognitive acceleration consisting of:

- *schema theory*: this is a general way of thinking, linked to Piaget's concrete operations, which can be utilised in a variety of contexts;
- *concrete preparation*: this is the context, including the language to be used, within which problems are set;
- *cognitive conflict*: the activities set contain challenges which are sufficiently difficult that pupils will be unable to achieve a resolution of the challenge without support (or scaffolding). In the process of assimilation aided by support new conceptual frameworks are 'constructed';
- *social construction*: cognitive acceleration approaches encourage pupils to describe and explain their thinking in relation to new ideas and to engage in group discussions in order to support individuals in reaching new understandings;
- *metacognition*: following the completion of a problem-solving activity pupils are encouraged to make their thinking processes explicit;
- *bridging*: once a new understanding has been reached within one context pupils are encouraged to consider other contexts into which this new understanding can be translated.

Implications for practice

Adey and Shayer (1994, 2002) argued that these 'six pillars' enable pupils to discover ways of thinking which will bring about solutions to problems. To achieve this teachers design a three stage action consisting of:

- *concrete preparation phase*: during this initial phase pupils are introduced to the problem-solving activity. Some construction may be necessary in terms of clarifying the nature of the activity or in making connections (bridging) with previous learning;
- *collaborative construction phase*: working in groups, pupils attempt to outline a solution to the problems using a variety of idea-generating techniques such as brainstorming, supported by tactical questioning by the teacher as they move around the groups;
- *presentation and distillation of ideas phase*: as each group presents their 'solutions' to the whole class group, many of which may be incomplete. They are engaged in discussion which seeks to identify the key elements of the learning experience as well as facilitating metacognition.

Summary

The objectivist perspective points to the importance of articulating the learning objectives, success criteria and providing pupils with feedback on their learning, that is, information which indicates pupils' progress in achieving the learning objectives. Gagné provides us with an insight as to how to design appropriate learning activities by chunking and sequencing tasks in order to enable all pupils to access learning. The Piagetian perspective provides a model of cognitive development whilst the Vygotskian perspective provides a model of the social aspect of this development. Adey and Shayer (1994, 2002) offer an insight into a teaching strategy, synthesising the Piagetian and Vygotskian perspectives, that is social and collaborative in nature with pupils internalising the mental processes initially made evident in social activities. The teacher has a crucial role to play in designing appropriate activities, involving discussion as well as providing support or 'scaffolding' for effective learning.

         Reflective questions

- The objectivist perspective suggests that it is possible for information to be broken down into bite-sized bits, sequenced and then taught to the whole class. What are the implications of this for teaching and learning in an inclusive classroom?
- The lesson plan is a basic route map through a learning experience rather than a detailed description of the terrain. Consider why it is important for teachers

to have a rough idea of where the lesson will take learning whilst at the same time having sufficient flexibility to accommodate teachable moments.
- Consider the implications of the (socio-) constructivist perspective for pupils who require support and structure to their learning experiences. Consider the implications of this approach for teachers in planning learning experiences.

Further reading

Jarvis, M. (2005) *The Psychology of Effective Learning and Teaching*. Cheltenham: Nelson Thornes.

Jordan, A., Carlile, O. and Stack, A. (2008) *Approaches to Learning*. Maidenhead: Open University Press.

Woolfolk, A. (2013) *Educational Psychology (Twelfth Edition)*. Boston, MA: Pearson.

CHAPTER 5

PLANNING FOR LEARNING AND TEACHING IN THE PRIMARY CLASSROOM

Maureen Farrell and A. Graeme Pate

> ### Key ideas
>
> **This chapter explores:**
>
> - the purpose of lesson plans, examines their history and considers who makes use of them;
> - how lesson plans fit into the current educational context and probes the strengths and weaknesses of some planning formats;
> - suggestions for what might be considered the essential elements of a lesson plan and links this to some views from practice;
> - the importance and place of learning intentions and an examination of the reflective practice required when planning a lesson.

Introduction

Planning for learning, or 'lesson planning' as it is usually called, is one of the elements which most beginning teachers are concerned about and often struggle to manage in the early stages of development. Almost all initial teacher education programmes will have developed their own lesson plan templates or guidelines for you as a student teacher to use on placement. Often these templates will be fairly rigidly imposed at the start of programmes but, as you become more familiar with the process, you will be encouraged either to develop your own planning templates or to employ those used in your placement schools. That said, it is true that even the most meticulously planned learning experiences can and do go wrong, and this can be discouraging. This chapter explores some of the most common planning mechanisms and discusses their role in the success of lesson implementation. It also considers some developmental changes which might provide more effective and less time-consuming alternatives while still providing the necessary information to help develop teaching and deliver engaging learning.

Thinking point

- We have all had experiences where something we have organised hasn't gone according to plan. Reflect on one of these experiences. What was the first indication something wasn't going according to plan? How did you react? What did you do?
- If you could go back in time and re-live that experience, what might you do differently?

A historical perspective

Lesson plans have featured in teacher education programmes since R.W. Tyler's 1949 work *Basic Principles of Curriculum and Instruction*. His predominantly linear lesson planning format stipulated four components: specifying lesson objectives; selecting learning experiences for attaining objectives; organising learning experiences and evaluating learning experiences. The result of this, perfectly logical, focus is that lesson planning templates or guidelines tend to look remarkably similar. While there is no difficulty with that in itself, one criticism is that it can result in unnecessarily rigid views of lesson structure and such templates could be considered as 'box-completion' exercises. This particular approach to lesson planning does not take account of recent changes to educational curricula, to the methods of teacher education, to advances in technology and to changes in teacher accountability and even to society itself. Recently, scholars have called for a much more flexible approach to planning (John, 1991, 1992, 2006). What is not called into question, though, is the need for some form of planning.

Undoubtedly lesson plans in an agreed format have a certain elegant simplicity. A further argument suggests that beginning teachers should be able to plan within traditional frameworks before attempting more ambitious or innovative planning methods. Lending weight to this is the fact that the professional standards for teachers which govern teacher education, now appearing in many countries, always include a planning element as a central requirement. As a beginning teacher you may also find it reassuring to have something written down on paper in advance of implementing the lesson. However, this can sometimes be seen as a means of ensuring effective classroom performance or even of mastery of a set of classroom management skills and teaching strategies which can be employed irrespective of curriculum content or the purpose of the lesson. Another common issue is that beginning teachers can often seem to be more interested in the product of lesson planning rather than the process. Of central importance in the process of lesson planning is that the practice of planning is as important as the practice of teaching. It is through planning that we learn to teach and through teaching that we learn to plan. You will also need to develop a realistic understanding of what lesson planning can and cannot achieve. A lesson plan meticulously prepared on paper and in advance is of little use if it cannot be implemented meaningfully in a classroom.

The current context

Before examining some planning formats in depth it would be useful to establish what we are taking as a set of 'givens'. Good teaching does not rely on one specific curriculum or another; good teaching is 'portable'. In other words, once you are able to plan, implement and evaluate good teaching in one context, it should be transferable to any other context. However, for that to happen skills must be developed which will allow you to plan for any eventuality and in any context, circumstance or location. Experience and research suggests that central to effective planning and teaching is the need for reflection at all stages. This will be discussed in some detail later in the chapter.

In Tyler's (1949) original book he refers to planning learning experiences and we have opted to use that terminology rather than talking about lesson plans. Learning experience plans (or LEPs) can cover single lessons or a combination of lessons which are linked in some way, either through curricular, topical or conceptual links and, therefore, allow both short- and medium-term planning. Central to the development of an effectively organised group of learning experiences are the elements of continuity, sequencing and integration.

The purpose of planning

Why should all the professional standards include a requirement for planning?

Most teachers, when questioned, will state that the level of planning they undertook while studying to *become* a teacher was far greater than the level of planning they currently do as *qualified* teachers. However, they had to go through the process so that such planning mechanisms could become embedded, allowing for an abbreviated but equally effective level of planning.

Let us now consider for whom plans are intended. Learning experience plans are useful to beginning teachers, teacher mentors and class teachers, university tutors, head teachers, classroom assistants and school inspectors, to name a few. Each of these people will use the LEPs for different reasons. For you as a beginning teacher, LEPs provide a mechanism which allows you to meet the needs of learners and the demands of curricular content. Such a plan, one which explicates associated pedagogical reasoning, is very different from simply 'doing teaching'. More practically, LEPs offer support in coping with the immediate demands of lessons, can contribute to improved confidence and provide an ability to deal with the unexpected elements which often happen in a classroom. Alternatively, if LEPs are not available, this can lead to teaching which loses direction or focus, inappropriate methods being implemented, time being wasted and possible class management issues. For other audiences, LEPs provide evidence of your understanding of lesson content as well as providing evidence of your ability to:

- identify appropriate lesson content for the learners;
- develop coherent and relevant lesson sequences;
- consider appropriate differentiated learning;
- convert theory into practice;
- match learning and assessment processes;
- reflect meaningfully on the learning.

This latter element cannot be over-estimated. Reflection can result in metacognitive awareness of planning, something which is particularly desirable in beginning teachers as it contributes to an understanding of the complexity and comprehensiveness of the planning process. Additionally, LEPs can be used by other teachers to cover for staff absences or to disseminate good practice within a learning community. For those in management or with a responsibility for evaluation and assessment in schools, LEPs can provide evidence of coverage of subject knowledge, coherence and cohesion in the development of learning, and illustration of whether the implementation of the learning matches the written plans.

 Thinking point

- It is likely you have already had some experience of planning and implementing a lesson. Review these plans and identify if you have evidence of the bullet points above. For each bullet point, reflect on what the impact would be if it was not evident in your planning.

Strengths and weakness of planning formats

The existence of lesson planning templates or guidelines has been mentioned earlier and for some beginning teachers these become lifelines which help them get through the very earliest of stages in their teaching career. If headings are given in the template, the learning experience can follow a structure which others have designated as satisfactory and can act as a useful aide-memoire at the implementation stage. Such templates are often particularly useful in the time management elements of lesson implementation. However, these same templates can also be regarded as formulaic, restrictive and over-simplified, closing down rather than supporting creative and imaginative approaches to learning. Using an LEP template could lead to ritualistic lessons and a narrow approach to the topic or subject which, in turn, can have the effect of limiting opportunities for responsive planning. Additionally, it is well known that actually implementing a learning experience often takes far longer than anticipated. If timings are included in LEPs, this can sometimes result in the balance of the learning experience being inappropriately skewed.

More appropriate and useful LEP formats should be more flexible and anticipatory, taking cognisance of the fact that there is often more than one way to solve a problem and more than one way that subject content can be learned. That lesson plans on paper seldom match the reality of the classroom is something most beginning teachers learn quite quickly. This is often the result of a discrepancy between the expectations of the planned learning activities and how they worked in practice. Consequently any effective LEP should take account of the diversity of learners and teachers and should consider the use of flexible curricular material and activities which provide alternatives for learners of different abilities. Research has shown that the rational planning model, while important theoretically, bears little resemblance to the thinking and actions of beginning teachers in the classroom (Zazkis et al.,

2009). More attention needs to be paid to the context of planning and how variations in context affect the type of planning chosen by the beginning teacher. Planning also has to be flexible enough to take account of learners' responses.

Contemporary planning mechanisms

In this chapter, lesson planning is presented as an all-inclusive concept which takes us from the learning context, the learning content, the strategies used and the assessment of the learning right through to the reflection on the learning experience. Writing an LEP is not something that happens in isolation. There is a process involved of preparation, implementation and reflection. Sometimes lesson planning can be regarded as a means of ensuring effective classroom performance rather than ensuring effective learning. This could cause you to lapse into a description of classroom procedures rather than presenting an outline of learning targets and the process of achieving them.

In current models of lesson planning, where reflection is included in the template, it is often a retrospective element which occurs after the lesson has been implemented. While retrospective reflection on lesson plans is an essential element, it is important to note there are other types of reflection which contribute significantly to the development of effective LEPs and thus contribute more substantially to the evolution of reflective practitioners in teaching. The first of these is 'reflection-before-action' (Van Manen, 1991).

Van Manen describes 'anticipatory reflection' which focuses on planning which is future-oriented. In terms of learning experience planning, this covers:

- consideration of what has to be taught – the lesson content;
- consideration of how it will be taught – the strategies; selection or development of resources to support the learning;
- consideration of the sequencing of the learning;
- consideration of the differentiation strategies which should be included;
- identification of both assessment purposes and instruments.

Such reflection anticipates the unexpected and acknowledges the need for flexibility. For example, what if the internet is down when you have identified its use as being essential to the learning? What if the interactive whiteboard is not working? Have you planned an effective alternative?

The next type of reflection occurs during the implementation phase of the lesson. Reflection-in-action could also be termed 'thinking on your feet' (Schön, 1983: 54) or contemporaneous reflection. You have an LEP guideline prepared, reflection-in-action occurs as the lesson unfolds and will take notice of:

- pacing and timing;
- management of behaviour;
- evaluation of the learners' understanding of the tasks;
- distribution and use of resources;
- evaluation of the lesson structure and management of the unexpected.

For instance, what happens if your lesson is disrupted because a fire alarm has sounded? This type of reflection will also contribute significantly to the next steps section of planning because you will have been taking note of the effectiveness of your planning as it happened.

The final type of reflection is termed reflection-after-action and this is the more traditional type of reflection which many lesson-planning templates utilise. This is the process of reflecting back on what happened and comparing it to what you had anticipated. As you become more familiar with the planning process you will inevitably find that your reflection-before-action and reflection-after-action will become increasingly close as you anticipate the learning experience with greater knowledge and skill. In this type of reflection it is helpful to consider:

- what happened from the perspective of the learner: what worked well and was successful/what did not work and could be achieved more successfully or differently;
- what happened from the perspective of the teacher: what worked well and was successful/what did not work and could be achieved more successfully or differently.

In each case this reflection should also include actions for the next steps both in the learning and the planning. Throughout the process of reflection, as a beginning teacher you should aim to make direct reference to academic reading and research and, in particular, to demonstrate how theory has been translated into practice, as well as evaluating the relative success of the learning experience in terms of learner behaviour. Looking back in the reflective sense is about gaining reflective distance to understand better the lived experience.

Thinking point

- Reflecting-after-action or 'after the fact' is the more traditional type of reflection. Reflection in action, however, is more challenging. What are the implications, both positively and negatively, if your reflection-in-action leads to an immediate change in what you are teaching (and what the children are learning)?

Essential elements of learning experience plans

While there has been relative stability and conformity in guidelines for lesson plans until now, current thinking seems to suggest that the time is right for change. Rather than thinking about what elements should be included in any LEP shell, let us begin by asking ourselves what essential information we would find useful to include in an LEP, remembering what has been said about rigid templates sometimes causing the creative, problem-solving, 'intelligent' aspects of planning and teaching to become lost. This becomes an example of reflection-before-action. It is essential that we are clear about the following issues:

- *What is being learned?* This includes both a general identification of the subject or topic or skill and a clear indication of the focus of learning. For example, the subject is mathematics and the particular skill being taught or developed is information handling. This also might include information about how this section of the learning fits in to a longer-term plan.
- *How are the learners going to learn this?* This encompasses both the organisation of the learning and the methodology, and will include information about the learning activities. For example, will your teaching strategy be expository, didactic, constructivist? Will your approach be teacher-centred, child-centred, authoritative or facilitating? Will there be active learning, collaborative learning or experiential learning? This will also require you to think about making the learning accessible to all the pupils so you may have to consider using several strategies.
- *Evidence of learning.* How will the learning be recorded? How will you (and they) know they have learned? What kind of evidence will you need? This suggests you should include information on success criteria. This might include specific information and 'threshold' information, such as learning intentions ('We are learning to say or recognise the numbers we write down...') and success criteria ('We can tell someone the names of all these numbers...'). In this example the threshold information might include whether the children have to get every example correct or whether they would still be considered to have achieved success if they only get the names of the numbers right half the time. In planning this section you will also have to judge how well your objectives have been achieved. Who achieved them – and who did not?
- *Assessing the learning.* Will the assessment be summative or formative, formal or informal? In this case you are identifying the specific element to be assessed as well as the type and purpose of assessment. You may also wish to include information about the instrument of assessment. For example, pupils may be asked to produce a newspaper report in a writing lesson. This is the product but what can be assessed using this, either summatively or formatively, is the pupils' ability to distinguish fact from fiction, the ability to sequence information and perhaps

the ability to incorporate quotations within a report depending on the aspects that you have targeted.

- *Next steps.* This section of the plan will make use of the previous two sections and will require you to think about what you are going to do with what you have found out and how this will feed into the learning and teaching cycle.
- *Evaluation.* This section requires you to step back and consider the way the lesson was implemented and allows you to comment on the effectiveness of the teaching for the children and for you. There is need for great care in this section because what can happen is that beginning teachers base their evaluation on fairly crude assumptions of what constitutes a 'good' lesson. These assumptions can focus on pupil enjoyment, behaviour management and 'smoothness' of delivery and are therefore rather superficial and utilitarian and not genuinely analytical.
- *Assessing your plan.* The final step at this stage of development is considering how well your planning worked. What changes would you make to both the planning – reflecting back on the LEP and the implementation – and the teaching? What effect will this have on any future LEPs?

  View from practice

A student teacher was asked by the class teacher to teach a lesson to 6-year-olds about Little Red Riding Hood.

The student teacher's learning intentions were for the children to:

- listen to the story of Little Red Riding Hood;
- draw a scene from the story;
- complete their work on time.

The student teacher determined that the learners would be successful if they had:

- enjoyed the story;
- concentrated on the drawing task;
- drawn a picture which showed a scene from the story.

The student teacher's plan was to remind the children of the story of the Three Billy Goats Gruff which had been read to them the previous week. Next, the story of Little Red Riding Hood would be read to them, after which the children would be given a sheet of A4 paper and some crayons in order to draw a picture depicting a scene from the story. At the end of the learning experience, the pictures would be collected and the best drawings would be displayed on the wall.

Having taught this learning experience, the student teacher recorded the following assessment:

> The children enjoyed the lesson. Almost all of them drew the wolf in bed dressed as the grandmother. The rest of them drew Little Red Riding Hood walking in the forest. For the next lesson, I will read the story of The Boy who Cried Wolf.

The student teacher wrote the following self-evaluation:

> The children enjoyed the lesson. They all concentrated on their drawings and I managed to go around to see all the children's work. Some of the children were very chatty. Once they were all on task I was able to go to the teacher's desk and mark the numeracy worksheets from this morning. I feel this was good management of my time. In future, I will make sure all the children are quiet when they are working independently.

In a subsequent discussion with the tutor, the student teacher was surprised to learn that the tutor was extremely concerned about the planning. If you were this student teacher's tutor, and based on what you have read in this chapter, what comments would you give about:

- learning intentions;
- evidence of success;
- the implementation of the lesson (i.e., the delivery of the lesson);
- assessment of the learners' learning;
- self-evaluation.

Fine detail

The previous section comprised of what we have called the essential elements – broad categories which should be considered when planning learning. Some of these can be broken down further. For example, in determining what is to be learned we need to consider whether we are thinking about one lesson or a series of linked lessons. Consequently we begin to think in terms of aims (longer-term goals for learning) and learning intentions (the targets for particular lessons). You may also see these referred to elsewhere as learning objectives or learning outcomes. The latter seems to us to presuppose success, which is not always the case, so we prefer the idea of identifying learning intentions.

Many beginning teachers find the formulation of learning intentions particularly difficult yet modern pedagogy recommends that these are shared with the learners, so getting them right is really important. Using learning intentions helps students develop a picture of what is expected of them from the learning. Black and Wiliam (1998a) suggest that students who have such an overview are more committed and more effective as learners and they also discuss their assessments with teachers and peers.

Another frequent issue with learning intentions is that beginners frequently express them in terms of action – what the learners are doing rather than what they are learning. Think back to the earlier example of writing a newspaper report. It is not the report itself that constitutes the learning but the skills involved in producing it; if the learning intentions are clearly and explicitly identified this focuses the learning and also makes identification of success criteria that much easier.

View from practice

A student teacher has been working with a class of seven and eight year olds on a project with a music focus. This has resulted in the children being exposed to many different types of music and in particular focusing on different instruments and the sounds they make. Recently they have been researching brass bands. The student teacher has arranged for a local brass band to come to the school to play for the children and let them see and examine the various instruments. The lesson plan for this lesson includes the following specific learning intentions:
The children will:

- listen to the music of a brass band;
- interact with the brass band;
- understand how brass band music is different from other kinds of music.

The children are assembled in the hall with their notebooks and eagerly anticipating the mini-concert when a message arrives that the band bus has broken down and the concert is postponed. As the learning intentions currently stand, the student teacher will need to postpone the lesson because of the way the specific learning intentions have been formulated. If the learning intentions

had been focused on the **learning** rather than the **doing**, the student teacher still might have been able to substitute a classroom-based learning experience with achievable learning intentions.
   Consider:

- How might the specific learning intentions be revised? (You may also wish to consider some of the verbs used and think about what the success criteria might be.)
- How could you quickly devise a classroom lesson to implement the revised specific learning intentions? What might such a lesson look like? How could you link it effectively with the re-scheduled brass band visit? How would you record the changed activity, linked to the specific learning intentions, in the lesson evaluation section?

As previously mentioned, it is easy, particularly for beginning teachers, to focus on what the children are doing rather than what they are learning. There are a number of difficulties with this approach.

During a lesson, you may realise that you need to make changes, perhaps because the work you have given is too challenging or because materials aren't available. If your plans focus on what the children are doing, it is very difficult to modify the lesson and have the same result. However, if your plans focus on what the children are learning, you can change the activity and still have the children learn what you intended.

Using the view from practice given above, if your planned learning intention focuses on what the children are doing (interacting with the brass band in the hall), the learning intentions cannot be achieved. If, however, the learning intention focuses on what the children are learning (identifying instruments in a brass band), a quickly organised classroom-based lesson using pictures of the instruments (found online along with some sounds, for example) would still allow the learning intentions to be achieved.

Here are examples of learning intentions stating what the children are doing followed by what the children are learning: 'The children will learn to draw a picture to explain the water cycle', or 'The children will watch a video in order to identify dangers in our community'. Drawing and watching don't focus on the learning; they focus on the doing.

Turning these sentences around to, 'The children will learn to explain the water cycle by drawing a picture', and 'The children will learn to identify dangers in our community by watching a video', provides a much clearer sense of what the children are learning. If the activity itself must be changed, such as the example of the brass band above, at least the focus of the learning intention is on the learning and such changes to the actual activity can be explained in an evaluation.

Thinking point

- If your learning intentions have been formulated as what the learners are doing rather than what they are learning, what impact will this have on the ability to formulate meaningful success criteria?
- If you have such a lesson plan, how would you/could you amend it?

Formulating learning intentions

Part of generating successful open learning intentions is the use of active verbs. There are a number of well-known sources of help for this. Perhaps the best known is Bloom's Taxonomy. This was a scheme of classifying learning objectives developed in the 1950s by an educational committee headed by Benjamin Bloom. Over the years, lists of Bloom's taxonomy action verbs have been generated and these can prove very useful in generating learning intentions. You will be able to find many examples online. In different documentation you may see learning intentions written in a variety of formats, such as:

- We are learning to …
- To be able to …
- To explain / discuss / demonstrate, etc.
- Today I am learning to …

If learning intentions are not written clearly the result may be a mismatch of lesson focus with activities, an inappropriate focus or awkward success criteria that do not fit the learning. More recently it has been suggested that by separating the learning intention from the context, learners can apply the skill or concept to a number of different contexts. It is also much easier to write success criteria for de-contextualised learning intentions.

Context-based and context-free learning

Not all learning is the same so not all learning intentions or success criteria are the same. There are: closed skills – the teaching of skills, concepts and knowledge, and

Table 5.1   Context-based and context-free learning

Learning intention in context	What students say they are learning	Context-free learning intentions	What students say they are learning
Write a newspaper report about pollution.	'I am learning about pollution.'	Write a newspaper report.	'I am learning how to write different kinds of report.'
To describe what happens during the festival of Diwali.	'I am learning about Diwali.'	Explain key features of a major religious festival or celebration.	'I am learning about world religions and how people worship.'

there are open skills – the application of skills, concepts and knowledge. Closed skills are either right or wrong. Success criteria for closed skills are either the steps involved or what you need to remember to achieve the learning intention. For example:

Learning intention

The children will learn to:

- convert a quantity into a ratio.

Success criteria

I can:

- add the parts;
- write each ratio as a fraction;
- multiply each fraction by the whole.

Open skills are neither right nor wrong. Learning intentions need examples and discussion about quality. For example:

Learning intention

The children will learn to:

- explain the use of musical instruments and elements in programmatic music.

Success criteria

I can:

- create a balanced three-section composition;
- use tone, pitch and dynamics to reflect the events and mood of the story;
- play instruments creatively.

The success criteria provide a 'menu' of devices which will help to produce quality work, where not all need to be included.

Learning how to formulate learning intentions may seem complicated but most teachers find that the ability to focus on the specific makes all planning more manageable. Learning to evaluate your LEPs and developing your reflective skills takes time and effort. But, as you become more skilled in planning the level of detail can be reduced. For example, over successive school placements you may find yourself moving from single LEPs to daily LEPs with consequent reduction in the number of words but without loss of attention to detail.

Summary

This chapter has explored one of the most important and yet perhaps one of the mostly hotly contested elements of learning to be a teacher: learning how to plan lessons 'on paper'. We have looked at the evolution of the lesson plan and examined some of the research that offers alternative solutions: we have identified and explored key elements of a learning experience plan. As teachers, our main focus must be to provide stimulating, imaginative and engaging learning contexts for our pupils. Doing this requires creativity, energy, commitment and … planning! Every successful teacher plans regardless of how much experience they have. However, not all planning will look the same. Some teachers may plan on paper in some detail, some may use Post-it notes; some may rehearse it out loud in the car on the way to work. But no matter how they do it, they will plan. The secret of successful planning? Lots of practise in whichever format you choose.

 Reflective questions

- If the best laid schemes often go awry, shouldn't the argument be for only planning a basic outline of a learning experience and having contingency plans if, for example, the IT equipment fails?
- 'It is through planning that we learn to teach and it is through teaching that we learn to plan'. Enumerate some of the steps showing how to learn to plan through teaching.
- Why are the elements of continuity, sequencing and integration central to the development of an effectively organised group of learning experiences?
- Creating lesson plans, or LEPs, is often considered by student teachers to be a chore which does not reflect what 'real teachers' do. Is this a fair assessment? What arguments would you make to a colleague who echoed these sentiments?

- Learning intentions and success criteria are only helpful if they are assessable. Action verbs such as explain, draw, demonstrate and measure are examples of assessable verbs. Is there a place in planning for learning intentions which use verbs such as understand, know and appreciate? Justify your answer.
- Most teachers will tell you there are times when you need to think on the spot and come up with alternatives and, as you have learned, even the most experienced and well-prepared teacher can, at times, have to 'think on their feet'. How does practice in planning learning experiences help for those times when you need to improvise?

Further reading

John, P.D. (2006) 'Lesson planning and the student teacher: re-thinking the dominant model', *Journal of Curriculum Studies*, 38, 483–98.

Rusznyak, L. and Walton, E. (2011) 'Lesson planning guidelines for student teachers: a scaffold for development of pedagogical knowledge', *Education as Change*, 15, 271–85.

Ruys, I., Van Keer, H. and Aelterman, A. (2012) 'Examining pre-service teacher competence in lesson planning pertaining to collaborative learning', *Journal of Curriculum Studies*, 44, 349–79.

CHAPTER 6

SOCIAL AND EMOTIONAL CONTEXTS FOR LEARNING

Margaret McCulloch

Key ideas

This chapter explores:

- social and emotional development;
- social and emotional wellbeing;
- implications for learning;
- building classroom relationships within a positive learning environment.

Introduction

Theories of child development offer different explanations of how children develop both socially and emotionally. It is important that teachers recognise that the learning process itself is impacted by social and emotional factors which relate both to the pupil and to the learning environment. Professional standards for teachers across the UK include an expectation that teachers will be aware of how children develop in the social and emotional domain and will be prepared to establish and sustain an environment which supports positive development in this area. It is therefore essential that as teachers we reflect on ways in which our own beliefs and values about children and education, and our own emotions, affect the classroom environment.

There is a growing focus on health and wellbeing in schools, arising from an increasing awareness of high levels of mental health problems amongst young people. This shifting emphasis, along with the perennial concern to support pupils identified as having social, emotional and behavioural needs, requires teachers to engage seriously with the crucial issue of relationship-building within their classrooms, between teacher and pupils, and amongst pupils. This chapter will consider some key aspects of social and emotional development, discuss their implications for behaviour and learning, and explore ways of developing positive classroom learning environments.

Social and emotional development

Although this chapter will use the phrase 'social and emotional development', it is important to note that social development and emotional development, while very closely linked, and often impacted by the same factors, are not entirely the same thing. The interactions a baby has with early caregivers are crucial in the development of interpersonal skills and emotional development. A baby learns at an early stage about the demonstration of emotions and the range of responses which these generate. Beyond this, there is a strong link between emotional development and the development of language and communication skills (Cross, 2011), which emphasises the importance of effective communication in the development of social skills. This section will consider theories which relate to both social and emotional development.

Theories of child development – social and emotional domain

In Chapter 3 we looked at some of the more common theories of child development across different domains. When we consider social and emotional development, the traditional focus on 'stages of development' is likely to lead to assumptions, and therefore expectations, that older children and adults will have more highly developed social and emotional skills than younger children. In the same way as we often make assumptions about cognitive abilities relating to children's age (see Chapter 11), delay in, or failure to, progress through identified stages of social and emotional development is likely to be seen as 'abnormal', with the responsibility for this often located in and around the individual, either the child or the family setting. On the other hand, more recent theories of development such as the ecological systems theory (Bronfenbrenner, 1979, 1994) recognise the potential impact of a wider range of social and environmental factors on children's development, including their emotional development, both directly and from a distance.

Our own experiences of nurture and education affect how we understand social and emotional development. Depending on our theoretical standpoint, personal experiences and beliefs, observed behaviours will be interpreted differently and different suggestions will be made to bring about change. There are five main theoretical approaches to conceptualising child development in the social and emotional domain (Trawick-Smith, 2013). Each of these has had a significant impact over the years on how our education systems are constructed, although each could be contested:

- *Maturationist*: In this view, proposed by Gesell (1925), development is seen as a purely biological process. Children move through stages as they mature. While more recent awareness of neurological development and environmental influences may make us sceptical about this approach, much educational policy is still based on a focus on the child's age, and on expectations of certain types of behaviour related to this.
- *Psychoanalytical*: This is also a 'stage approach' and describes social and emotional development in terms of resolving a series of conflicts, either successfully or not. For example, Erikson's (1959) theory of emotional development proposes a series of eight stages, from birth to old age, each characterised by a struggle between two emotional states, one positive and one negative. The first four key stages, relevant to primary educators, are:

  o during infancy, trust v mistrust;
  o during early childhood – 2–3 years – autonomy v doubt;
  o during pre-school – 3–5 years – initiative v guilt;
  o during primary school years – 6–11 years – industry v inferiority (see Trawick-Smith, 2013).

These will be referred to later in the chapter. It can be argued that this theory only *describes* development rather than providing any explanation of which experiences are more or less likely to provide a positive outcome. Nevertheless, it highlights a number of areas which can be used as the basis for reflection on children's behaviours in different contexts and it relates strongly to the notion of identity development.

- *Behaviourist*: From this perspective, children learn social and emotional behaviour from caregivers, by observing and copying and by having their own behaviour rewarded or not.
- *Cognitive-developmental*: This approach suggests that children's social and emotional development is linked to their cognitive development and to their reasoning skills.
- *Ecological systems* (Bronfenbrenner, 1979, 1994): This theory suggests that children's development is affected by interactions amongst four 'layers' of environmental systems, described as a set of 'nested structures' around the individual (Bronfenbrenner, 1979: 3). It also recognises that the child's own biological characteristics interact with these environmental influences, so may be better described as bioecological theory (Shaffer, 2009).

The microsystem, closest to the child, would include primary caregivers and others in the immediate environment, the home or the classroom, with whom the child regularly interacts (see Figure 6.1). The mesosystem involves systems connecting to the child or relationships amongst others in the microsystem such as schools, early years establishments, or a family doctor. The next level, the exosystem, includes structures or systems which are not directly part of children's lives but which may impact on them, such as legal or social welfare services which may affect the family's ability to support their development effectively. The most 'distant' system, the macrosystem, consists of the values and attitudes of the society or culture. In addition,

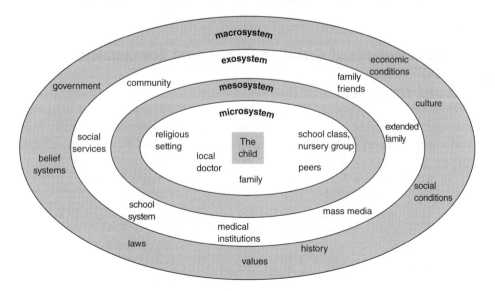

Figure 6.1 Bronfenbrenner's ecological model

Bronfenbrenner proposes a chronosystem which suggests that changes that occur through time, for example as the child matures, or as societal influences change, will also affect development differentially.

This theory is attractive because it challenges any potential 'simple' explanations for differences in children's development, which might refer, for example, to inherent characteristics in the child, or to 'poor parenting'. It recognises the impact of wider societal factors on the immediate interactions amongst care-givers and family and the child, and also their impact on the options available to care-givers, both financially and socially. For example, parents living in a society which invests in high-quality affordable childcare may be less anxious about their ability to earn enough money to keep their family and thus more likely to provide a calm home environment in which children can grow up than parents living in a society where less state funding is put into supporting families with young children, and there is constant anxiety about money. The interactions between the individual and environmental factors are fundamental to this model.

Thinking point

- Which of the theoretical approaches seems to you best to explain how social and emotional development 'works'?
- What 'common' ideas about children's behaviour are you aware of which you can link to one or other of the theoretical approaches mentioned above?

Some important aspects of social and emotional development

Trust and attachment

Erikson's (1959) theory suggests that the first conflict to be resolved in early childhood is that of 'trust or mistrust' and that trust will be developed when babies form a secure attachment with one or more caregivers who are sensitive and responsive to their needs for food, warmth and security. This attachment is based on caregivers' consistency and dependability, and their demonstration of affection, through physical contact. If, however, children experience inconsistent responses to their demands for food or attention, this can lead to a sense of mistrust.

Attachment has been an area of research for psychologists for many years since Bowlby and his colleagues' first investigations in the 1960s (for example, Bowlby, 1969). Ongoing research (for example, Allen et al., 2007) into the concepts of secure, insecure or disorganised attachment suggests that the impact of insecure attachment continues into later childhood and adolescence and affects relationships with peers as well as adults. Later in this chapter we will discuss how a 'nurture' approach may address some of the issues arising from this.

Autonomy/identity

Erikson's model suggests that children begin to develop a sense of autonomy from a very young age, and that a sense of 'self' continues to develop throughout the school years and beyond. How adults respond to children's growing independence is seen to be crucial in ensuring that they develop a positive and coherent sense of their own identity and self-concept in relation to others and to the world around them. If young children are not allowed opportunities safely to investigate their immediate environment or if they are sometimes encouraged and at other times chastised in that exploration, they may be left uncertain as to how adults will respond to them and their actions, which in turn may affect their social and emotional development. A positive sense of self is more likely to develop when caregivers respond consistently to the child's actions; however, consistency should not be confused with inflexibility as it is important to recognise that appropriate actions depend on context.

Social competence

Social competence has been defined as 'an ability to take another's perspective concerning a situation and to learn from past experience and apply that learning to the ever-changing social landscape' (Semrud-Clikeman, 2007: 1). The notions of social skills, social communication and interpersonal communication are included in the general term. It is connected to our ability to respond to and communicate effectively with others and to form appropriate relationships in different contexts. Children need opportunities to make (and break) friendships.

Social interactions must be considered in context; issues such as culture (what is expected, or the norm, in particular societies or situations), relationships (who is interacting with whom), situation and function (behaviour acceptable in one setting or for one purpose may not be appropriate in another) are crucial (Spitzberg, 2003). Social difficulties may arise when there is a mismatch between behaviour and context; teachers frequently comment on behaviour in the classroom which is more suited to the playground, and this will refer to aspects of physical contact and to communication. Children need to know and understand the different expectations of different contexts. Children and young people who are socially competent will be more comfortable participating in groups, clubs or events. Within the classroom, levels of social competence will affect learning.

Behaviour

In schools, the phrase 'social and emotional' is most frequently found in the context of 'social, emotional and behavioural difficulties' or 'needs'; this will be explored in more depth in Chapter 7. 'Inappropriate behaviour' in any context is often the site where issues of social and emotional development may be considered. However, it could be argued that the focus is often on the observed behaviour rather than on the potential social and emotional reasons for that behaviour. There is also, probably naturally, a tendency to focus on what might be described as 'negative' social behaviours that provoke a negative response from others. However, it is important also to identify that most children develop and demonstrate 'positive' social behaviours, which are those seen as acceptable and desirable by the culture in which they live.

In addition, the concept of pro-social behaviour, that is, behaviour which results in a beneficial outcome for another individual, whether or not it has some benefit for the person who instigates it, has become more prominent in recent years (see Wardle, 2011). This has highlighted the development of children's moral awareness and reasoning. While there is much more research into the area of anti-social behaviour, reflecting on how to create the conditions and an environment which will encourage the development of pro-social behaviour would seem to be of use for teachers who wish to develop productive classroom environments.

There is a range of social behaviours which would be termed 'negative' including being 'disobedient' to adults, or not being able to agree with peers. Arguably the most concerning behaviour, both for adults and for peers, is aggression of various kinds, including verbal and physical, both reactive and proactive.

Different theories suggest different reasons for aggressive behaviour, and again we can recognise how beliefs, values and policies have been affected by these. Maturationists explain aggressive behaviour by stating that some children are born with an aggressive temperament. While some historical research studies of identical and fraternal twins suggest that at least some tendencies towards aggression and irritability may be related to genetics, environmental influences also play a part in shaping responses. Behaviourists see aggressive behaviour as a result of copying observed behaviour, either on television, or from physically or verbally aggressive treatment by their parents or others; children may also have had their aggressive behaviour rewarded by getting what they want. A cognitive developmental approach suggests that children react aggressively because they do not understand the social situation and will learn to do so. The ecological systems view looks for wider causal relationships; for example, why are there so many television programmes involving violence? What are the reasons why children in our society watch so much television? Would higher priority given to supporting parents with high quality childcare ease stress on family life?

Whichever theoretical perspective is taken regarding any observed behaviour, positive or negative, as teachers we need to recognise that our personal response to the behaviour is crucial. Children entering the nursery playroom, or primary classroom, will be at different stages in their ability to form positive interpersonal relationships with adults and with other children. The classroom environment must allow space for teacher and pupil to work out an acceptable balance between the needs and wants of the individual and of the group, and to establish positive working relationships amongst adults and children based on mutual respect. A major element here will be how the teacher positions him or herself in relation to 'power' and control.

Thinking point

- Teachers cannot change what has happened in children's lives in the years before they come to nursery or school. What are the implications of this for teachers' work?
- What do teachers need to know in order to support all children's learning?

Social and emotional wellbeing

In recent years, the concept of wellbeing has become embedded in policy and practice in relation to children, not just in education but also in health, social work and other professional contexts. This has been partly in response to a number of international reports which suggested that children in the UK are less happy, less satisfied with life, and scored lower on scales of their own sense of wellbeing than children in most other industrialised countries (Bradshaw and Richardson, 2009). Internationally, the World Health Organization has been advocating the development of 'health promoting schools' since 2003. In addition, national reports have highlighted areas of concern. For example, recent research (Layard and Dunn, 2009; The Children's Society, 2012) included the frightening statistic that one in ten of 5–16 year olds in the UK has clinically significant mental health difficulties; reports into the effects of poverty and homelessness on children and families' health and wellbeing continue to be produced (for example, Shelter, 2006; CPAG, 2012). The policy focus on wellbeing has developed alongside a move to service integration and 'joined-up working' amongst different professionals concerned with children (see McCulloch, 2011).

Policy frameworks for children's services, including education, make significant reference to different aspects of 'wellbeing' (see, in England, *Promoting Emotional*

Health and Wellbeing (DfES, 2004b), *Every Child Matters* (DfES, 2005b); in Wales, *Thinking Positively: Emotional Health and Well-being in Schools and Early Years Settings* (Welsh Assembly Government, 2010); in Northern Ireland, *Our Children and Young People: Our Pledge* (Northern Ireland Assembly, 2006); and in Scotland, *Getting it Right for Every Child* (GIRFEC) (SG, 2012b). GIRFEC (SG, 2012b: 9) suggests that professionals working to support children and young people should consider the child's situation with reference to eight wellbeing indicators: how far is the child safe, achieving, active, responsible, healthy, nurtured, respected and included.

Wellbeing, then, can be seen to encompass all aspects of mental, emotional, social and physical health. While in many ways a desire to maximise wellbeing in young people could be seen to be an indisputably 'good' thing, it is important that this notion is critiqued.

One outcome of the developing focus on 'social and emotional wellbeing' was the development of a range of programmes across UK education systems focusing on social and emotional development, from a range of sources including local authorities and social agencies. Some of these focused on developing positive capabilities in young people such as resilience and self-esteem, while others attempted to reduce negative experiences or behaviour, for example, bullying, depression, etc. The terminology of 'emotional literacy', 'emotional intelligence' became pervasive although significant research evidence to support the concepts was not provided.

From 2005 onwards, the DfES promoted the use of *Social and Emotional Aspects of Learning* (SEAL) in primary and secondary schools in England, although this is no longer actively supported by the 2010 Coalition government. This programme was based on a rationale which linked the development of a positive school environment supporting emotional health and wellbeing with behaviour management. However, there are concerns that this type of approach, which identifies targets for, and requires measurement of, aspects of social and emotional development, is likely to lead to further suggestions of what is 'normal' and 'abnormal' and thus divide and potentially marginalise groups, rather than taking a more general approach to encouraging the development of all. It has been argued that the discourse of social and emotional wellbeing assumes a set of values, and 'good' emotions which are undebated (Watson et al., 2012).

This chapter cannot deal with the full range of programmes and strategies available; however, we would argue that it is vital that as teachers we should engage in critical analysis of programmes presented to us, interrogate the assumptions and beliefs on which they are based, and question the implications for the development of the young people in our charge.

There is a danger in treating social and emotional development as an area for teaching and assessment, with particular emphasis on those who appear to need 'remediation' as opposed to dealing with this as part of an inclusive approach. In the latter conceptualisation, social and emotional development occurs for all through engagement in a learning community which 'foster(s) a safe, caring, supportive, purposeful environment that enables the development of relationships based on mutual respect' (Education Scotland, online-b).

Therefore, we will focus on general areas of practice for which individual teachers are responsible and over which they have control. We will now consider the implications of what we have discussed so far for learning in the primary classroom.

The impact of emotions on learning

As teachers, we have no control over the experiences which children have already had in the years before they come to school, and while we will have communication with their family once they are in school, we are not responsible for wider aspects of their home life. We need to be aware that we have a particular professional role as an educator, rather than a psychologist or a social worker. However, it is vital that we recognise the importance of emotions in educational contexts, both for teachers and pupils. We must be aware of our role in organising and negotiating the complex interpersonal exchanges which are fundamental to learning in the primary classroom.

For many years, psychologists have debated the relative and connected roles of 'cognition' (thinking) and 'affect' (the experience of feeling or emotion, which will relate strongly to motivation) in learning (Pons et al., 2011). Engagement in any educational activity will produce some kind of affective experience which will differ for each participant. Whether this emotional experience is positive or negative may be crucial to successful learning (Schutz et al., 2011).

Neurophysiological research into how the brain processes information has established that emotional responses are processed in the part of the brain called the amygdala, sometimes referred to as the 'reptilian brain', which is concerned with the preservation of life. It overrides the functions of other parts of the brain at times of extreme stress of any kind. Humans have evolved in a way which means that when faced with a critical situation which feels threatening, the primitive 'fight-or-flight' reflex kicks in. The emotional memory of specific situations is long-lasting and often when we find ourselves in a similar situation again, we experience the same heightened emotional state. Many children and young people may be in this state for much of their time in classrooms. This may be as a result of previous experiences of inconsistent or stressful relationships with adults or peers, as discussed earlier, or as a result of specific classroom interactions or environments, such as failure to manage a task. This can have a seriously detrimental effect on their ability to learn.

It is also argued (Damasio, 1994) that emotion plays a key role in what and how we think, and how we behave, at all times, not just in times of stress.

It is also important to remember that as teachers we will also have emotional responses to particular contexts. Anxiety about working with a particular class, group or individual, or any unpleasant emotional memory of previous experiences, either as a teacher or a learner, may impact on our own behaviour and interactions with pupils. Teaching can be an emotionally charged situation, balancing the requirements of meeting different learners' needs and the pressures of administration, while recognising that parents and society in general have certain expectations of which kinds of displays of emotion by teachers are appropriate and which are not.

View from practice

Joanne was a student teacher on placement in a class of seven and eight year olds. When she arrived, the class was being taught by a supply teacher, the third since the beginning of term.

Mikey was constantly in trouble. By 10am most days he had been sent to the head's office, where he then spent most of the day, generally making little progress with his work and enjoying watching the life of the school around him. During her first days in the classroom, Joanne observed Mikey and was determined to find ways to avoid excluding him when she was responsible for the class.

She noticed that Mikey frequently got into trouble when the class was set to begin their independent maths work. He would engage in a range of irritating low-level behaviours which annoyed the children around him, for which he would receive a series of warnings until ultimately he was banished from the room, often after an argument with the teacher; other children were annoyed by him and he had few friends. She found out that Mikey had arrived in the school a few months earlier, having attended four other primary schools since he started his education.

Joanne drew up a plan of action as she began to take responsibility for teaching. Firstly, she spoke to Mikey at the end of the class and quietly informed him that she would not be putting him out of the room, no matter what he did. He would stay in the room to get on with his learning, but she would work with him on this. At the point in her maths lessons where the children would be sent to work independently she made sure that she spoke individually to Mikey to check that he knew what to do. She soon realised that he lacked understanding of some basic number concepts and needed to be given appropriate support, and work of an appropriate level, in order to achieve any success. She also established a set of procedures for Mikey to follow if he got stuck, including asking a carefully selected peer for advice, displaying a specific card on his desk so that Joanne would know that he was needing help, and providing alternative, appropriate activities which he could do while waiting for her to be available.

Over the next two weeks until the tutor visit, Mikey was not sent from the classroom once, and was observed working co-operatively with other children and engaging fully in the life of the class.

While this may seem a rather utopian example, it is a true story, with only names changed. Mikey's fear of being exposed as unable to do the maths led him to take avoiding action. When the fear was removed, and support offered, he was able to engage with the learning and form better relationships with his peers.

Building classroom relationships through positive environments

From this chapter so far, it will be clear that we are arguing strongly that the teacher needs to accept responsibility, as the adult in the classroom, for providing a safe environment for learning. This does not require detailed knowledge of individual children's levels of social and emotional development. It requires an empathetic approach based on thinking through how the classroom and interactions within it might feel to children and recognising the range of potential responses to specific situations. This kind of approach is both explicit and implicit in the statements of the professional standards in relation to social justice, integrity, trust and respect and professional commitment required of teachers across the United Kingdom and beyond.

Let us consider the three important aspects of social and emotional development identified earlier in the chapter in relation to classroom relationships and to in-school strategies for developing these.

Trust and attachment – a nurturing approach

From the 1960s onwards, researchers theorised that children who were entering school who seemed to be withdrawn, sad, afraid to mix, or aggressive, unable to follow class routines and unresponsive to teachers were insecurely attached. They held that this led to children being unable to form trusting relationships with adults or to interact appropriately with children, making it hard for them to cope with the demands of school. This would in turn have a negative impact on their self-confidence and self-esteem (Boxall, 2010).

The idea of nurture groups developed as a 'within-school' strategy to allow children to have time in a predictable, small-group environment, with consistent, reliable adults, who could respond to their specific needs and help them to experience positive relationships amongst adults and children. While it can be argued that the concept of nurture is based on a deficit model which tries to 'fix' children to fit a more 'normal' mould (Bailey, 2007), there is a clear aim to retain the children's membership of their own class while attending the nurture group, and children would normally be expected to spend no more than 15 months attending such a group before returning to their class full-time. From the 'nurture group' philosophy has developed the notion of 'the nurturing school' in both primary and secondary sectors, where the whole-school ethos is based on a nurturing approach and individual teachers are familiar with strategies which help children develop more positive relationships in class.

Autonomy/identity – encouraging resilience

We must avoid the dangers of focusing on negative aspects of social and emotional development. It would be too easy simply to assume, for example, that poverty or a difficult family situation in early childhood would necessarily imply the poor development of social and emotional skills and less successful life outcomes. We should remember that not all children respond in the same way to adverse life circumstances and many develop skills, attitudes and behaviours which allow them to be successful in learning and in later life. What makes some children appear more 'resilient' and to develop a strong positive sense of autonomy than others, has been examined by researchers.

View from practice

Staff in one primary school, aware that some children appeared more resilient to challenging life circumstances than others, decided to investigate the research into this area. They found that Newman and Blackburn (2002) had collated a list of factors which seem to promote resilience. These included:

- strong social support networks;
- a committed 'mentor' from outside the family;

- positive school experiences;
- a range of extra-curricular activities that develop competencies and emotional maturity;
- a sense of mastery and a belief that one's own efforts can make a difference;
- the ability – or opportunity – to 'make a difference' by, for example, helping others through volunteering, or undertaking part-time work;
- exposure to challenging situations which provide opportunities to develop both problem-solving abilities and emotional coping skills.

They considered each of these factors and created an action plan to address these, initially from within their own resources, by extending choice within their own after-school activities, and redesigning some of their cross-curricular topics to encourage children's independent learning and research skills. As the process developed, school staff established links with a number of voluntary agencies in the area who provided opportunities for young people to take part in a range of out-of-school activities, many of which encouraged engagement with the local community and parental involvement.

The experience of personal success in any aspect of life, including, but not only, learning in the classroom is seen to be key in encouraging the development of a strong sense of self-efficacy (Bandura, 1994) in young people; they feel that they are able to be successful in learning in general, and in certain aspects of that in particular.

Social competence – encouraging positive interactions

Primary classrooms by their nature require children to interact both socially and intellectually with peers and adults. A developing recognition of the 'social' component of learning (see Chapter 4), including the importance of opportunities to articulate ideas and learning, means that teachers are increasingly providing opportunities for children to work collaboratively. The drive to encourage engagement with learning through more active approaches, both physical and mental, has increased the level of interactions in the classroom. However, learning alongside others can only be successful if children feel secure in taking risks which are inherent in sharing their learning with others. They need to know that they will not be ridiculed for either not knowing something, or for knowing too much, and that their contributions will be valued by others.

Teachers must be mindful that approaches such as co-operative learning (Martin, 2007) cannot be successful unless children are supported to develop the necessary interpersonal skills. Some children with communication disorders including Asperger syndrome may find co-operative learning extremely stressful and this should be taken into account when planning learning experiences.

General principles

Building on the key issues arising from the theories of social and emotional development discussed earlier in the chapter, we would argue that teachers should, as far as possible, follow these principles:

- Expect to *like* the children in your class. Starting from this point makes a teacher more likely to smile and be pleasant, which is a necessary part in the development of any positive relationship. Positive classroom environments need to be based on evidence that teachers like the children and want to be with them.
- Be openly positive about all pupils in the class. Research suggests that negative language from teachers about pupils impacts on pupil perceptions of themselves and others. For example, 'you are always last to finish your work' has an impact both on the individual's self-concept and on the views that others hold of that individual (Smith, 2003).
- Provide a classroom environment that is calm, stimulating and welcoming, which offers challenge without stress.
- Respond consistently and fairly to pupils. Children need to be confident that a particular behaviour will produce a particular response.
- Avoid inviting confrontation. Be flexible - allow space for children to back down, or to negotiate. Might there be another way of reaching the goal?
- Find ways to 'make failure safe' (Smith, 2003) in learning. For example, use sand trays or whiteboards in early years when practising writing skills so that the less successful efforts can be easily removed.
- Use positive language to convey high expectations, both with pupils and in discussions with colleagues – for example, try changing 'he can't because ...' to 'he could if ...' (Smith, 2003).

This is not always easy. Research suggests that teachers whose morale is low, or who do not have supportive relationships with colleagues, may become less invested in classroom activities (Milkie and Warner, 2011: 18). Thus, sometimes in the face of very challenging circumstances, they become less able to take this positive approach and to work at creating engaging and interesting experiences for children. Some teachers may find themselves working in schools where the overall culture is not one of empathetic concern for pupil and staff wellbeing.

While school management teams should recognise the importance of developing and nurturing positive relationships amongst staff and pupils, as teachers we can help ourselves and each other by recognising areas of potential negative impact on our own emotional health, and creating opportunities for mutual support, both in and beyond the workplace.

Power and control

Many difficult classroom situations involve the issue of power and control. Teachers often feel that they need to establish that they are 'in control', and fear 'losing control'. This can lead to heightened emotional states on both sides and thus to confrontation and anxious responses to situations. While this is not a major focus of this chapter, we would make two general suggestions.

Firstly, focus on learning, rather than behaviour (Head, 2007). If conversations in the classroom centre clearly on how the children's learning is progressing, as opposed to whether or not they are 'behaving' then this changes the 'feel' of the conversations and may defuse potentially explosive situations. Many confrontational situations arise when children find themselves unable, for whatever reason, to complete the learning tasks expected of them.

Secondly, be prepared to negotiate whenever possible. Coming to a compromise, or offering choice, does not indicate a loss of control. It shows that the teacher is a reasonable human being who can consider options, within certain constraints, and also encourages pupils to learn important critical skills.

Summary

In this chapter we have argued that social and emotional issues are strongly connected with learning and therefore teachers must have a good understanding of how children progress in this domain in order to support their development. Knowledge of the different developmental theories should allow teachers to recognise why different responses to particular situations might be more or less successful, both in the long and the short term, and to make informed judgements about how to react in any given circumstances. We have noted recent societal concern around wellbeing, including social and emotional wellbeing, referring to pressure on schools to address these issues. While it may seem almost self-evident that positive experiences in school and good relationships with teachers and peers should enhance children's social and emotional development, we have recognised that maintaining a positive classroom atmosphere can be challenging, and that our own emotions are crucial in understanding any set of circumstances. However, we would maintain, as stated at the outset, that the teacher, by dint of being the responsible adult, has the professional and moral duty to ensure that a positive, nurturing classroom and school environment is established and sustained.

 Reflective questions

- In what ways has this chapter challenged any assumptions about children's social and emotional development that you may have previously held?
- How could you organise learning in your classroom to enable children to experience some of the nurturing experiences or resilience-promoting factors noted above?
- What might be some of the challenges involved in doing this?
- What aspects of your own emotional responses to classroom situations should you be considering?

Further reading

The Nurture Group Network at http://www.nurturegroups.org. Access to resources, publications and general information about theories underlying and practice in nurture provision.

Information on self-efficacy at http://www.uky.edu/~eushe2/Pajares/self-efficacy. html. Background to social cognitive theory and Bandura's work on self-efficacy.

Kohn, A. (1999) *Punished by Rewards: The Trouble with Gold Stars, Incentive Plans, A's, Praise, and Other Bribes*. Boston: Houghton Mifflin. (The author critiques the behaviourist approach to motivation in a humorous but compelling and challenging way.)

CHAPTER 7

IDENTITY, RELATIONSHIPS AND BEHAVIOUR

George Head

Key ideas

This chapter explores:

- identity and relationships;
- behaviour;
- pedagogy.

Introduction

Behaviour in schools has been an enduring issue since the introduction of universal education. Approaches to dealing with behaviour can be understood as either broadly pastoral or punishment based. Within and between each of these categories a range of approaches has emerged; some have been based on psychological theories of behaviour, others on the interactions among social systems that surround schools and children, and a third group focused on learning as a means of addressing behavioural issues.

Following an exploration of the underpinning, and often competing, concepts that inform policy, this chapter will take a critical look at these psychological, social and pedagogical approaches, teasing out the theories, values and beliefs that will contribute to your understanding of how and why each operates as it does. In turn, this will inform our capacity as professionals to create approaches appropriate for pupils whose behaviour is found to be problematic.

Terminology

The terminology used to identify children whose behaviour schools find difficult has altered considerably over the years and reflects sometimes subtle shifts in thinking on how they are viewed by schools and teachers. In the late twentieth century, the term 'maladjusted' was in commonplace usage to describe individual pupils. This term was replaced by 'social, emotional and behavioural difficulties', which indicates a category rather than an individual. More recently, 'difficulties' has been replaced by 'needs' or 'skills' (DfES, 2001; SG, 2009c) in some contexts. A premise of this chapter, however, is that behaviour in classes is dependent on the identities which learners and teachers create for each other and the relationships between them. These identities are constructed in large part by the three adjectives of social, emotional and behavioural in the umbrella category. An examination of each of these describers provides the basis of a critical consideration of the overall category.

Social

This term suggests a difficulty that has its roots not in school, or not only in school. There may be many reasons for a child experiencing a social difficulty, ranging from deprivation and crime to disaffection with the education system or society in general. In such circumstances, the child may, in fact, have become disengaged from the education system as they may see it as irrelevant and ineffective in meeting their needs. Alternatively, by the time they reach upper primary, they may simply consider that, within the community in which they live and intend to go on living, they have learned enough.

Whatever the reason, it seems reasonable to assume that a social difficulty requires a social solution. Since school is an important part of society, it has a role to play in any solution. However, we should recognise that there are other professionals who are better placed to deal with social difficulties, for example, social workers. The information gained from social reports can be helpful for schools and teachers in that it encourages a more holistic picture of the young person and their circumstances, thereby encouraging a more sympathetic approach to their education. However, perhaps the same information is more directly useful to colleagues in social work. The role of the school in such cases is more of a supportive one, addressing educational issues in a way that complements or reinforces measures being taken at home or in the community. An understanding of children's difficulties as 'social' is reflected in policies related to referral to social work and education in segregated special schools for children whose behaviour has been considered socially inadequate or disruptive.

Emotional

An emotional difficulty may or may not have its roots in school. As with social difficulties, there may be a range of causes. The child may well be interested in education but cannot connect or 'acts-out' as a result of the prominence of their emotional difficulty.

Knowing that a young person is troubled in this way may help us to understand classroom outbursts and to be more sympathetic towards their plight. It also helps teachers and colleagues to be more understanding of what it is realistic to expect and demand of such young people. However, perhaps an emotional difficulty suggests a response directed towards feelings, and possibly counselling or some other therapeutic measure is seen as the most effective response. Once again, whilst such background information is helpful for teachers, it may, in fact, be more useful for other professionals such as counsellors and psychologists.

One definition of an emotional difficulty, therefore, might be that it has its roots in the psychological wellbeing of the pupil and that psychological approaches such as anger management or therapy are the most appropriate interventions. An understanding of behaviour as an emotional difficulty is reflected in policies such as referral to psychological or even health services and, as with social understandings, ultimately education in segregated provision, including nurture groups.

Behavioural

In recent years, it has become increasingly recognised that behavioural difficulties are not simply attributable to poor upbringing or inherent character traits. As more is learned about autism, Asperger syndrome, and attention deficit hyperactivity disorder (ADHD), for instance, the more these difficulties can be understood and addressed through a range of programmes, including medication. In addition, the recognition of the relationship between behavioural difficulties and dyslexia, dysphasia (impaired language and communication skills) and dysgraphia (impaired writing skills), has created a perception of behavioural difficulties as being part of, or arising out of, learning difficulties. A range of programmes has been developed for use in schools but again, the expertise of others such as speech and language professionals may well be more important as a first step in addressing some difficulties.

The term social, emotional and behavioural difficulties (commonly referred to by the abbreviation SEBD) does not imply a homogenous group of children but is arguably, rather, a convenient term for pupils whose difficulties are either less tangible or socially less tolerable than others. More significantly, it could be argued that the term has acted as a barrier to the development of approaches in schools for dealing with children who have attracted the label. The use of SEBD to describe a section of schoolchildren has, possibly, reinforced the approach that suggests that before teachers deal with the learning of such young people, they need first of all to deal with their behaviour. Unlike learners with other disabilities, for example visual impairment, hearing impairment or learning difficulties, teachers are expected to 'sort' the difficulty as a pre-requisite to dealing with learning. It could be the case, therefore, that the system in which they work, in which children who might be experiencing SEBD are sent to separate schools, units and bases, or are dealt with in school as part of the discipline procedures rather than through learning and pastoral support, forces teachers, whatever their opinion, to approach some children as 'different'.

Theories of behaviour

Theories of learning and theories of behaviour help us to make sense of what we do with, and for, children as part of their learning. The theories described could be categorised broadly as being either authoritarian or authoritative and democratic. The language used here is interesting as both terms describe a relationship between learner and teacher that is based upon power. Even within democratic theories, such as humanism, choice theory and systems theory, the teacher's voice is the authoritative one. It is the teacher who has the ability to facilitate learning and to create the conditions in which student learning meets their intellectual, social and emotional needs; it is the teacher who can make it possible for the student to make better choices; and it is the teacher who is able to change student-teacher relationships by altering their interactions with students. In each of these approaches, the teacher is the one who instigates action to address behaviour and the child is essentially passive, at least up to that point.

There are a number of theories that aid understanding of behaviour and for the purposes of this chapter they have been grouped into two broad categories; those that are *authoritarian* and assume a pathological or 'in-child' deficit, and those that do not and can be described as *authoritative* (Ayers et al., 2000; Porter, 2000). These theories can be said to hold different perspectives on children's behaviour, and can be understood by a consideration of their ontological positions. Ontology can be seen as 'what there is that can be known' or, quite simply, *the what to know*. There are basically two views of ontology and the one that is relevant to this first set of theories is a realist ontology.

Realist (authoritarian)

Realist ontology is based on the premise that there is a fixed body of knowledge that learners must come to know. This knowledge exists in the world and is separate from the individuals who have to learn it. In terms of behaviour, a realist ontology assumes that there are fixed, or relatively fixed, ways of behaving. These will include what is normally considered to be polite, obedient behaviour; those forms of behaviour which children do not necessarily 'know' are appropriate for different contexts, but have to be taught. Having been taught appropriate behaviour in the classroom, it becomes the child's responsibility to display that behaviour at all times. When they do not, their conduct is considered to be 'mis'-behaviour and some action has to be taken by the teacher and/or another professional to remedy the situation. The first set of theories that can broadly be understood in realist terms are those based on biology, some forms of psychology and cognition (Ayers et al., 2000; Porter, 2000).

Biological and psychodynamic theories are based on beliefs that there is some antecedent or continuous cause of children's behaviour. The causes may be neurological, physiological, genetic or the result of early childhood experiences that require to be resolved. The obvious way of addressing behaviour which is perceived to be the result of biological or psychological events is medication and therapy. Historically, one of the implications for children whose behaviour could be understood in such terms has been that when their treatment has been ineffective, or when going through particularly difficult experiences, they have been considered as 'not fit for class' or even mainstream school itself, sometimes resulting in exclusion to segregated provision. The development of the inclusion agenda, however, has encouraged local authorities, school governing bodies, schools and teachers to reconsider the appropriateness of such measures.

Other deficit-assuming theories of behaviour are those related to behaviourism. According to these theories, while children's behaviour may or may not have biological or psychological sources, individuals are considered to have perceived personal deficiencies. Broadly speaking, these theories are based on the belief that children need adults to inform them of what is expected of them and that teachers have the right to impose order on children. Furthermore, when children display persistent 'inappropriate' or 'mis'-behaviour, they do so because it works. Approaches which can be considered as understanding behaviour in terms of behaviourist theories normally entail positive and negative consequences under the assumption that these will encourage pupils to comply with teachers' expectations. These theories leave little or no room for children to assume responsibility for their behaviour as it is externally controlled by the teacher and the school discipline policy. Head (2007) and Kohn (2006) argue that the most common outcome of rewards-based strategies is that they teach children how to get rewards.

Furthermore, by addressing only the observable and measurable aspects of behaviour, such as shouting out or getting up out of their seats, and not addressing underlying contributory factors, they actually work against what they are trying to achieve. Children learn that when they 'mis'-behave they are entered into the rewards and sanctions regime; thus, they gain a level of attention they otherwise might not have had, and they can gain rewards for behaving 'not too badly'. Moreover, teachers' experiences of behaviourist approaches indicate that whilst they may be effective in the short term, over a longer period the reward loses its novelty and sanctions cease to hold a threat.

Some theories in this category, however, while assuming deficit and a rewards and sanctions approach, also suggest a more active role for children. While still maintaining a focus on obedience and compliance, they also recognise that there are both cognitive and emotional aspects of behaviour. Working through these to develop, for example, cognitive skills or self-efficacy, is an important element of what, later in this chapter, is termed learning behaviour.

Relativist (authoritative)

Theories that move away from deficit-laden understandings include humanism, choice and systems theories. Ontologically, these theories can be understood as encompassing a relativist position. Relativist ontology is based on the premise that there are multiple realities that are personal to individuals, groups and cultures and we make sense of them through interaction with others. Teachers who hold a relativist ontology are likely to view behaviour differently. In the same way that they see knowledge as multi-faceted and created socially, so will they view interpretations of behaviour as social constructs and will want to investigate the multiple realities that lie behind any behaviour. Approaches that can be understood in terms of these theories do not seek blind obedience and compliance but autonomy, emotional self-regulation, cooperation and integrity. When a pupil's behaviour causes disruption to their own or others' learning, therefore, teachers will seek to resolve the conflict that may be at the root and they will examine the choices that they and pupils make in their classes generally and in response to conflict and disruption in particular. Most importantly, they will adopt an ecological understanding of their pupils, their classrooms, schools and wider communities. Teachers using approaches based on these theories will adopt a collaborative approach involving themselves, their students, other professionals and other adults in order to help students make informed choices regarding their learning and behaviour. An ecological understanding is also underpinned by a belief that what happens in one area of a child's life will have an impact through all parts of the child's ecosystem. The skills a teacher possesses are, of course, those related to teaching and the area of children's lives with which they are best equipped to deal is their learning. Teachers' approaches that can be understood in terms of humanistic theories, therefore, do not consider children's behaviour in class as 'mis'- or inappropriate behaviour and a matter of discipline but as a context of learning to which they can bring their skills of teaching and their values and beliefs regarding children and how they learn; in other words, pedagogy.

Thinking point

- What strategies to address behaviour have you seen or used in schools?
- Which strategies would you describe as authoritarian and authoritative and why?

Pedagogy, relationships and behaviour

Compensatory pedagogy

As argued in the critique of SEBD at the beginning of this chapter, children so labelled can be perceived as 'exceptional' and the teaching strategies developed for them have tended to assume that they have special or additional needs. These are then compensated for through, for example, differentiation of materials, asking for less demanding outcomes or through lowering expectations, generally. This is the case when considering both learning and behaviour. This compensatory approach is underpinned theoretically by behaviourist principles which assume that the appropriate classroom behaviour is obedience and compliance as demanded by the teacher. One consequence of a compensatory approach, therefore, is to regard children as being in deficit in terms of both learning and behaviour and to construct an authoritarian identity for teachers. Authoritarianism is usually reinforced through adopting a pedagogical practice aimed at normalising children's behaviour. As a result, compensatory pedagogies tend to take learners' confusion, anger and lack of understanding and treat them as ignorance that is dependent on the teacher (or other external source) for a remedy. When normal practice related to a deterministic view of behaviour has been exhausted with little or no success, teachers turn to the systemic approaches available to them, normally the discipline system, often consisting of behaviourist approaches of rewards and sanctions. A compensatory approach can thus lead to a cycle of punishment, exclusion and other measures which serve to mark out pupils who might be experiencing social, emotional or behavioural difficulties as different and to question the extent to which they belong alongside their peers within the mainstream of education. A compensatory pedagogy, therefore, can be understood as a pedagogy of ignorance, dependency and despair (Head, 2011).

Complementary pedagogy

Recent studies on behaviour in schools emphasise the importance of relationships (Addison, 2012; Mowat, 2010). In this section it is argued that a complementary pedagogy reconstitutes the relationships among learners and between learners and teachers through the building of trust and respect. A complementary pedagogy begins with and maintains a perspective based on ability and the value of children's own experiences, thoughts and beliefs. Consequently, rather than compensating for a perceived deficit, it invites an approach to learning, teaching and behaviour that complements the skills, abilities and knowledge that children already have and provides a context in which they can be developed in collaboration with others, including their teachers and other adults such as learning and behaviour support assistants. In collaborative tasks, children come to realise that they and others have ideas, opinions and beliefs that are valid and valuable. Similarly, learning behaviours entail a range of functions from planning, justifying, and challenging to ordering, structuring and making sense of what is being learned.

If such experiences are to be sustainable, however, they must be understood both in practical and theoretical terms. While the goal of compensatory pedagogies is normalisation, the goal of complementary pedagogies can be understood in more humanistic terms as autonomy within broadly communitarian principles. Addison (2012) refers to this approach as one of 'academic care' and, in reference to Lingard et al. (2003) 'making hope practical'. Teachers and children find themselves in a condition of unknowing; that is, while they experience difficult behaviours they are unlikely to consider them as mis- or inappropriate behaviours but rather as the manifestation of often unknown circumstances that require to be understood from a range of perspectives including that of the pupil, other children and the teacher. Since the focus of the teacher can be understood as the development of children's autonomy, emotional self-regulation and integrity, the appropriate approaches are those in which the teacher is most skilled, teaching. Learning therefore becomes the medium through which children generate insight into and understanding of their social, emotional and cognitive selves. Within a complementary pedagogy, the teacher does not seek to normalise learners' traits, thoughts and behaviours but to recognise and affirm them as attributes, to enliven them and seek to give them expression. In this regime, the relationship between the teacher and children is authoritative, that is, the teacher gains trust and respect through who she is and what she does. Children come to school expecting to learn and engage with other children, not be punished, rewarded or segregated from their peers. When they learn, especially in collaboration with others, they develop the skills and abilities they need to address current and future issues in all areas of their lives. While school as a feature of the ecosystem that constitutes a child's life and development through childhood and into the adult world constitutes a relatively short time, it is nevertheless of major significance as what happens in school will impact on other areas of the child's life, including their future. The part that teachers play in children's progress, therefore, may be modest but is extremely important. Adopting a focus on learning rather than behaviour through complementary pedagogy can be understood, therefore, as a pedagogy of participation, trust and hope.

Thinking point

- What teaching approaches have you experienced, used or observed in schools?
- Which would you describe as compensatory or complementary and why?

Making hope practical: metacognition as a learning process

View from practice

One possible way of creating an enhanced learning context, in which children develop the skills, abilities, aptitudes and dispositions they will require to address cognitive, social and emotional issues throughout their lives, is to adopt a metacognitive approach to learning. Head and O'Neill (1999) describe how one metacognitive programme operated in a special school for young people who had been excluded from mainstream school as a result of issues related to behaviour. They used Instrumental Enrichment, a metacognitive programme developed by Reuven Feuerstein to support a variety of learners with a range of difficulties and used in Israel. (See Head and O'Neill, 1999.)

A metacognitive approach to learning entails children generating the knowledge they need to attempt and complete any task they are set. The information required to generate that knowledge may come from a variety of sources including the pupils' previous experiences, the teacher, books, the internet, and

(Continued)

(Continued)

other learners. Having generated this knowledge, pupils then embark on planning behaviour. The first step is to define the task to be undertaken. This makes obvious sense as, if the children know exactly what they are supposed to be doing before they begin to do it, they are more likely to get it right. Again, the knowledge is generated by the pupils with the teacher asking a series of questions that prompt pupils into thinking about the task.

The next step is to generate a strategy for carrying out the task. Once the strategy has been developed and put into place, it can be evaluated. So, when a strategy has worked, pupils are encouraged to investigate why it has worked and to anticipate where the same or a similar strategy might be useful in the future. Similarly, when a strategy does not work, they are encouraged to consider why and to modify it or form another strategy.

Having engaged with the task (but not necessarily completed it) the children are then asked to reflect on what they have learned whilst carrying out the task. Some of what they have learned will relate directly to the task but other, perhaps more significant information, will relate to the learning process itself. For example, whilst carrying out some of Feuerstein's exercises, pupils noted that one of the things they learned was that when they have a task to perform, it can be helpful to look for clues to assist them. The importance of identifying what has been learned becomes apparent in the next part of the process that Feuerstein refers to as bridging. Bridging helps children make the links between what they are currently learning and the wider world, thereby giving their learning a value and significance beyond the immediate context. So, for example, children who learned that it is helpful to look for clues when completing a task could be asked to think about when else it would be helpful for them to look for clues, whose job would require them to search out clues, and how they, as young learners, would use this strategy in a range of contexts.

The significance of this process for children who may be experiencing SEBD is twofold. First, whilst they are doing all of the above, they are exhibiting learning behaviour. In other words, not only has inappropriate or 'mis'- behaviour been eliminated, it has been replaced by a range of behaviours that enhance the learning experience. This goes much further than behaviour modification programmes that stop at the point of elimination of unacceptable behaviours and assume that the quiet, or polite or compliant behaviours that follow will automatically ensure that learning is taking place. Learning behaviour may be a much more secure indicator that learning is taking place. If it is, then this is the kind of behaviour that would be appropriate for all children in classes. Other learning behaviours which form part of a metacognitive approach include: comparing, justifying, challenging, sequencing, summarising, analysing, criticising, conceptualising, hypothesising and working systematically. These are the skills and abilities that all children can employ to address the issues in their current and future lives. Moreover, a fundamental proposition related to metacognition is that developments in the cognitive sphere of the human mind have an equal impact on the affective domain. In simple terms, the argument is that it is impossible to think without feeling or feel without thinking. As children increasingly engage with their learning in this way they begin to challenge identities related to ignorance or bad behaviour and to generate the most appropriate identity for school, that of the effective learner. An approach to learning understood in terms of humanistic systems and choice theories can be more effective in addressing social and emotional issues than those aimed at observable and measureable behaviour.

A mediational style of teaching

In terms of classroom learning, mediation is the act of the teacher placing her or himself between the child and the world in such a way that it helps the child interpret the world meaningfully. The teacher-mediator is always searching for explanations, reasons, causes and is constantly exploring possibilities. The mediator realises that giving a learner information is not the same thing as the learner generating the information for him or herself as the result of probing, questioning and challenging.

View from practice

A teacher asks a pupil to carry out a task such as, 'Can you close that door, please?' This is a request, and no matter how polite, the child is left with only two choices: to comply or to refuse. If requests are only ever given in this way, then the options never alter and the child will comply or not depending on a number of other factors that probably remain unstated.

However, if the request is expanded a little to include something like, 'There's a lot of noise out in the corridor and I can't concentrate on what I'm doing and it's disturbing our work', then the teacher has begun a process of mediation. The request is still there to be carried out or refused, but this time the pupil has been given a reason for carrying out the task, and the task

(Continued)

(Continued)

therefore carries a purpose beyond pleasing the teacher. Moreover, the teacher has introduced an element of cause and effect, thereby justifying the request. The pupil may still refuse to carry out the task but having been given a reason for doing it, may feel obliged to offer a reason for refusal. Moreover, as pupils become used to this process they engage in it themselves so that in some future occasion where they wish to not comply, they are likely to offer legitimate reasons for their decision without the teacher having to probe (Head and O'Neill, 1999).

Mediating mechanisms

Process questioning is the most commonly used means of mediating learning experiences. A teacher-mediator rarely accepts an answer at face value. Where the answer is right, the mediator wants to know how the learner knew that, how they came to that conclusion, what other possible answers there were and why they were rejected. In other words, they ask lots of 'how' and 'why' questions.

In addition, teacher-mediators want to challenge their own and learners' learning and behaviour. They want others to justify their answers and they are prepared to justify their own actions. Teacher-mediators mediate for the regulation of behaviour by having a clear focus on learning and having respect for the people in their class as learners. In addition, mediation helps create a sense of mutual respect and dignity through recognising the creativity in even the most obscure of responses and being prepared to explore them. In such cases, even pupil actions that begin as 'mickey-taking' can turn out to be the source of significant learning experiences.

Summary

One of the main arguments throughout this chapter has been that it is unhelpful to look at behavioural difficulties as in-child deficits that have to be dealt with as a prerequisite to learning. Another has been that it is simply not enough to eliminate unacceptable or inappropriate behaviour and to assume that learning will naturally follow.

One of the privileges of working with young people who may be experiencing SEBD is that their needs and rights encourage teachers to think how best to support them. The form of support that teachers are best equipped to provide is to help them become better learners. Through being better learners, they will be able to generate the knowledge, insights and strategies they require to deal with the difficulties and problems that we all encounter through life.

Reflective questions

- What are the implications of dealing with unwanted behaviour as a matter of indiscipline?
- What are the identities you wish to construct for the children whom you will teach?
- What approaches to learning and teaching do you consider to be most appropriate for all pupils, including those whose behaviour you find difficult?

Further reading

Daniels, H. (2001) *Vygotsky and Pedagogy*. London: RoutledgeFalmer.

This is a comprehensive study of the implications for schools and teachers of Vygotsky's theories on learning and development. These theories form the basis of learning and teaching that can be understood in terms of complementary pedagogy.

Head, G. (2011) 'Inclusion and pedagogy', in M. McMahon, C. Forde and M. Martin (eds), *Contemporary issues learning and teaching*. London: SAGE. pp. 60–71.

This chapter contains a more detailed discussion of compensatory and complementary pedagogies in relation to inclusion.

Kohn, A. (2006). *Beyond Discipline: From Compliance to Community*. 2nd edn. Ohio: Merrill Prentice Hall.

This text constitutes a critical account of behaviourist approaches to dealing with behaviour, especially those based on rewards and sanctions.

Mowat, J. (2007). *Using Support Groups to Improve Behaviour*. London: SAGE.

This book reports on the effectiveness of a collaborative peer group strategy to address learning and behaviour.

CHAPTER 8

DEVELOPING A CAPACITY FOR LEARNING

Vivienne Baumfield

Key ideas

This chapter explores:

- the emphasis on self-efficacy and self-regulation in learning;
- the importance of developing practical tools to support innovation in learning and teaching;
- the demands that developing a capacity for learning makes on the teacher and the implications for their professional values and identity; and
- the benefits of engaging in collaborative inquiry, with pupils and with other teachers, as part of a community of inquiry.

Examples are drawn from the experiences of the teachers in the Learning to Learn in Schools project, involved in annual cycles of action research into their own practice.

Learning and learning how to learn

Developing learning capacity is not a new idea but it has become more prominent as the pace of change in society accelerates and research expands our understanding of the interplay of philosophy, psychology and sociology in the learning process. In recent years there have been two major projects on developing classroom approaches that focus on raising learners' awareness of how they are learning: the Learning How to Learn project based on the principles of Assessment for Learning (James et al., 2006) and the Learning to Learn in Schools project, which built on research into learning dispositions (Higgins et al., 2007).

Developing a capacity for learning uses ideas taken from recent developments in cognitive psychology that suggest that intelligence is not innate or fixed. If learners are given the opportunity to participate in rich learning environments with appropriate support then their potential to learn is increased. The difference between successful learners and those who may struggle in the classroom is the extent to which they are able to understand what is required of them and are aware of the strengths and weaknesses of their existing strategies for learning. Advocates of approaches designed to develop learning capacity tend to draw upon the work of socio-constructivists who emphasise the benefits of learning by engaging in the active construction of meaning through social interaction with more knowledgeable peers or adults. Close parallels exist between these approaches and interventions designed to develop thinking skills. They are also linked to the idea that in a modern society, where knowledge is changing rapidly, it is important for students to leave school ready to participate in life-long learning. The result is a proliferation of different but overlapping programmes aimed at improving learning in schools, which can be confusing.

In 2005 the UK government asked the independent research group Demos to conduct a review of approaches to developing learning capacity in school classrooms and their importance in enabling students to become better learners. Demos convened a working group consisting of three headteachers and three cognitive scientists chaired by Professor David Hargreaves, who had established an international reputation for his work on the knowledge-creating capacity of schools. The group concluded that whilst teachers tended to be over-reliant on 'common sense' views of learning and lacked a professional vocabulary with which to discuss learning, with either their colleagues or their students, contemporary circumstances provided an ideal opportunity to redress this situation. The working group highlighted two enabling factors in the current educational context: firstly, the advances being made by cognitive psychologists in developing deeper understanding of how we learn; secondly, the promotion of closer relationships between research and practice through the development of evidence-informed policy. Consequently, teachers were open to new ideas and more willing to experiment in the classroom.

However, whilst phrases such as 'learning to learn' were in common use, pinning down what was actually meant by developing a capacity for learning could be more challenging and make the evaluation of the evidence base for some of the approaches difficult. The working group highlighted the need to elucidate the link between learning to learn approaches and learning in a more general sense, and the generation of criteria by which to determine learner progression and identify good practice (Hargreaves, 2005).

Thinking point

- Do you agree that teachers tend to rely on 'common sense' views and lack the vocabulary to talk about learning as professionals?
- What are the opportunities for discussing learning in your school with colleagues or students?

Cognitive psychologists emphasise that developing a capacity for learning requires the development of metacognitive awareness, understanding how you learn, and self-regulation so that you can recognise and seek remedies to address any problems in learning. For Claxton (2006), expanding the capacity to learn is a more radical proposition than simply improving learning. Preparing students for an uncertain future requires more than simply ensuring the effective acquisition of what is already known and involves the development of a theory of learning in which knowledge is seen as rapidly changing. He talks about developing an 'epistemic culture' in classrooms and schools in which learning capacity is understood as being a combination of philosophical, psychological and sociological factors. Learning to learn then becomes as much a matter of values and character as it is of acquiring greater cognitive skill, and the formation of 'habits of mind' that promote resilience and resourcefulness is important. The Demos working group concluded that it is more productive to think in terms of a 'family' of learning practices that enhance students' capacity to learn by integrating psychological descriptions of individual skills with philosophical reflections on personal dispositions. This focus on the co-ordination of a set of practices is consistent with the final stage in Claxton's description of four generations of teaching learning (Claxton, 2006) and by establishing a relationship between student learning and teacher learning locates the discussion more firmly in the context of pedagogy:

First generation

- Raising attainment
- Good teaching is the effective delivery of content knowledge

Second generation

- Developing study skills
- Hints tips and techniques

Third generation

- Emotional and social factors
- Characteristic ways of learning
- Concerned with the 'how' of teaching

Fourth generation

- Involvement of students in the process
- Concerned with how students can be helped to help themselves
- Teachers themselves involved in becoming better learners
- Developmental and cumulative

Integrating research and practice

The development of criteria for evaluating the impact of approaches to building learning capacity through closer integration of research and practice was the focus of two major school-based research and development projects in the UK: Learning How to Learn (LHTL) and Learning to Learn (L2L).

The Learning How to Learn project

'Learning How to Learn' was a four-year project funded as part of the Teaching and Learning Research Programme (TLRP) and involved 40 primary and secondary schools in seven different local authorities in England. At the beginning of the project, there was no satisfactory, agreed definition of what developing learning capacity through learning how to learn might look like, beyond the assumption that it would involve the self-monitoring and self-regulating aspects of metacognition (James, 2013). Consequently, the focus was on embedding and spreading what had been learned regarding strategies that could support and develop learner autonomy and agency from previous research into formative assessment. Teachers in the partnership schools participated in a session demonstrating tools to promote the four key aspects of Assessment for Learning (AfL):

- rich classroom dialogue and questioning to elicit students' understanding;
- formative feedback to help students know how to improve;

- sharing learning objectives, criteria and exemplars of what counts as quality learning in specific subject domains with the learner;
- peer- and self-assessment.

LHTL's emphasis on what can be done in the school classroom to develop learning capacity challenged the idea that there is a set of distinct learning to learn study skills and concluded:

> ... that LHTL cannot be separated from learning itself, i.e. learning something. Rather it is an activity involving a family of learning practices (tools) that enable learning to happen. This explains our preference for 'learning how to learn' over 'learning to learn' – the how word is important. (James, 2013: 141)

They found that the key to the promotion of LHTL with students is the development and support of teacher learning, as teacher beliefs affect how they use the AfL tools and their willingness to promote student autonomy. In the current climate, the pressures on teachers to adopt practices at odds with their educational values, a situation that has become acute in the years since the publication of the Demos working group report, also needs to be considered. Closing the gap by re-aligning practice with core values requires support for teacher dialogue, the possibility of reasoned dissent and encouragement to take calculated risks in order to further professional learning. The LHTL project also identified the need to develop a better understanding of the different types of networks and links in and between schools so that new ways of thinking about teacher learning can thrive. Teachers in the schools that participated in the LHTL project, for example, were very positive about the benefits of engaging in collaborative inquiry into their practice:

> Opportunities to work collaboratively, in an atmosphere of trust and mutual respect, will help to build the social capital needed for teachers to share, reflect upon, and develop their ideas and practices. These constitute the intellectual capital of schools. (James, 2013: 152)

The Learning to Learn in Schools project

The Campaign for Learning's 'Learning to Learn in Schools' (L2L) project investigated practical approaches for the development of learning capacity in 32 schools in three local authorities in England over a period of four years. The Campaign for Learning had adopted the 5Rs model of dispositions developed by Guy Claxton (readiness, resourcefulness, remembering, resilience and reflection) as a useful basis for developing approaches in schools and the project began by using the following working definition of L2L:

...(it is) a process of discovery about learning. It involves a set of principles and skills which, if understood and used, help learners learn more effectively and so become learners for life. At its heart is the belief that learning is learnable. (Campaign for Learning, online)

At the same time, it was important to explore what this concept might mean and understand how the teachers in the project were interpreting 'learning to learn' in their practice. Teachers' conceptions of developing learning capacity in classrooms and schools were explored in each year of the project by eliciting responses to three questions:

- What can a L2L pupil do?
- What can a L2L teacher do?
- What is a L2L school like?

Analysis of the responses from all of the teachers involved in the project elicited three broad overlapping categories summarising the teachers' views of pupils: they were aware of the process of learning; they were prepared for learning; and they were good communicators about their learning. L2L teachers were characterised by their emphasis on the quality of relationships with pupils; their ability to make the process of learning explicit; their skill in creating inclusive learning environments. The strongest theme with respect to the features of a L2L school was the creation of a learning school culture with common aims but diverse means; the importance of the pupils' role in shaping the school culture was also highlighted, as was the willingness to experiment. The final report of the L2L in Schools project identified four overarching themes linking the teachers' descriptions of pupils, teachers and schools engaged in developing a capacity for learning:

1. A shift of responsibility for learning away from the individual teacher or learner towards more inter-dependent learning roles where individuals take responsibility, seek help, support others, make mistakes, reflect and revise their plans.
2. An exploration of a range of successful approaches for different learners: accessibility of learning to learn techniques which may support difference and which emphasise the acquisition of a broad repertoire of learning skills, approaches and active knowledge.
3. A focus on communication skills – pupils, teachers and schools – discussing learning explicitly, where the strategies and motivations which underpin learning become part of everyone's overt understanding, as well as the development of each learner's personal repertoire of tools and techniques.
4. An approach which accepts the benefits of change and which acknowledges that the process should be challenging but which provides support for both pupils and for teachers (Higgins et al., 2007: 22).

Thinking point

- How similar do you think the definitions of developing learning capacity from the two major UK research and development projects are?
- Is it either feasible or desirable to try and identify a capacity for learning to learn, or learning how to learn, that is distinct from learning as commonly understood by teachers and students in schools?

The L2L in Schools initiative aimed to investigate three aspects: whether, and if so how, learning to learn approaches support the development of confident and capable lifelong learners; the relative importance of different learning to learn approaches in raising standards; the impact of the adoption of learning to learn approaches on teacher motivation and capacity to manage change. L2L in Schools adopted a model of professional inquiry whereby teachers in the participating schools were supported in completing classroom-based empirical investigations of the approaches and strategies they believed would enhance learners' skills, knowledge and attitudes for learning to learn. Teachers were supported by their local authorities and by the university-based team of researchers in carrying out annual reports of their inquiries explaining what they had learnt. During the lifetime of the initiative a total of 85 case studies were written by teachers and an analysis of these enabled emerging themes from across all of the participating schools to be identified. Significantly, whilst some schools started out using specific 'off-the-shelf' learning to learn skills packages, by the end of the project they were more likely to develop their own approaches to meet the needs of pupils in their class. At the same time, there was a move away from 'stand-alone' learning to learn lessons towards infusing strategies into subject teaching as teachers became more confident about 'tinkering' with and adapting the approach to suit the context in which they worked. The approaches to developing a capacity for learning used most frequently by teachers focused on talk-based aspects of learning. Pupils and teachers valued opportunities for the development of a language for learning and communicating about learning to others (including parents and other people outside of the classroom). Formative assessment strategies were found to be particularly effective in providing a strong focus on talk for learning through self and peer evaluation activities.

In both the LHTL and the L2L project, having access to practical strategies, tools, to support teaching was identified as an important aspect of developing a capacity for learning. Tools are designed to make a particular activity different, faster, slower, richer, more focused, more efficient, more sustained, and carry with them the rules for how they are used. In this sense, tools are part of the implicit learning of a professional culture, since they frame practice and new tools and technologies can facilitate or enforce change (Hickman, 1990). When a teacher is using a new tool in the context of their pedagogical practice, the experience will have aspects of familiarity (since the tool is grounded in the territory of learning), and of novelty (since something is being added to the repertoire). This combination of security and novelty creates the conditions for the teacher to experience 'positive dissonance' (Baumfield, 2006), whereby as the tool opens up new channels for feedback, routines and expectations are disrupted without the teacher feeling vulnerable. The teacher then has the opportunity to engage in a re-framed experience. This refocusing

Pupil response record: Circle time

Name: Rachael

Age: 8

Circle time...

Figure 8.1 Pupil View Template

of attention away from the teacher's performance to a greater awareness of the process of learning is reported by many teachers and is an important feature of the use of the tools.

In the L2L project, tools such as Pupil View Templates were used to promote learning through a cycle of inquiry for students, and also became research tools when used by teachers for the systematic gathering of evidence.

A Pupil View Template (PVT) is a visual method for collecting data around a cartoon image of a learning situation in a classroom; the template prompts the students to reflect on their responses to different aspects of the experience. The speech bubbles focus their attention on what the students portrayed in the cartoon might be saying, whilst the thought bubbles are intended to elicit what they might be thinking. PVTs permit a range of responses from simple descriptions to more sophisticated accounts of abstract thinking processes or complex emotions. Research into their impact on students shows that they are an effective tool in developing metacognitive awareness and skills, and teachers also report that students are more likely to listen more carefully to their peers and to be more supportive of each other (Wall and Higgins, 2006). The feedback from the PVT is immediate and context-specific, which makes them very relevant to the needs of both learners and teachers. They work 'in the moment' as a tool for learning and for teaching whilst also having the capacity to function as a research tool for the investigation of differences between individuals or groups, changes over time in discourse patterns or evidence of metacognitive processes. PVTs can provide an evidence base for the sharing of successful interventions between teachers, leading to more extensive and systematic use across a school and, as confidence in their use grows, creative adaptations to suit the context.

The following vignettes illustrate how teachers in the L2L in Schools initiative developed their understanding of how to develop learning capacity through classroom enquiry.

View from practice

Will involving pupils in reflecting on learning through the use of e-learning logs increase motivation and resilience?

Two teachers in a small primary school in the South West of England wanted to explore the question of whether involving pupils in reflecting on their learning increases motivation and resilience. The pupils in Y6, 10 to 11-year-olds in the last year of primary school, were encouraged to keep electronic diaries throughout the year, recording reflections on their own learning using words and photographs. Evidence of the impact of this intervention on the pupils' capacity for learning was collected by analysing the reflections in the e-learning logs and by teacher observations.

It became obvious to the teachers that the pupils were finding it difficult to articulate their learning as opposed to describing what they had done. To help this process a series of questions relating to the e-learning logs were displayed in the classroom as prompts. However, most children still found developing the concepts behind these questions hard and it became clear that the concepts needed to be introduced to them earlier, discussed and revisited frequently to make a difference. The fact that there was a whole-school approach to assessment for learning was beneficial in so far as the children were familiar with the language used in the evaluation of learning, but further reinforcement by the teacher was needed to connect this to the use of the e-learning logs.

The initial intention to use the logs regularly through the year did not develop as much as the teacher hoped as the preparation for end of Key Stage 2 tests dominated most of the summer term. However, looking back on the project, the teacher realised that many opportunities to continue with the e-learning logs once the tests were over had been missed. In hindsight, children had not been encouraged to reflect on such valuable learning experiences as outdoor education, visits to the new secondary school and participation in the school production. Despite these limitations, the pupils' reflections recorded in the e-learning logs were encouraging in so far as they showed how they were beginning to recognise the value for their learning:

I like looking back at my slides to remember what we did.

I had forgotten about converting fractions to decimals but then I saw them in my log.

The laptops help me add in other things and it looks colourful.

If I hadn't put the photo in my log I wouldn't have remembered the An Gof tapestry and how good I felt we had done.

We did dance with another school and worked together really well as a group.

The teachers concluded that one tangible benefit that came from the intervention was the support for pupils to refer to past learning and remind themselves of particular strategies or positive experiences of learning.

(Continued)

(Continued)

Analysis of the teachers' observations of the class suggested the following outcomes of the intervention:

- The pupils were motivated by the opportunity to be involved in the assessment of their own learning and it had a positive effect on their self-esteem.
- The older children appeared to be motivated by their success and not by extrinsic rewards.
- Those pupils who made most use of the opportunity to record their reflections also had a more explicit understanding of the role of the teacher and their own responsibilities as learners.

The teachers decided to continue with the initiative but to try to make stronger connections with assessment for learning throughout the school. They also recognised the need to reinforce the language of learning as an integral part of subject-based tasks as well as in terms of the actual recording of reflections in the e-learning log. Finally, the teachers themselves learned not to ignore the powerful learning opportunities that non-classroom based, more informal activities can provide.

View from practice

To what extent is the development of speaking and listening skills a prerequisite for children to become more efficient learners?

Two teachers in a large four-form-entry London primary school, with a transient pupil population in which over 30 different home languages were being spoken, chose to focus on the relationship between developing speaking and listening skills and the capacity to evaluate learning. They realised that a key factor necessary for success was the development of the children's ability to talk about how, as well as what, they were learning. This led to the primary focus being on analysis of the development of speaking and listening through the collection of evidence from teacher observations, the use of pupil views templates and attainment and behavioural data routinely collected throughout the year.

The teachers developed a programme of skills to encourage talk and improve the quality of paired work and feedback. The programme was used with one of the four Year 3 classes, of pupils aged between 7 and 8-years-old, and the other three classes acted as a comparison group. During the year positive, supportive paired relationships were seen to develop in the project class, with a reduction in negative comments and a greater understanding of how to work together. Evidence for this could also be found in the pupil views templates completed at regular intervals as well as in discussions with the teacher. By the year's end children of all ability levels were found to be using sentences of greater length and of greater complexity. The children were also able to complete observations of one another's talk and to identify key features of feedback.

At the start of the year the project class was seen as the class with the lowest attainment as adjudged by statutory Standardised Assessment Tests (SATs) results, yet by the end they were the class who had made the most progress.

Table 8.1 Comparative attainment results

	Project Class [30 children]	Comparison Classes [90 children]
Reading	5.6	2.2
Writing	5.4	3.3
Mathematics	2.5	2.0

The teachers involved drew the following conclusions:

- The strategies used improved children's speaking and listening skills as well as giving them the language and ability to talk about their own learning.
- There would seem to be a clear link between this development of speaking and listening and the raising of attainment.
- The development of a positive ethos within the class, inherent in the L2L approach, may have supported improvements in the children's behaviours.
- Underlying any of these successful outcomes was the need for the teacher to be knowledgeable, enthusiastic and committed to L2L approaches.

(A version of these vignettes can be found as case studies included in Baumfield et al., 2013.)

Thinking point

- What do you think might be the advantages and disadvantages of teachers engaging in inquiry into their own practice?

Many teachers started off as isolated innovators within their schools, but for most participants there was a process of expansion as the innovations were disseminated within and beyond their schools. Scaling up, however, was challenging as teachers found that although evidence based on their own practice was compelling it was not simply a case of 'spreading the word', as supportive professional development was also required. Effective implementation of approaches across a school needed time to be given to the development of new skills for both pupils and staff and for sustained dialogue about pedagogy to be encouraged.

There is considerable diversity in terms of the impact of learning to learn on schools. It is evident that the structures and cultures of some schools are a better fit with such innovations as learning to learn. In some schools learning to learn has offered a set of practices which are consonant with the senior leaders' values. Where there has been success it has been because of the motivation of such leaders, the enthusiasm and commitment of key individuals in the school (not necessarily in [formal] leadership roles) and their willingness to experiment, share experiences across the school and to trust one another to improve the quality of learning taking place through professional enquiry (Higgins et al., 2007: 82).

Summary

Developing a capacity for learning requires the development of a set of practices that can support the formation of effective learning habits and dispositions. In both the LHTL and the L2L in Schools projects it was found that such practices cannot easily, or productively, be separated from learning itself as they are the tools that enable it to happen. Where there is a slight but significant difference in emphasis between different approaches to developing a capacity for learning is in the conceptualising of the dynamic of the relationship between common principles, generic tools and specific, diverse, practices. In some approaches there is more reliance on the power of the tools themselves to create opportunities in the classroom for the elicitation of understanding of the principles underpinning developing a capacity for learning. Whilst a tool or approach may not have a particularly sound theoretical basis, it can still have the potential to change what happens in classrooms; it has catalytic validity. In the L2L in Schools project, for example, there was a greater tolerance of ambiguity initially as some teachers opted for stand-alone learning skills strategies and the teaching of separate 'learning skills' lessons. Over time the teachers developed sets of practices and a depth of understanding that led them more towards integrated, dialogic teaching and formative assessment; an example of theory emerging out of practice. Essentially this is a question of understanding the relationship of theory to practice in developing professional knowledge. If a sound theoretical understanding is seen as a prerequisite for any innovation rather than being emergent in practice then there is a risk of not valuing the expertise of teachers. Such a view also begs the question of whether we do know in advance what will be best in practice given the very specific and volatile contexts of individual classrooms. As Dewey advised, the solution is to deny any dichotomy between theory and practice by placing greater trust in teaching as an intellectual activity through which we can learn by participating in a community of inquiry. Both of the major research projects in the UK looking at developing a capacity for learning reached this conclusion.

Reflective questions

- If learning has to be learning about something, then what should be an appropriate balance between content, subject knowledge, cognitive skills and the development of positive learning dispositions in the primary school curriculum?
- To what extent do you think current developments in education policy can sustain the ideal of the teacher as an inquiring professional advocated by the LHTL and L2L projects?

Further reading

For more examples of the work of teachers involved in the L2L project, annual reports and case studies can be found at www.campaignforlearning.org.uk.

Further details of the LHTL project with examples of some of the tools that were used can be found in M. James, P. Black, P. Carmichael, C. Conner, P. Dudley, A. Fox, D. Frost, L. Honour, L. MacBeath, R. McCormick, B. Marshall, D. Pedder, R. Procter, S. Swaffield, and D. Wiliam, (2006) *Learning How to Learn: Tools for Schools*. London: Routledge.

Practical examples of how the principles of AfL can be used in classrooms to promote the development of learning capacity can be found in the DVD and booklet *Principles to Practice* distributed to all schools in England by TLRP, which can be downloaded from: http://www.tlrp.org/pub/documents/Principles%20 in%20Practice%20Low%20Res.pdf.

CHAPTER 9

COLLABORATIVE LEARNING

Mike Carroll

Key ideas

This chapter explores:

- collaborative approaches to learning;
- Vygotsky's perspectives on learning and the use of these in the classroom;
- structural elements of collaborative learning;
- the nature of talk during collaborative activity;
- collaborative grouping.

Introduction

There has been a gradual growth in the use of group work in primary schools in the United Kingdom as schools have grown in their awareness of the academic and social benefits to be gained as a result of children working together and helping each other (Gillies and Ashman, 2003). Group work is seen as an alternative to the teacher-as-single-authority, chalk-and-talk approach to teaching and learning. The type of learning taking place in modern manifestations of group work makes use of co-operative learning in order to promote the active involvement of children in their learning and allow for more appropriate 'personalisation' through differentiation. Co-operative learning is seen as 'an instructional technique that is peculiar among teaching strategies because of its ability to aid teachers not only with teaching subject matter but also with teaching certain social skills and dispositions that pervade the school curriculum' (Schul, 2011: 88). Consequently the argument that emerges is that a co-operative approach to learning in the primary classroom is one which will provide children with opportunities not only to learn about curricular content and develop a range of thinking skills to support this learning but it will also support children in the development of social skills and dispositions vital for functioning in contemporary democratic society.

A confusion of terms: co-operative or collaborative?

The terms 'co-operation' and 'collaboration' are often used interchangeably although attempts have been made to differentiate between them; however, it is not entirely clear whether there is any substantive difference between these terms with respect to how this language is used within primary classrooms. At a very basic level there is a commonly-held view amongst primary teachers that co-operative learning is any type of group work (Schul, 2011); but group work can often involve little more than the arrangement of classroom furniture to enable children to share resources. Co-operative learning is designed by the teacher to enable children to go beyond the sharing of resources in order to nurture social interdependence. In co-operative learning, groups are assigned a task for which each child's contribution is essential for the good of the whole group; consequently co-operative learning involves children working together, sharing ideas and resources, taking part in discussions during which they explore different ways to achieve the task being undertaken. More concisely these pedagogical approaches can be defined as teaching strategies in which two or more learners are expected to depend on and be accountable for their own and each other's learning.

Co-operative learning is a structured approach to learning, with the task and structure being largely determined by you as the teacher. The group can sub-divide or 'jigsaw' the task in order to identify individual sub-tasks and then share their outcomes with other group members in order to complete the work. Collaborative learning tends to be more focused on joint activity, typically with the objective of creating a shared understanding along with the possibility that the children can determine what the final product will look like, albeit with guidance from the teacher. Thus whilst co-operative learning involves children working together to achieve individual goals, and this may include learning from others, collaborative learning involves children achieving a shared goal (Watkins et al., 2006). In order to achieve a shared goal children need to engage in a greater degree of discussion and exchange of information and ideas, set within the group environment. The realisation of a 'shared understanding' leads to much deeper and potentially more effective learning than that which can be achieved by individual children working within a co-operative learning framework.

Although the terms are used interchangeably, most primary classrooms tend to operate within a co-operative rather than a collaborative frame as it is often assumed that primary school children do not have the social skills necessary for collaborative working. Consequently collaborative learning is a more all-encompassing concept which offers the possibility for the redefinition of the teacher-pupil relationship. Collaboration requires role shifts for children, including:

- from passive observer to active problem-solver;
- from private to public presence in the classroom;
- from low to high risk as a result of expectations set by oneself and the group;
- from competition with peers to collaborative work with them;
- from learning independently to learning interdependently; and
- from seeing teachers as the source of authority and knowledge to seeing oneself and the community as important sources of authority and knowledge (adapted from Perumal, 2008: 328).

Thinking point

- A defining characteristic of collaborative learning is that the balance of ownership and control of the work shifts from the teacher to the children themselves. Consider groupwork in your classroom and/or school. To what extent is there a discernible role shift?

Some theoretical ideas

The socio-constructivist perspective on learning stresses the importance of knowledge construction taking place within the social context in which the individual is acting; knowledge construction is said to be 'situated' within the context of activity (Kumpulainen and Wray, 2002). Social interaction lies at the heart of collaborative activity; consequently teaching and learning activities need to be constructed in a way that supports the creation of a 'dialogic space' (Wegerif, 2007). Vygotsky (1978) argued that language is critically important in learning as it enables participants to share experiences and create a joint understanding of the learning task. In collaborative activity children are encouraged to think and act collectively to share and merge their understandings as part of a process of meaning-making and knowledge construction. Kumpulainen and Wray (2002: 10) suggest that in involving children as active participants we transform 'classroom interactions from structured discourse patterns to dynamic teaching and learning conversations more typically found in everyday settings.'

Central to this (sociocultural) perspective on teaching and learning is Vygotsky's (1978: 57) concept of internalisation, which defines learning as moving from the social (interpsychological plane) to something 'inside the child' (intrapsychological plane). The movement from the social to the individual, although complex, is facilitated by active participation, particularly when assistance is provided by other 'more knowledgeable others' (MKOs) in the classroom. Clearly you are a MKO but this also includes other more able children supporting their peers. Vygotsky's (1978) notion of the 'zone of proximal development' (ZPD) is helpful in understanding how active participation brings about learning. The ZPD is defined as 'the distance between the actual development level as determined by independent problem solving and the level of potential development as determined through problem solving under adult guidance or in collaboration with more capable peers' (Vygotsky, 1978: 86). The Vygotskian perspective suggests that learning takes place when a child interacts with a MKO who is able to support them to participate in activities that are just above the level where children can perform activities independently. The MKO facilitates and extends learning for a less competent peer by providing scaffolding for their learning. Scaffolding occurs through dialogue involving, amongst other things, the exchange of ideas, clarifying, probing and challenging each other's thinking, acknowledging good ideas, and tentatively offering solutions to problems which lead all participants to transform information into new cognitive and metacognitive understandings.

Asymmetrical relationships (high-low ability) within the cognitive domain can be seen as a concern as there appear to be no discernible gains for high ability children acting as MKOs. For all participants to benefit it is necessary to formulate tasks which cannot be completed by more able children by themselves. Only through working together can the task be achieved. Collaborative work has both socio-emotional and socio-cognitive dimensions to learning; consequently asymmetrical pairings are more likely to result in positive interaction if the more able children are encouraged to see themselves as helpers. However, asymmetry within the cognitive domain can, in some cases, be reversed within the socio-emotional domain so presenting the possibility of the collaborative experience being mutually beneficial.

Structural elements

The acronym PIPER describes the basic elements of collaborative learning:

- Positive interdependence;
- Individual accountability;
- Promotive interaction;
- Extension of social skills; and
- Reflection on performance.

Positive interdependence

This involves setting a task that children working by themselves would find difficult to complete. A common strategy is to facilitate positive interdependence through the task structure by setting a task with a single outcome or product which must be accomplished within a specified time frame; consequently the task can only be achieved if children working as a group coordinate their efforts. Group members can 'jigsaw' the task into sub-tasks with individual group members working independently on their different sub-tasks. Alternatively group members can perform different roles (such as leader or checker) with each contributing to the completion of the task. In this way the group goal can only be achieved by the collective contributions of all of the group members. The practice of sharing and constructing perspectives through collaborative interaction generates an intellectual and social synergy that promotes reflection, planning and metacognition (Kumpulainen and Wray, 2002). Johnson (2003) also argues that goal interdependence can be amplified by linking it to reward, such that successful completion of the task within the specified time frame leads to a reward being distributed to the members of the group, for example, by giving additional golden time.

Individual accountability

There are a number of potential problems that you as a teacher will need to be aware of, as some children can effectively become 'collaborative ghosts', drifting in and out of engagement, whilst others function as 'collaborative workhorses'. This is often acceptable to highly able 'workhorses' as they are often content to dominate and marginalise other members of the group in order to complete the task. This is often rationalised by some children in terms of differences in their respective abilities being deployed to achieve the task. It is critically important to ensure that each group member not only has a responsibility for completing and sharing their own part of the task but that there is an expectation that they will take responsibility for learning all parts of the task; consequently each group member has responsibility for their own learning as well as for helping other group members to learn. In evaluating performance it is important to take account both of the overall attainment of the group as well as each individual member within the group.

View from practice

An NQT in an upper primary class used variations of a technique called Numbered Heads Together which involves randomly selecting a group reporter in order to preserve individual accountability. The basic approach adopted was to ask the children in each group to secretly number themselves, that is, 1, 2, 3, and so on. The teacher would then call out a different number for each group and the child selected would then be expected to report back to the class of the findings of their group. Alternatively the teacher used a random name picker (sourced online). Numbered heads was invariably used to identify the group reporter for more extended problem-solving tasks, for example, talking the class through a poster presentation. The teacher believed that identifying the reporter at the end of the activity ensured that all the children remained actively involved in supporting each other in understanding the material as every child knew that potentially they could be named as the reporter. This acted as a powerful motivator to ensure individual accountability. The same teacher also used 'Listening pairs'. Children worked in pairs sharing their responses to the questions set. Children would then be randomly selected to share the paired response to the wider group. Having children respond in this way encouraged them to listen more attentively to each other and so promoted active participation and reinforced the idea of learning as a shared endeavour.

Promotive interaction

Collaborative learning within the classroom is predicated upon Chen and Looi's (2011) notion of cognitive proximity, which has two key dimensions: interaction and dialogue. Cognitive proximity is contrasted with non-collaborative classrooms in which teachers strive to control the structure and content of classroom interaction by creating a 'quality audience' which typically means that the teacher controls the dialogue with children being invited to respond to questions posed by the teacher so reducing children to 'active listeners'.

According to Kagan (1994), the collaborative classroom requires children to be grouped in order to facilitate face-to-face interaction, largely independent of the teacher. Johnson and Johnson (2004) refer to this as promotive interaction as it involves children helping each other in achieving the task set, and ultimately improving performance, by exchanging information, clarifying understandings, explaining thinking and providing constructive feedback.

The social experience of participating in dialogic interaction serves to motivate children into deeper engagement with the task set. Children taking ownership of the dialogue is illustrative of Chen and Looi's (2011: 679) notion of 'socio-linguistic proximity (children communicating to one another in their own language)'. Essentially, face-to-face dialogic interaction is at the heart of this process; consequently group members support each other in terms of cognitive performance as well as the development of interpersonal and group-work skills.

Extension of social skills

Collaborative engagement creates a 'social space' which supports children's socio-emotional and socio-cognitive development. All the children have a role to play in undertaking the task set; they learn to ask for support from, and to offer support to each other and in so doing they build a sense of responsibility and belonging. Children will not necessarily develop and extend their social and communication skills by virtue of being placed in groups without planned interventions (Johnson, 2003). Group-work skills, including relational and communicative skills, need to be developed over a period of time in order to support the process dimension of collaboration, requiring a degree of perseverance from you as the teacher. Teaching interpersonal and group-work skills is likely to enhance the process of collaboration. Gillies (2007) outlines a range of interpersonal and group-work skills which can include:

- contributing ideas;
- taking turns in sharing ideas, tasks and resources;
- creating an atmosphere of trust and respect for each other;
- actively listening to each other using appropriate body language;
- suspending judgement;
- asking questions to clarify meaning and verify understanding;
- giving reasons for their views and being able to change their views;
- planning and organisation;
- conflict management; and
- providing constructive feedback.

Thinking point

- Consider groupwork in your classroom or school. How are children prepared for groupwork so that children can develop and extend their social and communication skills?

Reflection on performance

Finally as a teacher you should build into the process opportunities to evaluate the product, or cognitive results of children's teamwork, and to consider what learning can be gleaned from the process of collaborative interaction in order to identify adjustments that can be made to bring about improved performance. This can be either teacher-led or group-led evaluation and assessed at group or individual level. Involving the children in this evaluative process (self and peer assessment) can be highly productive as it supports metacognitive thinking by enabling them to identify strategies that bring about positive outcomes to collaborative activity. For example, providing constructive feedback on the positive contributions that individual children make to group work is more likely to increase the incidence of such positive behaviours and thus reinforce the likelihood of improved outcomes to collaborative group work. Furthermore, the process of sharing views and perspectives within and across groups can support children in discovering different ways of approaching tasks and solving problems.

Planning collaborative learning experiences

There are three different phases for you to think about in planning collaborative learning experiences, namely:

- the introduction phase:
  - exposition – you outline the challenge, nature of product to demonstrate learning and the time frame set aside for task completion;
- the processing phase:
  - children work as a team to actively solve meaningful problems or work on open-ended tasks following principles of PIPER;
  - children produce designated product and publicly exhibit (present) the outcomes of their learning;

- the plenary phase:
  - o debrief – children reflect on their learning with respect to the challenge set;
  - o assess outcomes of collaborative product and process.

A defining characteristic of collaborative learning experiences is that the balance of ownership and control of the work shifts from you as a teacher to the children themselves. As a teacher you still exercise control in the set-up of the activity; however, some teachers are nevertheless wary of collaborative learning as, at a practical level, it generates more noise in the classroom but more importantly they are unsure about 'giving away' power. We will look at what this 'noise', or rather what talk entails later but the reality is that you will still continue to exercise 'power', albeit more diffusely, as 'a guide on the side, not a sage on the stage' (Blatchford et al., 2003: 168). The collaborative activity is designed to provide children with a collective space in which to share their understandings, negotiate and construct rules for working together and identify solutions to problems among themselves, under your gaze. In stepping back there may be a sense of 'redundancy' as you appear to remain largely on the periphery during the processing phase of the lesson; however, in another sense you become even more active as you guide the children when required; neither too much nor too little help and support so that the children retain as much responsibility as possible for their own learning. Gillies and Boyle (2005: 244) also note that there is a linguistic shift in the pattern of teacher-child interaction as you move from more formal and impersonal interactions, typical of whole-class lessons, to more personal, friendly and supportive interactions with children in their groups.

According to De Lièvre et al., (2006) there are five different guiding roles for you as a teacher during collaborative learning experiences:

- *cognitive*: focusing on the content of the task by assisting children in linking, clarifying and analysing their contributions through prompting and probing using open-ended questions;
- *relational*: dealing with the children's feelings about working together so that they can develop their group-working skills;
- *metacognitive*: helping children develop their understanding of how to plan their learning and organise their work;
- *motivational*: supporting, encouraging and praising the children for their efforts; and
- *organisational*: helping the children orchestrate their efforts so that they can work together efficiently.

It is evident from these guiding roles that you will be actively involved in providing support for the cognitive and the socio-emotional processes. Furthermore in 'walking the talk' you should be actively involved in providing constructive feedback and conducting informal assessment of group and/or individual performance.

Your organisational role will involve ensuring that children, when working within groups, work well together. Conflicts can arise for a number of reasons, such as inappropriate division of time, with some children preferring to spend their time on process (talking) at the expense of product (producing materials illustrating outcomes of learning). A sense of injustice can arise as a result of unequal division of labour with some children emerging as 'loafers and shirkers', whilst others become collaborative 'mules' by taking on almost all of the work. There is also the possibility of unequal cognitive loading, sometimes as a result of misplaced good intentions, with able children taking on tasks which have a high cognitive load, such as gathering information using the internet, whilst other children are relegated to menial tasks, for example, gluing pictures onto poster paper. There is also the possibility that relational bias in the classroom and playground or socio-emotional discomfort, as exhibited by quiet and withdrawn children, may hinder the work of the group. Essentially it is your role to ensure that different personality types are not allowed to dictate the success, or failure, of collaborative group work (Blatchford et al., 2003: 167).

The level of talk within the collaborative classroom is also illustrative of the teacher's ongoing internal dialogue as they oscillate between different identity positions, particularly with respect to how directive they should be in controlling the classroom environment. Mercer's (2000) work on talk suggests that you as a teacher have a crucial role in 'talking into being' the collaborative classroom as there are three ways of talking and thinking within the classroom which are significant to collaborative group work:

- *disputational talk*: which tends to be individualised, competitive rather than cooperative with a tendency to lead to disagreement as individual voices seek to dominate;
- *cumulative talk*: which involves more sharing and agreement although there is little by way of constructive criticism or critical engagement; and
- *exploratory talk*: which involves the sharing of ideas being subject to more critical scrutiny as there is active and supportive engagement by the participants as they build on each others' contributions in order to reach a shared agreement presenting the possibility of joint construction of new knowledge.

The collaborative classroom is one in which we wish for children to engage in exploratory talk; however, it cannot be taken for granted this will emerge as a natural consequence of a teacher designing a collaborative learning experience. For exploratory talk to emerge, you will need to model communication and thinking skills so that children can use these skills to enrich their own discourse and learning. You can scaffold the children's learning through creating a discursive environment which involves probing and clarifying ideas to extend thinking, acknowledging and validating ideas and understandings, reframing statements to consider alternative perspectives, focusing on key contributions, confronting discrepancies in thinking, challenging understandings and tentatively offering suggestions towards a solution (Gillies and Boyle, 2008). For the 'social pedagogic' potential of collaborative work to be fully realized the nature of discourse needs to be 'taught and caught' through a careful integration of teacher-led discourse and dialogic interaction amongst the children (Blatchford et al., 2003).

Thinking point

- Using Mercer's (2000) three ways of talking, how would you describe the discursive environment of your classroom, particularly with respect to groupwork?

Collaborative grouping

Think-pair-share

This technique often provides the starting point for teachers who are new to collaborative learning. You can create a relatively low-risk 'social space' providing children with an opportunity to state their own views and to hear from others so enabling children to move from a private to a public dialogic space. The administrative 'costs' of paired work are minimal, that is, time spent assigning children to pairs. Furthermore, paired work makes it difficult for children to avoid participation. The simplest way to form pairs is through proximity, that is, the shoulder partner. Think-pair-share consists of you posing a challenging or open-ended question which the children are asked to think about, and perhaps record their thoughts, independently. Each child is then connected to form a pair in order to discuss their respective responses to the question, so facilitating active construction of knowledge through dialogic interaction. You can incorporate think-pair-share into your planning as a 'structural bridge' between phases of a lesson, moving from one phase to another whilst building upon the children's responses to a key question. Pairing can be extended through the 'Think-Pair-Square' technique which involves two pairs joining together to form a temporary group. This provides the children with an opportunity to gain more insights by extending the number of people involved in the discussion.

Three-spoke pinwheel

This would involve you forming the children into trios and giving them a task to undertake which involves three roles, for example, talking, listening and recording. The roles are rotated with the pinwheel being complete when each child has performed all three roles. This technique allows children an opportunity to practice different roles as well as ensuring that no one is 'left out' as a result of the formation of a 'buddy pair', that is, two of the trio form a pair and then effectively exclude the remaining member of the trio from any discussion. By creating three distinct roles, with each role being vital to enable task completion, the integrity of the trio is maintained.

Home group

The home or base group is a micro-managed group of between 4 to 6 children; this is the group in which children spend most of their time, but not all, whilst engaging in collaborative activity. In forming a home group strive for a blend of gender, ability (cognitive and socio-emotional), motivational levels, learning and behavioural needs. The 'six-pack' group is best suited to provide a degree of flexibility in terms of forming pairs and trios within and across home groups; however, the size of groups will depend on a range of factors such as age, ability and experience of working collaboratively, the availability of time for group work, the purpose of group work and the nature of the task to be undertaken. As the home group is the most stable grouping it is a good place to practise social skills and rotating team roles which can include:

- *Leader*: to keep the team on task and to moderate discussion;
- *Resource manager*: make sure resources are available and time is monitored;
- *Motivator*: to ensure that everyone participates;
- *Checker*: to ensure everyone understands the task and that the group's response meets the criteria set for the task;
- *Recorder*: to record discussion and to ensure that there is full agreement;
- *Prompter*: to ensure understanding by seeking clarification of ideas being suggested;
- *Artist*: if artwork is needed as part of any presentation; and
- *Reporter*: to explain the group's response to the task to the rest of the class.

Jigsaw

The basic principle of jigsaw is to divide a problem into sections, one for each group member. The group divide a task into several components with the children volunteering to gather information on one sub-task and report back to the group in order for all of the information to be integrated as part of the group's response to the task. Each home group can appoint an 'intelligence officer'. The role of the intelligence officer is to periodically go on an 'intelligence mission' – three stay; one stray – to gather insights from the other home groups. The information that they gather is then reported back to their home group. The 'reporter' should be identified once the task has been completed using the 'Numbered Heads' technique. Assigning the role of reporter at the commencement of a task will compromise the principle of individual accountability as it enables children to effectively sign off on any learning outwith the boundary of their 'expertise'.

Expert groups

This involves temporarily dissolving home groups in order to create new or 'expert groups'. Each expert group is formed from children from each home group who have responsibility for a specific sub-task. These children work together to master their aspect of the task and also to discover the best way to help others learn it. All experts then reassemble in their home groups where they share the findings of their expert group. Each home group uses the report back session to formulate their collective response to the overall task. A variation of this is the Rainbow Jigsaw (spin out/spin back in) with the home group forming their response to the task. New rainbow groups are then created consisting of representatives from each home group (spin out) where the findings of each home group are shared. The home groups are then reformed (spin back in) for all group members to report back. There is a further integration of the ideas gathered. At the spin out phase each rainbow group can be asked to consider another dimension to the task before reforming into home groups.

View from practice

An NQT in an upper primary class commenced the year with the carousel brainstorming technique on the topic 'our learning environment'. The teacher explained that they would be working in groups during the forthcoming year and she wanted to know what factors would help them work effectively in their groups. The children were divided into four roughly equally-sized groups. Four questions were written on flip chart paper and posted on the wall space around the classroom:

- What does an excellent learning environment 'feel like'?
- What does an excellent learning environment 'sound like'?

- What does an excellent learning environment 'look like'?
- How would you wish to be treated by others?

The activity had three phases: brainstorm, distillation and presentation. During the brainstorm phase the groups rotated around the pre-prepared posters spending about three minutes at each poster during which time they wrote down bullet points in response to each question. All contributions were recorded without qualification and comment from other members of the group. The teacher circulated between the groups keeping her contributions to a minimum in order to allow the children's 'voice' to emerge. During the distillation phase each group was given one question each and they were asked to evaluate the ideas listed in order to identify five key elements. Each group then presented their findings to the rest of the class who discussed whether they agreed with the points raised. The teacher then prepared the collective response; each child was given a copy, and an A3 laminated poster entitled 'Our Learning Environment' was placed on the wall space. This became the social contract that the children had with each other for working in groups.

Summary

You will encounter teachers who remain unconvinced about the benefits of collaborative group work for a range of reasons such as: loss of control, increased noise levels, lack of available time, children lacking in the necessary social and communication skills, and that the more able children are hindered in their learning. These concerns may not have been fully dispelled by this chapter but I hope that there is sufficient food for thought such that you will be encouraged to experiment with collaborative group work. The points raised in the chapter may help you to construct a learning environment within which collaborative group work can take place in order to integrate the socio-emotional and socio-cognitive dimensions to learning.

Providing children with opportunities to engage in collaborative learning should be part of all teachers' pedagogical repertoires; however, it is equally important that this approach should not be overused. Rather, collaborative learning should form part of a rich tapestry of learning experiences which includes opportunities for whole class (All), collaborative (We) and independent (I) learning. Collaborative learning is one of the ways in which you can create an inclusive classroom by encouraging children to work together, so building social bridges amongst and between peers. Activities designed to enable children to work towards achieving a common goal whilst preserving the essential principle of individual accountability facilitates the real goal of collaboration, namely that of interdependence amongst peers.

Reflective questions

- What are the benefits of adopting an eclectic approach to teaching and learning by providing children with opportunities to engage in whole class (All), collaborative (We) and independent (I) learning?
- To realise the 'social pedagogy' of classroom groups it is not enough merely to place children in groups. What do you see as being the prerequisites for effective group work?
- Planning collaborative learning experiences characterised by high levels of dialogic engagement can, for some, result in a 'cacophony of voices'. To what extent would you agree and/or disagree with the proposition that this is a managed risk worth taking?
- What do you see as the advantages and/or disadvantages of taking on a guiding but non-directive role in the classroom?

Further reading

Education Scotland (online)

- o Dylan Wiliam's views on the benefits of learners working in group situations and the importance of group goals and individual accountability.
- o http://www.journeytoexcellence.org.uk/videos/expertspeakers/collaborative-learningdylanwiliam.asp (accessed 14 December 2012).
- o Carol McGuinness reflects on how learners develop collaborative thinking skills through working with others towards achieving group goals. http://www.journeytoexcellence.org.uk/videos/collaborativethinkingcarolmcguinness.asp (accessed 14 December 2012).

Gillies, R.M. (2007) *Cooperative Learning: Integrating Theory and Practice*. London: SAGE.
Mercer, N. and Hodgkinson, S. (2008) *Exploring Talk in School*. London: SAGE.

CHAPTER 10

INTERDISCIPLINARY LEARNING

Mike Carroll and Fiona McGregor

Key ideas

This chapter explores:

- tensions between subject-specific and interdisciplinary learning;
- different pedagogical approaches to interdisciplinary learning;
- models of curriculum integration;
- planning integrated learning experiences.

Introduction

A curriculum organised exclusively in terms of the traditional school subjects will not be sufficient to meet the emerging needs of society. The process of globalisation coupled with rapidly changing technology has resulted in the need for us all to acquire new skills so that we can adjust to ever-shifting political, social, economic and environmental demands; consequently the curriculum needs to provide children with opportunities to develop the lifelong skill of 'learning to learn'. Within a rigid subject-based curricular framework there is a danger that children will adopt a silo approach to their thinking and find it difficult to apply ideas and ways of thinking taught within one subject to another area of activity. To prepare children for an unknowable future, schools are required to put in place a more complex curricular structure blending a subject-based curriculum with opportunities for more integrated learning experiences.

Interdisciplinary learning (also referred to as cross-curricular or integrated learning) recognises the need to build bridges between the different subjects in order to bring about a synthesis of the knowledge and understandings, skills and informed attitudes that the discrete subject areas can offer. In the primary school this often takes the form of a 'topic' (area of study which draws upon several curricular areas to reinforce conceptual and content links) or 'theme' (area of study guaranteed a time and a place in the curriculum according it the status of a separate 'subject').

Curricular integration implies wholeness and unity rather than separation and fragmentation (Beane, 1991). Curricular integration provides an opportunity to construct an enriched pedagogical experience for children, a pedagogy of connection (Dillon, 2006). Teachers identify meaningful connections and relationships across the subjects in order to apply ideas, concepts, skills and develop informed attitudes in a more in-depth and relevant learning experience, particularly through the use of problem-solving skills that are transferable throughout the children's curricular experience and their lives.

Educational policy and the integrated curriculum

The 1960s saw movement towards a child-centred philosophy with the publication of two influential reports, namely *Primary Education in Scotland* (SED, 1965 – The Primary Memorandum) and *Children and their Primary Schools* (DES, 1967 – The Plowden Report). Both these reports advocated holistic and rounded education through an extension of the concept of the 'child-centred' curriculum, asserting that 'at the heart of the educational process lies the child' (DES, 1967, Para. 9). The child was seen as an 'agent of his own learning' (DES, 1967, Para. 529). Learning was viewed as taking place through individual exploration and discovery as a result of first-hand experience.

These reports advocated an integrated approach, as 'knowledge does not fall into rigidly separate compartments' (DES, 1967, Para. 503) and 'it is quite impossible to treat the subjects of the curriculum in isolation from one another if education is to be meaningful to the child' (SED, 1965: 37). Accordingly, learning should be facilitated through 'topics' or 'centres of interest' (SED, 1965) which link with children's interests both within and outside the classroom as long as that interest is maintained by the children. The systematic teaching of single curricular disciplines was seen as a teacher-centred pedagogy that was dull and remote from children's interests and, as such, less valuable than the more global approach advocated through centres of interest and a variety of projects. However, even with the Primary Memorandum it was acknowledged that beyond Primary 5 (9–10 year olds) differentiation into discrete subjects was seen as appropriate in order for children to engage in more systematic study.

The re-emergence of curricular specification

From the 1980s onwards UK-wide educational policy increasingly began to reflect central government policy. The curriculum in Scottish primary schools, unlike those in England, Wales and Northern Ireland, was not determined by statute or regulation but by advice from the then Scottish Executive Education Department (SEED), using working parties of teachers and educationalists. However, in the lead-up to the development of the 5–14 Programme (SOED, 1993) there were significant shifts within Scottish education. Firstly, there appeared to have been a shift in policy-making style from 'debate followed by consensus to consultation followed by imposition' (Hartley and Roger, 1990, cited in Adams, 1999: 369). Indeed in the consultation paper (SED, 1987) the Minister left the Scottish educational community in no doubt that the introduction of statutory powers was not ruled out if there was a failure to implement the new curriculum.

The guidelines set out a greater degree of curricular definition with a shift in emphasis from the epistemological (the 'how to know') to the ontological (the 'what to know'). The 5–14 Programme that was developed was based around an 'objectives' model of curriculum with a greater degree of specification in terms of knowledge and attainment targets with specified levels of attainment. Primary schools organised their curriculum through a series of curriculum areas (subjects) in order to ensure that pupils' learning progressed from stage to stage, building on what they had learned before. At the level of government there was an apparent rejection of integration and topic work and an emphasis on a subject-centred approach, particularly in the upper primary stages (SOED, 1991).

Ultimately the 5–14 Programme was introduced as a set of 'curricular guidelines' without requiring recourse to legislation. Although there are similarities with respect to policy developments elsewhere in the UK the absence of statutory powers to codify the curriculum nevertheless represents a point of divergence.

In England, curricular reform was backed by statute with the Education Reform Act 1988 heralding the introduction of the National Curriculum (NC). Teachers in

English primary schools are familiar with the basic framework of the NC with its Key Stages, Attainment Targets and Programmes of Study for a number of 'core' and 'foundation' subjects along with arrangements for assessment, SATs. Whilst there have been changes since 1988, these general structures have largely been maintained. During the consultative phase, prior to the introduction of the NC, it was evident that government intended that 'clear objectives for what pupils should be able to know, do and understand will be framed in subject terms' (DES, 1987: 9) with 'the majority of curriculum time at primary level... devoted to the core subjects' (DES, 1987: 6) and that 'the degree of definition will be greatest for the three core subjects' (DES, 1987: 6). The detailed programmes of study for individual subjects reinforced a move towards discrete subject teaching in primary schools, particularly for core subjects (English, Mathematics and Science). There was some scope to develop integrated work, particularly with respect to the foundation subjects.

The greater emphasis on teaching discrete subjects was further reinforced by contributions from leading educationalists such as the 'Three Wise Men' Report by Alexander, Rose and Woodhead (1992) which criticised poorly-planned topic or thematic work in primary schools for producing superficial learning:

> We consider that a National Curriculum conceived in terms of distinct subjects makes it impossible to defend a non-differentiated curriculum. This does not mean that all the National Curriculum subjects must necessarily be taught separately: curriculum conception and modes of curriculum organisation must not be confused. But, whatever the mode of organisation, pupils must be able to grasp the particular principles and procedures of each subject, and, what is equally important, they must be able to progress from one level of knowledge, understanding and skill to another within the subject. (Alexander et al., 1992: 22)

The fact that this report acknowledged that, when well planned, topic work produced work of a high standard tends to be overlooked:

> This is not to deny that the topic approach can, in skilled hands, produce work of high quality. There is evidence to suggest that some schools, recognising the problems outlined above, are planning carefully structured topic frameworks for Years 1 to 6 which map the attainment targets and programmes of study of the subjects involved. (Alexander et al., 1992: 22–3)

A divergence in the policy landscape

More recently, it would appear that there has been further divergence across the constituent parts of the UK in terms of the degree of flexibility available to schools and teachers in delivery of the school curriculum. In Scotland, flexibility is central to meeting the purposes and principles of education as outlined in *A Curriculum for Excellence* (CfE) (Scottish Executive, 2004). The intention is to create a single, coherent Scottish curriculum for children and young people from 3 to 18 so that they may develop the four key capacities of becoming successful learners, confident individuals, responsible citizens, and effective contributors. The aim of the curriculum is to support the development of knowledge, skills, attributes and informed attitudes children and young people will require so that they may 'flourish in life, learning and work, now and in the future' (Education Scotland, online-c).

CfE consists of eight curriculum areas: expressive arts, health and wellbeing, languages, mathematics, religious and moral education, sciences, social studies, and technologies, with a continuous focus on literacy, numeracy, and health and wellbeing across learning (the cross-cutting themes). The curriculum areas are organisers for setting out the experiences and outcomes that describe the expectations for learning and progression in all areas of the curriculum. The experiences and outcomes describe progress in learning through curriculum levels; consequently they describe stages in acquiring knowledge and understanding, along with the development of skills and attributes. The framework is designed to be less detailed and prescriptive than previous curriculum advice, to provide an opportunity for professional autonomy and responsibility when planning and delivering the curriculum in order to meet the varied needs of all children and young people (SG, 2008a).

Discrete subjects continue to be an essential feature of the curriculum, particularly in secondary schools as they provide an important and familiar structure for knowledge. Progression will facilitate study in greater depth with subjects increasingly being the principal means of structuring learning and delivering outcomes. However:

> The curriculum should include space for learning beyond subject boundaries, so that children and young people can make connections between different areas of learning. Interdisciplinary studies, based upon groupings of experiences and outcomes from within and across curriculum areas, can provide relevant, challenging and enjoyable learning experiences and stimulating contexts to meet the varied needs of children and young people. Revisiting a concept or skill from different perspectives deepens understanding and can also make the curriculum more coherent and meaningful from the learner's point of view. (SG, 2008a: 21)

In England, the Rose Report (2009) commissioned by the government, proposed that in order to reduce the number of subjects requiring to be taught the curriculum should be organised around six broad areas of learning:

- understanding English, communication and languages;
- mathematical understanding;

- scientific and technological understanding;
- historical, geographical and social understanding;
- understanding physical development, health and wellbeing;
- understanding the arts.

These six areas map onto the subject-based curriculum that children will follow as part of their secondary education. Within this curricular framework the significance of a blended approach to the curriculum comprising discrete subject teaching and well planned cross-curricular themes was advocated:

> Subjects remain as recognisable, powerful organisers of worthwhile curriculum content in the areas of learning. Subject 'labels' are clearly visible within the areas of learning in the middle and later phases of the curriculum. (Rose, 2009: 14)

and

> There are times when it is right to marshal content from different subjects into well-planned, cross-curricular studies... because it provides opportunities across the curriculum for them to use and apply what they have learned from the discrete teaching of subjects. (Rose, 2009: 15)

It has been argued that schools are keen to take more responsibility for producing a 'creative curriculum' that is relevant, engaging, flexible and innovative by blending some of the 'foundation subjects into cross-curricular themed teaching and learning experiences' (Blair and Francis, 2011: 26). The consensus and momentum to embrace a more flexible and devolved curriculum may well have been dampened, but hopefully not extinguished, by the UK Coalition Government's rejection of the Rose Report on the grounds that it lacked rigour and did not place sufficient stress on the importance of studying academic subjects, which is a key aim of the revised 2014 National Curriculum for England.

The terminology of integration

An assortment of prefixes including multi-, cross-, inter- and trans-disciplinary have all been deployed to describe the process of making connections between disciplines and in so doing creating new possibilities for learning involving one or more disciplines. Each prefix imparts 'a subtle but related change in meaning. To add to the confusion, the terms are used interchangeably and without precision' (Dillon, 2008: 256).

The basic building block for curricular integration is a framework of individual disciplines. A discipline is defined as a field of study linked to a knowledge base that has been systematically built up over time in accordance with agreed principles, methodical rules and procedures (Kockelmans, 1979). This disciplinary framework is deeply entrenched within our (Western) educational psyche, being linked to notions of knowledge hierarchies. In our schools this largely explains the subject-based curricula familiar to all teachers. Beane (1991: 12) suggests that the legacy of a curriculum organised in terms of subjects is so ingrained in our thinking that is we can find it difficult to imagine a different curricular framework, so limiting broader understandings to help explain the complexity of real life.

Different terminology helps describe different degrees of connection among disciplines towards an integrated curriculum:

- *Multi-disciplinary*: this suggests that elements of the curriculum are loosely combined to explore a theme; however, there tends to be little by way of connection between the disciplines involved.
- *Cross-disciplinary (or cross-curricular)*: elements of the curriculum are combined to help solve a problem that would not be possible if there was no connection between the disciplines. No single discipline by itself would be able to provide a solution to the problem. The application of knowledge, skills and informed attitudes of the different disciplines brought together to solve the problem may not be transferable to other problems as these would require different cross-disciplinary configurations.
- *Inter-disciplinary*: (often used interchangeably with cross-disciplinary) this approach indicates that it involves creating a new and potentially narrower field of study that lies between two disciplines. To achieve this it is necessary for there to be a transfer of specialist knowledge and methodological understanding between the disciplines to facilitate integration, to solve particular problems. This is not usually something that individual teachers will be capable of doing alone as it implies collaborative effort between participants with the necessary disciplinary expertise.
- *Trans-disciplinary*: the previous approaches all describe curricular connections so remaining firmly attached to a disciplinary framework. Trans-disciplinary learning starts with a real-life problem and sets about realising a solution, so minimising the weaknesses of starting from a disciplinary perspective. The strength of this approach is that the group should be able to transfer their learning in order to solve a variety of different problems. This approach is not common in primary schools.

A continuum of integration

A number of writers have attempted to develop a typology or continuum of integration with limited curricular connections at one end of the continuum leading to a greater density of connections. Before looking at one of these it is important to be aware that the concept of different positions along a continuum is not meant to suggest that one approach is better than another, just that they are different. However, depending upon the learning objectives that you are seeking to achieve it may be that a particular approach is more appropriate than others. Ultimately it is the quality of planning that validates whatever approach you utilise to support the learning activities that you design.

Fogarty (2009) describes 10 levels of curricular integration:

- Within single subjects:

  o *The Fragmented Model*: the curriculum consists of discrete subjects timetabled separately, leaving children with a fragmented view of the curriculum.
  o *The Connected Model*: the curriculum still consists of discrete subjects but there is a greater emphasis on establishing internal connections within each subject. There is a deliberate effort to link ideas, concepts and skills within the subject rather than assuming that children will be able to do this.
  o *The Nested Model*: this targets and makes explicit knowledge, content, social skills and thinking skills linked to particular subject.

- Across subjects:

  o *The Sequenced Model*: the subjects remain discrete but activities are identified that are sequenced across several subjects to provide a coherent framework for learning.
  o *The Shared Model*: this involves bringing together two subjects to focus on shared knowledge and understanding, concepts, skills and abilities as well as the development of informed attitudes.
  o *The Webbed Model*: a theme is identified and used to integrate subject content. The theme may extend beyond one classroom so leading to the formation of a cross-curricular team who seek to identify relevant subject matter to develop the theme. Time is set aside for the children to work on the theme. A common approach is for the teacher to set up 'stations' or 'learning centres' covering different linked activities relevant to the theme. The children rotate through the different stations and they are expected to make the connections across the subject areas rather than having these taught. In adopting this approach you would need to ensure that the connections form part of your planning otherwise the children will struggle to see the relevance of the linked activities.

o *The Threaded Model*: thinking skills, social skills, multiple intelligences and study skills are threaded throughout the connected subjects.

o *The Integrated Model*: blending subjects by finding overlapping concepts, skills and informed attitudes by process of collaborative sifting; these are then made explicit to the children.

- Within and across learners:

o *The Immersed Model*: integration takes place within children with little or no outside intervention. The child integrates their learning by viewing this through an area of interest.

o *The Networked Model*: the integration process is directed by the children providing them with different avenues of exploration linked to a real-life problem. The curriculum is negotiated and planned collaboratively between the teacher and the children. This involves discussion aimed at identifying what both teacher and children know and what they would like to know, how to learn it and how to assess it. Subjects are selected on the basis of the contribution that they can make to the learning.

Thinking point

- What models of curricular integration (a) are you most familiar with and (b) do you work with in your classroom/school?
- What determines the type of model that you may deploy at any given point in time?

Planning for integrated learning

There are two broad types of interdisciplinary learning which, in practice, often overlap:

- learning planned to develop awareness and understanding of the connections and differences across subject areas and disciplines;
- using learning from different subjects and disciplines to explore a theme or an issue, meet a challenge, solve a problem or complete a final project (Education Scotland, online-d).

Both of these broad types emphasise the importance of subject-specific knowledge, not simply content knowledge but an understanding of the distinctive forms of knowledge these subjects provide and how the unique perspective offered by these subjects, set within a coherent pedagogy of connection, helps children to understand the world more fully. Blending a subject-based curriculum with opportunities for more integrated learning experiences, in which the connections across different subject areas are explicitly and frequently articulated, will not only strengthen the children's understanding of the distinctive contribution that the subjects have to make to their learning but will also provide a vehicle for the development of generic skills about learning how to learn.

Working in schools during a period of educational reform will require you to make sense of national curricular frameworks in terms of what already exists within the school and what is contained within any new framework documents. The complexity of the task that you will face should not be underestimated. The planning task with which you will be confronted consists of producing a structured programme incorporating an interlinked balance of subject-specific learning and opportunities for interdisciplinary learning, taking into account curriculum design principles (challenge and enjoyment; breadth; progression; depth; personalisation and choice; coherence; relevance) and the stage of development of the learners in your classroom. The blending of subject-specific and interdisciplinary learning must also be balanced across a term, year and stage (or phase). An element of flexibility is built into the curricular framework as schools are best placed to decide what the right balance is for them as they respond to their context and to the needs of their learners.

This challenge may persuade you that it is preferable to go along with planning documents as they currently exist rather than attempting to find creative and imaginative approaches to teaching and learning which will inspire the children in your class. Even as a newly-qualified teacher it is important to provide the children in your care with a curricular experience that is 'socially transformative'; consequently it is essential that your role is that of a leader of learning both within and beyond your classroom. This requires you to become instrumental in inspiring colleagues within the school and beyond as well!

Creating effective interdisciplinary learning experiences will require you to go beyond consideration of the content of the curriculum, typical of plans that merely combine aspects of different subjects together as part of some contrived jigsaw. Planning for interdisciplinary learning 'requires individuals to conceptually connect ideas across the disciplines, which involves exploring the meanings embedded within the content' (Brand and Triplett, 2012: 383). Ideally this is an endeavour that should not be undertaken alone but rather as part of a collaborative approach to planning. No matter how competent you may be (or become) as a teacher, perhaps even specialising in a particular area of the curriculum, it is unlikely that you will ever possess a detailed grasp of the culture of all subjects in terms of knowledge and understandings, skills and informed attitudes that each of the discrete subject areas contribute to learning.

Attempts to create interdisciplinary learning experiences without calling upon the range of expertise that exists within and beyond the school can lead to a shallowness of connection, what Gardner (2007) calls 'disciplinary juxtaposition'. It is important that you pay careful attention to the value of bringing together elements of each subject in order that the sum of the parts makes a meaningful contribution to the children's learning, so providing insights not possible within single-subject approach.

Planning for learning within an individual classroom should not take place in isolation. It should be an integral part of a school's improvement planning in order to develop programmes of work that provide for progression across the full range of learning objectives (NC attainment targets and CfE experiences and outcomes). Collaboration is a prerequisite for the development of interdisciplinary initiatives. Clearly this can be problematic if you find yourself in a school that lacks a collaborative culture, as it may be difficult to motivate colleagues. In particular, as a new member of staff you will lack the power to influence in the same way as more experienced colleagues. So, fostering collaboration requires a willingness to persevere and to trust colleagues to reach professional judgements. It is important that you seek the support and advice of the school's management team in order to ensure that planning documentation and the resulting teaching and learning activities are continually monitored to determine the appropriateness of the balance between subject-specific and interdisciplinary learning over the course of a term, year and stage (or phase).

Thinking point

- One of the challenges in planning interdisciplinary learning is maintaining an appropriate balance between the subjects which contribute to the study, so having a clear rationale for including subjects in the topic or theme. How can you ensure that learning is not superficial and fragmentary (Alexander et al., 1992) and that the links made between the subjects are rigorous?
- Harris (2008: 266) argues that an ever-increasing emphasis on performance measures creates a school culture which leaves teachers little time for the collaboration necessary for planning interdisciplinary learning experiences in order to make a positive impact on student learning. Consider whether this is the case in your school.

Seven-step design and planning process

A useful model for curriculum planning in primary schools is offered by the (now defunct) Qualifications and Curriculum Development Agency (QCDA) (2010). This model is shown at Figure 10.1.

- Identify priorities
- Record starting point   } What are you trying to achieve?
- Set clear goals
- Design and implement   } How will you organise learning?
- Review progress
- Evaluate and record impact   } How will you know when you have been successful?
- Maintain change or move on

Figure 10.1   Seven-stage model of curriculum planning (adapted from QCDA, 2010)

These are useful broad principles; however, when developing coherent 'topics' or 'themes' it is also necessary to find ways to connect learning objectives across programmes of study. There are a variety of standards-based approaches to planning that involve the following steps:

- identify a topic or theme that will arouse curiosity and interest;
- build upon prior learning to take account of progression and coherence;
- identify connections across different subject areas rather than simply linking content;
- select learning objectives, identify appropriate learning intentions and success criteria;
- decide on the necessary knowledge and understanding, skills and informed attitudes for the children to achieve;
- identify suitably challenging activities and resources;
- determine the pedagogical approach ensuring diversity of teaching and learning experiences;
- determine a pattern ('challenge' days timetabled for integration activity, activity weeks or ongoing permeation of formal curriculum), location (specific thematic areas) and personnel involved in delivery (subject specialist supporting the development of theme, formation of curricular team all contributing to aspects of learning);
- choose appropriate assessment instruments to generate evidence of learning required as part of the assessment process; and
- leave space and opportunity to respond to children's learning and their proposals for further learning.

View from practice

An NQT developed a Space topic that initially involved discussion with other class teachers and the children. The NQT was particularly interested in what the children knew and wished to learn.

A 'topic web' plan was developed to help provide an overview of the balance of curricular coverage set within the wider context of the stage appropriate curriculum. Eight curricular areas were initially targeted but this was subsequently reduced to five once the conceptual links had been established.

The web plan was then further developed by identification of learning objectives, activities and resources. The plan as used to identify the pattern of delivery to facilitate a coherent 'flow' to the learning experiences. The NQT was clear that planning should not be done one activity at a time due to a concern that this would present the children with a 'disjointed' set of learning experiences.

Thinking point

It is not unusual for a limited amount of curriculum time to be made available for interdisciplinary learning. Morrison (1994) suggests that you need to consider four characteristics of school time:

- quantity – time available for specific curricular areas;
- structure – best way of organising time;
- quality – when time is made available;
- flexibility – facility to rearrange time to meet evolving needs.

For an interdisciplinary learning topic or theme that you have been involved in planning or delivering in the past consider these four characteristics of time. What supported/hindered interdisciplinary learning?

The learning objectives identified with respect to an individual topic or theme normally sit within a 'matrix plan' whereby the structure of the curriculum is mapped to help specify and detail curricular coverage (Morrison, 1994). The matrix plan will enable you to identify the learning objectives to which you need to return in order to ensure consolidation, continuity and progression in learning. Creating the matrix plan usually falls within the remit of the management team and serves to provide an overview of the 'big picture' to ensure that statutory responsibilities to deliver the curriculum are being met.

Assessment should be an integral rather than a 'bolt on' part of the planning process. Through planning learning, teaching and assessment together and ensuring that there are opportunities to gather a wide range of evidence of learning, you will be in a position to reflect on what has been achieved and agree next steps in learning and progression. Finally the balance between child-initiated and teacher-initiated learning opportunities needs to be carefully considered and monitored. Hayes (2010: 384) states that too much pupil choice may allow 'children to avoid areas of learning that they find hard, thereby inculcating poor work habits and attitudes'.

View from practice

Theme: Connecting learning inside and out.

This was a whole-school initiative that formed part of school improvement plan with the aim to create progressive learning experiences that would span all levels. The goal was to link opportunities for outdoor learning with classroom learning in such a way that they became mutually reinforcing, making learning real by utilising and developing the skills learned.

A collaborative working group was formed which set about identifying appropriate experiences and outcomes, having first gathered information from children about what they would like to learn, to help inform activities. Education Scotland's Curriculum for Excellence experiences and outcomes guides for outdoor learning were used to support the curricular mapping exercise in order to ensure that the experiences and outcomes for interdisciplinary learning complemented the curricular plans at each level.

Once weaving a thread of progressive outdoor learning experiences, linked directly to 'indoor' learning, had been completed, staff worked to create activities and resources for outdoor learning appropriate to several curricular areas, for example, health and wellbeing, numeracy and science. The range of activities included the creation of 'Buzz Boxes' containing resources and learning activities to support outdoor learning. The knowledge and understanding provided by the different curricular areas were in turn linked to skill development including enquiry, teamwork and critical thinking. Consider whether this an example of interdisciplinary learning.

(Guides available at: http://www.educationscotland.gov.uk/learningteachingand assessment/approaches/outdoorlearning/about/experiencesand outcomes.asp)

Summary

The concept of a 'creative curriculum' (Rose, 2009) continues to exercise a hold over the imagination of many primary schools in their ongoing attempt to inter-link subjects not as an end in itself but a means to accomplish educational goals. Interdisciplinary learning is appropriate if it facilitates progress towards educational goals by providing opportunities for children to revisit a concept or skill from different perspectives to deepen their understanding as well as making the curriculum more coherent and meaningful from the children's point of view.

Working across and between subjects is inherently creative as it will require you to make imaginative links between one subject's knowledge and understandings, skills and informed attitudes, and other subject areas:

> Effective cross-curricular practice places particular demand on teachers' subject and pedagogic knowledge to combine disciplines such that they are able to draw out the common body of knowledge, skills and understanding in order to identify the ways in which they might provide opportunity for development, reinforcement, application and generalisation in learning. (Parker et al., 2012: 713)

Curricular integration will require you to blend together subjects effectively to enable children to make productive links between subjects. The complexity of the pedagogic task before you should not be underestimated; however, curricular inte-gration offers an opportunity to provide a richness and relevance to the children's curricular experience by connecting their learning to real-life experiences.

Reflective questions

- Is it necessary for children to have grounding in subject knowledge and under-standings, skills and informed attitudes before embarking upon interdiscipli-nary learning? What are the implications of this across the key stages in the primary school?
- Some teachers may feel they lack the necessary content knowledge and abil-ity to employ a range of teaching and learning approaches appropriate to the developing interdisciplinary learning experiences. What are the implications of this with respect to your continuing professional learning?

Further reading

Further information on interdisciplinary learning can be found at the Education Scotland website: http://www.educationscotland.gov.uk/.

Barnes, J. (2011) *Cross-curricular Learning 3–14*. 2nd edn. London: SAGE Publications.

Fogarty, R. (2009) *How to Integrate the Curricula*. 3rd edn. Thousand Oaks, CA: Corwin.

CHAPTER 11

CREATING CHALLENGE IN THE CLASSROOM

Margaret Sutherland and Niamh Stack

Key ideas

This chapter explores:

- the multi-faceted and contested nature of ability;
- how our beliefs and practices as educators are shaped by our own experiences, perceptions and understandings;
- how our knowledge of developmental milestones may impact negatively on the level of challenge we provide;
- planning and providing challenge for all students, including highly able pupils.

Introduction

The belief that we need to stretch and challenge our students is not a new one. Key educational and developmental theorists such as Vygotsky and Piaget have spoken about the importance of a rich and stimulating environment which draws children out of their comfort zone and on to further learning and development. Challenge should be integral to the planning of all activities, at all levels, for all abilities. Every child should be challenged within their development and learning, although what constitutes challenge may differ among learners.

Challenge is an integral feature of an inclusive approach to education and it is not, as is sometimes misunderstood, only the prerogative of highly able learners. However, our perception of what constitutes appropriate challenge will greatly depend on our personal beliefs about ability. We will be influenced by what we think ability is, how we believe it can be identified and what we understand as the limits to our capacity as educators to progress children's ability using elements of challenge. So before we begin to talk about challenge we must first talk about ability.

The contested nature of ability

The term 'ability' is used in a variety of ways within educational literature. It is multifaceted and engenders much debate. For example, some authors argue for the importance of ability groupings, placing children with other children with the same kinds of abilities, to stimulate learning, while others argue that mixed ability groups provide an effective learning environment (Smith and Sutherland, 2006). We have devised developmental milestones or norms at which we predict children and learners will achieve particular tasks so that we can identify when development is not progressing as expected. However, these discussions focus on normative expectations or perceived deficits in expectations; there is rarely any discussion of abilities in *advance* of normative expectations. In discussing these norms and expectations we often focus on cognitive ability but we have also expanded our understanding of ability to encompass a much broader range of skills such as verbal ability, spatial ability, musical and interpersonal abilities (Gardner, 2000). We have developed numerous measures to test this diverse range of abilities, which we use to make comparisons amongst different groups and to identify individual areas that need support and areas of strength which need encouragement. However, there is much debate about what the essence of ability is and what might be the most appropriate method to measure it.

As educators, our own understanding, experience and perceptions of ability and intelligence can impact on our classroom provision and on our learning interactions with children (Dweck, 1999). It can determine how we identify children in need of challenge, what challenge we offer and what power we feel we have as educators to facilitate developmental change.

Thinking point

- In one sentence write down what the term 'ability' means to you.
- What would a child with ability in a particular subject (say for example mathematics, but it could be any subject you choose) be doing in your classroom?
- Share your definition and thoughts with someone else. Do they match? Are they different? In what ways are they the same/different?
- How do your definition/examples shape what you do in the classroom?

Ability in practice

Ability is often associated with concepts related to skills or to intelligence, which can lead to rather narrow expectations of what it is and how it can be demonstrated. Rather than trying to define ability it may be more helpful to talk about particular behaviours in which learners engage. This way we can start to visualise how ability is demonstrated in the classroom and perhaps most importantly how we begin to provide opportunities which allow students to demonstrate these behaviours.

Even in nurseries we can see differences emerging in relation to learning as children engage in diverse ways with the range of activities on offer, some gravitating towards the physical release and expression provided by outdoor play, others embracing the creativity and imagination allowed by the craft table. As discussed in Chapter 3, early education is important as it is here that children begin to explore and develop skills and abilities across a range of subject areas through play, practice and direct input from adults. A fundamental key to the powerful influence of early education is the daily opportunities for agency and choice. A sense of ownership in our own learning is hugely motivating (Bruner, 1996) and a quite simple way to ensure challenge in an inclusive classroom at all levels is to begin with the principles of agency and choice. Of course children already bring many prior experiences with them to the nursery. Their education begins well before they encounter their first formal educational institution. Children will have already developed a range of abilities through the experiences they have had since birth and in response to the feedback they have received from their early implicit educators such as their parents, family and peers.

The adults around them may have been comparing what their child has achieved to that of other children and may have started thinking about and gauging their child's ability in relation to age and stage. One of the problems with this kind of approach is that we begin to see children's learning as compartmentalised and highly dependent on, and linked to, age. Parents and educators often have this prescribed timescale in their heads and so are looking for children who meet or do not meet the descriptions.

Learning, however, is messy and we know that children do not progress in a linear fashion through the learning stages. Chapter 4 has already outlined the theoretical standpoints in relation to learning and highlights some of the key frameworks that have emerged and influenced practice. In this chapter we will consider the needs of a specific group of learners, namely the highly able, and consider how, through an inclusive approach to pedagogy, we can not only create challenging learning experiences for them but create challenging learning experiences for all.

Defining high ability

Many 'highly able' children will have reached and overtaken the developmental milestones mentioned earlier well in advance of their peers. These children are often referred to in the literature as 'gifted and talented' or 'highly able'. This area is a contentious one and so it is important for teachers – both beginning and experienced – to have thought explicitly about this cohort of children and considered how best to provide for them in their classrooms.

Already we can see that a range of terms have been used in relation to this area – highly able, ability, gifted and talented, to name but a few. No single definition of the concept exists and many writers and researchers have spent years debating how best to define and subsequently measure ability. Indeed there are debates as to whether we should, or if it is even possible to, define and measure ability. Historically, intelligence quotient (IQ) tests have been used in an attempt to quantify ability (Herrnstein and Murray, 1994). An IQ score is considered by many to be a reliable indicator of ability. This uni-dimensional relationship between IQ score and ability has been challenged (Lucas and Claxton, 2010). As we saw in Chapter 6, our emotional wellbeing impacts on our readiness to learn and engage. Researchers have sought to move the debate beyond IQ suggesting that a more 'highly efficient – and, ideally also highly explanatory – prognostic model for achievement excellence' is required and that 'IQ …is …not up to this job' (Ziegler and Stoeger, 2012: 130).

Related to the IQ debate is the role of nature and nurture in the development of abilities. Is it all about genetics or does environment play a part too?

In the following vignettes we are introduced to two children. Read the scenarios carefully and then consider the thinking points that follow.

View from practice

Peter

Peter is seven years old and has a challenging home background, with his parents' substance abuse having played a significant role in his life. The family are receiving substantial support from social services and Peter has been under the care of social services for brief periods of time. The open door policy of the school means that they too are able to offer the family support and advice. Peter is physically small for his age, has quite a poor pallor and is prone to ill health which results in regular absences from school. When in school, staff work with Peter to ensure he develops strong inter and intrapersonal skills through a range of activities. Peter has not achieved all the academic learning expectations at the same time as his peers and he is behind in both reading and writing. However, his teacher has noted a quiet curiosity in his manner and has been surprised by some of the insightful questions he has asked during some activities. When unhindered by his delays in reading and writing Peter shows real engagement in tasks and has on occasion completed them to a higher standard and with deeper understanding than those identified as highly able.

Jessica

Jessica started school at age four and a half and is now seven years old. She is the youngest of four children. Jessica's parents are both highly qualified professionals. Mum is a 'stay at home mum' who ensures that the family regularly engage in interesting activities and trips to museums and parks. Jessica is perceived by her teacher as highly inquisitive, knowledgeable, articulate and she uses advanced vocabulary. During storytelling activities in particular she is very keen to examine the books and illustrations in detail. She has a good understanding of print and phonics. She has a strong general knowledge and can see relationships between aspects of the different activities, her own experiences, her knowledge about real life and her imagination. She is beginning to ask questions of a philosophical nature. She is a popular girl and gets on well with her peers

(Continued)

(Continued)

and can often be seen in the middle of a game or group task directing activities and making suggestions.

- How have the differing life experiences Peter and Jessica bring to the classroom manifested themselves in terms of their evident abilities?
- How can schools/teachers ameliorate the impact of different family circumstances on the learning experience?
- What kinds of activities/opportunities might be required to identify potentially able underachievers such as Peter?

An inclusive approach to high ability

These scenarios highlight some of the issues relating to the 'nature versus nurture' debate. Is Jessica 'highly able' or has she just had appropriate experiences that have allowed her to develop particular skills that are valued within the learning context and within society? They also leave us asking questions about identification and the role of this in exacerbating restricted views of ability. If particular assumptions are made about Peter and his readiness to learn then he may not be offered more challenging experiences and may never be provided with opportunities to demonstrate his abilities. Equally, if assumptions are made about Jessica and her abilities she may continue to be offered challenging experiences, thus confirming the view that she is highly able. The experiences which children have outside school will clearly influence the skill set which they bring with them to school in terms of knowledge, readiness to learn and wider understanding of the world. If we make assumptions about a child's potential ability based only on the skill set they start with then we are at risk of limiting the opportunities for children like Peter to demonstrate what his true abilities are. If we fail to provide learning opportunities which allow for a diverse range of abilities to shine, and which allow for a range of different levels of difficulty and complexity to stretch and challenge children with different levels of ability, we may fail both Peter and Jessica, as Jessica may not be getting the extension she needs beyond her already rich environment.

A criticism often posed of gifted education is that it panders to an already elite group of already advantaged children like Jessica. Certainly, American research has shown that gifted education programmes are in reality dominated by children already enjoying social advantage and familial support (Borland, 1989). In contrast, within mainstream education we have tended to focus on the needs of those perceived as disadvantaged: minority groups, the under-privileged and those perceived as having learning difficulties. The groups are mistakenly perceived as being mutually exclusive. Consequently, within a mainstream inclusive context less attention has been directed to the development of able achievers. There is a fear that providing for highly able pupils might suggest that teachers are making judgements about children, with some deemed more important and valuable than others, and this is not considered to fit within the egalitarian ideals of an inclusive system. The current global financial climate has impacted negatively on education with significant reductions in available budgets and staffing; this means that schools are being forced to make difficult decisions about how to spend money and staff time. In this contracted financial climate there may be a tendency to direct the limited resources to those perceived as most in need, and spending money and resources on highly able pupils might be seen as increasing social division. These commonly-held views are based on a series of misguided assumptions and need to be challenged. If we are to achieve excellence and equity for all then we need to think about equality of challenge for highly able pupils (Winstanley, 2010).

Consider this scenario:

- Emily is doing very well across all subjects in school. She consistently scores in excess of 85 per cent on all class tests.
- Chris struggles with some aspects of the curriculum, particularly reading and mathematics. Her scores on class tests are poor and she works on a personalised learning programme for reading.

The obvious response to the scenarios outlined above is to support Chris in order that her test results improve and that as Emily is doing fine, we do not need to worry about her or provide her with any support. However, if Emily is ready to work on more challenging concepts then she is in fact working well below what she is capable of. There is the possibility that if Emily continues to be given work which she can complete easily and we fail to provide her with adequate challenge then she may become bored, demotivated, engage in challenging behaviour or just simply disengage from education. We would argue that both children need support and challenge appropriate to their needs and abilities.

Shaping our beliefs and practice

We believe it is important to explore our beliefs about ability because literature suggests there is a link between what we believe and what we do in our classrooms (Malm, 2009).

Many experiences will have influenced our thoughts and beliefs about ability and learning and teaching. Included in these will be:

- our experiences within our family when we were growing up;
- our experiences of learning and of school and university;
- reactions from our peers;
- exam results;
- things we have read and heard about in the media.

Throughout our careers as teachers and educators we need to engage in professional development. Chapters 19 and 20 of this book consider this in more detail but professional development is important if we are to hone and develop our skills and understanding. Using the chart in Figure 11.1, think about what has influenced your beliefs about high ability. Using the seven-point scale, consider whether, and, if so, how far, the statements have influenced your beliefs about ability.

In the context of this chapter, we are asking you to begin to think about the ways in which research has influenced you. Research offers us the tools to examine and critique our practice but also more widely our inherent beliefs.

	1	2	3	4	5	6	7
My family were supportive of me when growing up and always encouraged me to do my best.	☐	☐	☐	☐	☐	☐	☐
I worked hard and did well at school.	☐	☐	☐	☐	☐	☐	☐
The group I was in for maths and language at school.	☐	☐	☐	☐	☐	☐	☐
Comparing myself to others around me (at school or at University).	☐	☐	☐	☐	☐	☐	☐
Working with the diverse range of learners in my classroom has helped shape my beliefs.	☐	☐	☐	☐	☐	☐	☐
Listening to the views of other teachers.	☐	☐	☐	☐	☐	☐	☐
I have read a lot of research about current understandings of ability.	☐	☐	☐	☐	☐	☐	☐

How to score:
Didn't influence my beliefs at all (1)
Influenced my beliefs a little bit (2,3)
Influenced my beliefs to a certain degree (4)
Influenced my beliefs quite a bit (5,6)
Influenced my beliefs a lot (7)

Figure 11.1 Influences on beliefs about high ability

Creating room for challenge

Highly able pupils will often require something in addition to the standard curriculum and activities. There are a number of recognised ways of addressing this including acceleration, enrichment and differentiation. Bearing in mind that one size will not fit all and that the needs of highly able learners are as diverse as the needs of any other group, this section outlines possible ways of creating a context for challenge, all of which will suit different individuals at different points in their learning journey.

Acceleration

Earlier in the chapter we argued that some highly able children will reach some of the predetermined milestones much earlier than their peers. If this increased pace of learning continues then it is not unreasonable to assume that some highly able children will require accelerated learning experiences. Acceleration of learning can take many forms:

- a child may start formal schooling earlier than their chronological age suggests;
- a child might move year groups so that they work with children one or more years ahead of them;
- a child might work with older children in particular subject areas and at particular times of the day or week;
- a child might work alongside a mentor who guides and supports the learner through advanced work;
- a child might work at an accelerated pace through the regular curriculum.

If acceleration of any sort is being considered then the welfare of the child has to be kept at the forefront of planning. Children and their parents should be part of the planning process as acceleration is much more likely to be successful if the child has been fully involved. Hymer and Harbron (1998) argue that children need to be mature and secure emotionally, socially and physically as well as intellectually if acceleration and in particular radical acceleration is to take place. It is equally important that the groups of learners the child may leave and join are aware of the situation, as their self esteem and motivation to learn may be affected. It is also important that the appropriateness of this approach is constantly reassessed. Is the speed of acceleration appropriate? Does it need to be adjusted, to ensure that the challenge does not overtake the child?

Enrichment

Enrichment involves modifying the curriculum in a way that allows pupils to explore topics in greater breadth and depth. This also allows them to use the advanced skills they may have and in addition it offers opportunities for higher-level thinking and investigation. The idea of interdisciplinary learning is covered in more detail in Chapter 10 of this book. A strength of this kind of project work is that it is often situated in the real world. Crucially the topic under scrutiny can be the same as that for the rest of the class, with the content and materials used with highly able pupils being in advance of the expected age range.

Differentiation

As the name suggests, differentiation is about making something different. There are many ways that a teacher can differentiate learning for pupils and one of the most common ways is by task and outcome. For example, the teacher can ask a basic question such as: Where do you find volcanoes? We can then differentiate for highly able children by setting different tasks and outcomes. Most children will look at maps and list the countries where volcanoes are found. Highly able children could be asked to identify the tectonic plates around the globe and match the coordinates with the occurrence of volcanoes.

There is nothing wrong with these kinds of activities and indeed matching up the two results from the activities will offer opportunity for further questioning to develop. However, differentiation by task and outcome is not enough. Teachers need to ensure that other methods of differentiation are also used:

- *Differentiation by resource*: highly able pupils will benefit from having access to a range of texts and information. The texts and sources of information should incorporate increasingly complex information. Highly able pupils may also benefit from having access to an expert. The expert may be available to offer face-to-face tutorials and discussion sessions or may do this 'virtually'.
- *Differentiation by interest*: highly able children can be encouraged to self-select activities in areas that are of particular interest to them. Offering opportunities to increase particular skills they wish to develop through their interests is also beneficial.
- *Differentiation by pace*: some highly able children will need less time to complete activities and some children will not require to complete every activity. Alternatively some children may need more time to complete an activity in order that they can analyse the topic in depth.
- *Differentiation by amount of support on offer*: some highly able pupils may not require support for their learning, for example they might not need concrete

mathematics material if they have grasped the concept and can work in the abstract. Some children will relish being given freedom to explore a topic or concept in the way that interests them most. Some children may enjoy working alongside an expert who can offer guidance and advice.

Thinking point

- You are the teacher of a class of 8-year-olds. The class topic is the Romans. Two of the children in your class have a reading age of 11. Looking at the ideas outlined above, decide which ones you could employ during the topic and why.

A topic such as the Romans allows for cross-disciplinary learning to occur. Through such an approach we might be able to challenge children who not only have an advanced reading age but we might also begin to identify children who are also budding historians or geographers. The table outlined below has been developed with West Dunbartonshire Education Authority, Scotland. It is a template that offers guidance to teachers as they plan activities whilst at the same time allowing for local differences in resources. It demonstrates how you might answer the question in the thinking point above and how we might plan activities for all children which provide them with the challenge they require but also the opportunity to demonstrate abilities we may not yet have identified.

Table 11.1   Planning sheet – Topic: The Romans

Activity	Resources	Focus of activity	Observation	Development	Next steps
Historical investigation into Pompeii. Key points to cover: 1. What happened in Pompeii 2. What evidence can we gather about everyday life.	Pictures Film Books Magazines Newspapers Internet	Literacy and English (listening and talking). Tools for listening and talking. Finding and using information. Understanding, analysing and evaluating.	Knowledge of topic. Retention of facts. Type of question asked. Choice of which ones to try. Showing the interconnection and relationship between the events being studied.	Direct to materials for further knowledge.	Investigate life in modern day Pompeii. Explore the likelihood of another eruption that would cause the same devastation.

If these activities are suitable for all children, what are our expectations of how the two pupils who have already been identified as demonstrating advanced reading ages will perform on this task? Here are some things that some highly able pupils might do. These lists are not exhaustive but are helpful as we think about challenge.

Children who are highly able in language and literacy will often:

- have good close reading skills;
- pay great attention to detail in a text;
- understand the nuances of language;
- read fluently, confidently, constantly and with understanding;
- be able to read between the lines.

Children who are highly able in history will often:

- consider historical interpretations and think about their accuracy;
- understand an historical timeline;
- ask good historical questions based on what they have learnt;
- be able to make connections between historical events;
- consider historical events from multiple viewpoints.

Children who are highly able in geography will often:

- enjoy representing information in a variety of ways such as maps, graphs, diagrams, etc.;
- have a wide general knowledge about the world;
- be able to link knowledge from one subject to another;
- be able to 'think' and 'see' in three dimensional form;
- understand the relationship between the physical and human elements of geography.

The example planning sheet in Figure 11.1 demonstrates that it is possible to plan activities for all which incorporate challenge for those who need it and support for those who may struggle with the task. But we need to be careful not to cap the learning opportunities within an activity by allowing for the possibility that some children might on some tasks work beyond our expectations of that age and stage. In planning we need to ensure that we are not planning just for the middle group, we need to incorporate low threshold activities that provide easy access to the topic for those who need it and high ceiling activities for those who need to stretch their learning so they are not always immediately hitting a barrier to progress their learning. Barriers to learning are equally frustrating and demotivating for children whether they have a particular learning difficulty or if they are highly able. Barriers are doubly frustrating and debilitating when children are both highly able and have a learning difficulty or difficulties (Montgomery, 1990).

Thinking outside the box

Often approaches are not specifically labelled as being good for highly able students but many approaches incorporate aspects of challenge that are good for all learners including the highly able ones. In addition to the activities in this chapter there are many others that are discussed in previous chapters in this book that, with a bit of tweaking, pre-planning and careful consideration, offer ideal challenging learning opportunities for highly able learners.

In particular:

- Chapter 9 – Collaborative learning. Highly able pupils also need opportunities to work collaboratively with other intellectually highly able pupils.
- Chapter 10 – Interdisciplinary learning. Highly able pupils are often experts at making the connections between disciplines. How to make the connections is not the starting point for able pupils.
- Chapter 13 – Global citizenship and development education. Highly able pupils may be very interested in the world and in the 'big issues' such as global warming, sustainability, renewable resources, etc. These topics offer great opportunity for highly able pupils to engage in in-depth activities.
- Chapter 14 – Spiritual and moral development. Highly able pupils can sometimes have a heightened understanding of existentialism. This needs to be considered at the planning stage.
- Chapter 15 – Teaching for creativity; creative teaching. Creativity is included in many of the models for giftedness. This is an important aspect when catering for high ability.
- Chapter 16 – Digital learning spaces. The development of digital learning spaces and the opportunities they offer have an important role to play when creating challenging experiences for highly able pupils.

Summary

In this chapter we have considered the contested nature of ability and the complexity involved in trying to identify and develop children's abilities. We have discussed how important our own beliefs and practices are and the importance of continually reviewing both through engagement in continuing professional development and educational literature and research. We have discussed how we might create, plan and provide challenging opportunities and considered whether the focus is perhaps more appropriately placed on the learning need rather than simply labelling the learner. While there is much debate around what it means to be highly able, there is no doubt that we meet young people in our classrooms who absorb and process information quickly, make connections between different parts of their learning, grasp new concepts quickly and are capable of working ahead of their peers. We also need to remember those in our classrooms who for one reason or another may not be as easy to spot but still need to be challenged. In creating inclusive classrooms the needs of this group of learners must be considered in the same way as any other group.

Reflective questions

At the beginning of the chapter we asked you to write down in one sentence what the term 'ability' means to you.

- Having read this chapter, do your original ideas still hold true?
- Do you want to change your definition in light of your reading and reflection?
- If your thinking has changed, how will you now incorporate this into your practice?

Further reading

Winstanley, C. (2010) *The Ingredients of Challenge*. London: Trentham Books.
Ideas on how to embed challenge in everyday school life.
Smith, C. (2005) *Gifted and Talented in the Primary School*. London: SAGE.
An inclusive approach detailing whole school, class and group activities.
Sutherland, M. (2012) *Gifted and Talented in the Early Years* London: SAGE.
Lots of photocopiable ideas for things to try out in your setting.

Web resources

www.nrich.maths.org – 'The NRICH Project aims to enrich the mathematical experiences of all learners. To support this aim, members of the NRICH team work in a wide range of capacities, including providing professional development for teachers wishing to embed rich mathematical tasks into everyday classroom practice.' This website contains a wealth of activities for pupils and guidance for teachers.
www.londongt.org – 'London Gifted and Talented offers continuing professional development, resources and consultancy to improve the quality of gifted and

talented teaching and learning.' This website contains practical advice and activities and excellent resources for CLPD events.

www.ablepupils.com – This website contains information on resources for teachers, podcasts from key speakers in the field and perhaps most usefully a set of guidelines for addressing the needs of highly able pupils, which include current information from research and practical experience that will be useful to teachers and schools as they seek to meet the needs of all learners.

CHAPTER 12

ASSESSMENT FOR LEARNING

Louise Hayward and Ernest Spencer

Key ideas

This chapter explores:

- assessment as integral to all effective learning;
- the idea of independent learning, involving intellectual challenge (from the curriculum), thinking and collaborative working;
- how assessment for learning contributes to development of independent learning abilities;
- important factors in making assessment for learning work.

Introduction

Assessment for learning is very simple in one sense. It means finding out what has been learned, by any and every means that provides good evidence about this, and using the information to decide on next steps in learning and what needs to be done to help learners take these steps successfully.

Assessment for learning is also complex. It does not consist simply of a series of 'assessment techniques'. The spirit of assessment for learning (Marshall and Drummond, 2006) involves clear understanding of what learning *is* and how it is best developed, generally and in varying ways for different individual learners and in different aspects of the curriculum. Learning is certainly defined in terms of the important outcomes specified in the formal curriculum. It also involves another kind of development, promoting reflectiveness about the very process of learning and its applications and the ability to learn independently. This understanding of learning is crucial to identifying learning goals, designing learning activities and obtaining evidence about what is being learned. Curriculum, learning, teaching and assessment for learning thus form a complex whole.

The whole set of assessment for learning processes essentially comprises a sequence of three recurring activities: stimulating learners to think about the topic, the learning goal, or goals, and the criteria for success; finding out, often through dialogue, what and how they are thinking; on the basis of this evidence, identifying with them next steps for more effective thinking and fuller, more certain grasp of what is being learned.

Assessment for learning is thus itself a means of learning – assessment *as learning*.

Thinking point

- When we think about assessment for learning, should we ask 'Assessment for learning what?' Are we considering the processes of learning the formal curriculum or a broader kind of activity which might be called learning how to learn? Or both?

Learning the formal curriculum

The obvious answer to the question 'what is to be learned?' might seem to be: 'what the curriculum specifies'. Certainly, the curriculum is meant to be learned, whether it is a national, or regional, definition of what pupils should know and be able to do or one created by a school or an individual teacher. It typically spells out important ideas, information and skills to be developed in the various aspects of school work. In some cases, it may identify attitudes or orientations to be promoted, such as enjoyment of reading for pleasure, an investigative approach to science or social sciences, a problem solving one in technologies or a creative one in expressive arts areas. Some curriculum statements also identify much broader, generic aims, like the 'four capacities' in the Scottish Curriculum for Excellence, which intends to enable each child or young person to be a successful learner, a confident individual, a responsible citizen and an effective contributor. Comparable broad aims in the National Curriculum in England and Wales include, for example, enabling pupils to think creatively and critically, to solve problems and to make a difference for the better; and to become innovative, enterprising and capable of leadership in their future lives as workers and citizens.

However, the formal curriculum statement is never, on its own, all that matters.

Learning how to learn

A curriculum statement comes alive only when it is put into action. The experiences designed by the teacher to enable young people to 'learn the curriculum' can and should achieve more. They should develop reflectiveness about learning and its applications and the ability to learn. Self-determination is a key factor in learning of the highest quality and in relation to emotional and social influences (Dweck, 1999). Learning to learn helps pupils to perceive what they can do and be.

Learning how to learn includes understanding information and ideas (these are often specified in curriculum statements) and following clear explanations about them. Making personal sense of them in one's own words and in relation to things already known is a crucial part of the process. As well as information and ideas, important components of the skill of learning how to learn are curiosity, engagement and self-confidence, reflective thinking, hypothesising, investigating, problem solving. These capacities lead to a sense of continuous change in oneself, a continuous potential to engage with new ideas, contexts and groups of people and to become a confident and fully accepted member of one's community or of several communities. These abilities, and, indeed, all skills, develop in collaborative activity with other people – teachers and other learners. They become internalised, personal, through imitation, 'apprenticeship' and purposeful practice of them.

So we can sum up very effective learning in relation to any aspect of the curriculum at any stage as involving three key ideas:

- intellectual challenge;
- thinking;
- collaborative working.

Intellectual challenge means experience of significant ideas, grappling with real intellectual challenges which matter in the subject areas studied. Expectation of ability to understand and think about significant ideas should be high, though there will often be a need for the teacher to present them in language or other representation which is accessible to the pupils. Nobody, at any level of abilities, should be asked to think about or work towards trivialities. The learning processes relating to these ideas include analysis, critique, comparison and incorporation in each pupil's own fashion in her or his own set of values and constructs.

Thinking is as important as the ideas. Really effective teaching stimulates an excitement of mind, a desire to get a grip, work things out for yourself, find out more, experience more, try to solve problems. The cause of this excitement is complex: it includes the nature of the ideas and tasks presented and the teacher's relationship with the pupils, in particular his or her expectation of independent thought on their part and his or her skill in supporting them in the process.

Two kinds of thinking, both of which would be happening continuously in really good school work are:

- Understanding in one's 'own words' new ideas and information in relation to what one already knows and reflection on what one is learning. Requirement to write or talk is often a valuable means of stimulating thinking for understanding – the kind of thinking needed to clarify understanding is the same kind needed to speak or write clearly about a topic. Clarification and communication of understanding can be achieved in other media, too: art, drama, music, video production … The principle is the same: production of an ordered statement requires hard thinking about the topic, as well as skill in and thinking about the means of communicating it.
- Critical thinking, application of doubt, questioning of assumptions and assertions, others' and one's own. The uncertainty and permanent testability of knowledge and value positions should be a key concept in young people's minds. There should be constant encouragement in discussion and in the general work of any course, to question assumptions and test assertions and hypotheses, one's own and those discerned in, for example, reading, radio and television programmes, political, social and moral arguments. This principle also implies that pupils should frequently be dealing with problems (of various types, according to the subject area) which require them to make decisions for which the correct basis is not obvious – decisions which involve grappling with and resolving one's own

uncertainty about, for example, a practical or social problem, a commitment to a view or a policy or an interpretation of a text.

Collaborative working, as discussed in Chapter 9, is a central idea in the 'social constructivist' model of learning derived from the work of Lev Vygotsky (1978). This recognises that learners meet ideas first in the external 'social' plane. They then internalise them through *dialogue* with others (including, in school, teachers and other learners) and with themselves in formulating their 'own words' grasp of them. Teachers recognise the importance to deep understanding of having to articulate ideas in ways that make them clear to other people. We understand much better what we have had to make explicit in order to help others to learn.

The idea of independence in learning is sometimes misinterpreted as 'individual learning'. Nothing could be further from the truth. Assessment for learning is set within Vygotsky's theory of social constructivism and more recent socio-cultural theory (Pedder and James, 2012), which recognise learning as an interactive process. Learners learn from the teacher and from one another, from having opportunities to express their ideas and to develop them in discussion with others. The skills of reflective thinking, hypothesising, investigating and problem solving are all developed in interaction with others.

Thinking point

- How does assessment for learning contribute to independent learning?
- What are its characteristics which develop learning abilities?

Assessment for independent learning

Black and Wiliam (2009) provide very helpful guidance for thinking about assessment for learning. They define it, drawing on earlier definitions (Black and Wiliam, 1998b, and the Assessment Reform Group (ARG), 2002), as the process in which teachers, learners or their peers elicit, interpret and use evidence about pupil achievement to make decisions about the next steps in learning 'that are likely to be better, or better founded, than the decisions they would have taken in the absence of the evidence that was elicited' (Black and Wiliam, 2009: 9).

They identify five key strategies:

- clarifying and sharing learning intentions and criteria for success;
- engineering effective classroom discussions and other learning tasks that elicit evidence of understanding;

- providing feedback that moves learners forward;
- activating students as instructional resources for one another; and
- activating students as the owners of their own learning.

These activities are central to the rich educational process described above as characteristic of learning to be an independent learner. Assessment for learning is an integral part of planning very good learning and putting it into practice, not an additional element.

If we are committed to a social constructivist learning approach derived from the work of Vygotsky, we should think of formative assessment as 'assessment for development' rather than just 'for learning'. Vygotsky distinguished between learning and development, describing the latter as involving changes in psychological functions available to the learner, not just acquisition of new knowledge or new skills. Black and Wiliam (2009: 19) argue:

> The zone of proximal development (ZPD) is not, therefore, just a way of describing what a student can do with support, which might be simply learning; it is a description of the maturing psychological functions rather than those that already exist. A focus in instruction on the maturing psychological functions is most likely to produce a transition to the next developmental level and 'good learning' is that which supports the acquisition of new psychological functions.

Assessment for learning contributes significantly to such development, because the quality of reflection, interactive feedback and dialogue are critical features in learning activity. It develops the reasoning resources, commitment, confidence and orientations that a learner can bring to independent and collaborative learning in any future task.

Black and Wiliam (2009) argue that any teacher using interactive dialogue for normal subject teaching and feedback that encourages self-regulated learning (targeting one's own understanding, feelings, motivation and action) is engaged in a form of thinking skills programme in each curricular area. She/he is helping young people to become independent learners.

Thinking point

- The central purpose of assessment for learning is the empowerment of learners, enabling them to be active participants in the processes of learning. How can we make that happen?
- What are the key factors to consider as you seek to build assessment for independent learning in your school or classroom?

Key factors in making assessment for independent learning work

Curriculum and progression – what matters

What does 'assessment is an integral part of learning and teaching' really mean? Good assessment begins from the curriculum, from having a clear understanding of what matters in it and what progression for learners might look like. This understanding is crucial, to guide the learning goals that are established.

For example, if you think about progression in macro terms, what are the differences between someone beginning to learn about an area and someone who has significant expertise? What pathways might there be from early stages to expertise? In relation to a particular topic, you might reflect on what the main differences might be between evidence of knowledge and understanding that you would expect from a learner just beginning work on it and from one who has gained a great deal from it. The learning goals set should always relate to important ideas in progression.

Decisions about what matters in the curriculum are key – they form the basis of the learning tasks, the criteria of success and next steps in learning. Clear understanding of what matters in the curriculum thus underpins the whole continuous learning process.

How do teachers and pupils share understanding of what does matter in a given topic?

A crucial activity is the identification and sharing of the particular *learning goals* for a block of work. In a traditional classroom what matters in learning would be identified by the teacher, who would be likely to build in ideas of what was important from national or school curriculum guidance. In a classroom concerned with assessment for independent learning the identification of what matters would also involve the learners. If learners are to be engaged in learning and to be motivated to learn as a community, they need to have a stake in what is to be learned. The 'Energy' case study in 'Views from practice' below offers a good example of one way of engaging pupils with the teacher in designing learning goals.

Tasks are important and perhaps in the past too little attention has been paid to them. Good tasks engage pupils in thinking and activity that broaden and deepen their knowledge and understanding in the curriculum topic, with all its challenges. Tasks therefore have to be designed to enable pupils to demonstrate that they understand and can explain and apply what they have set out to learn. If the tasks are too narrow or too simplistic then the teacher defines and constrains what the pupil is able to demonstrate. Essentially, good tasks provide a framework for pupils to develop their thinking and the opportunity to demonstrate that thinking. The history case study in 'Views from practice' shows examples of such tasks. Evidence about how thinking has developed can be collected in many ways, for example, through observation of artefacts, drawings, actions, role play, performance, concept mapping, spoken explanation/account, and written answers. Different pupils are likely to produce their best evidence in different ways: it is thus important to make sure that plans to collect evidence are varied and responsive to individual learners.

Assessment for independent learning also involves opening up what Black and Wiliam (1998a) refer to as the Black Box of learning. How will learners know how much and how well they have made progress in learning? Both teachers and learners need to understand what counts as evidence of learning. *Clear success criteria* are statements that identify crucial evidence: what you and the pupils need to see happening to be sure the learning has been successful – what pupils should be aiming for. These criteria are likely to be derived from curriculum statements, but also from professional understanding of the subject area. When success criteria are negotiated with learners (what do we think a really good performance would look like?), they are likely to be more meaningful to them and the focus of their attention as they think about their own work.

Criteria, jointly developed and relating to what matters in the curriculum, then become the focus of evidence obtained. Both teachers and learners can use criteria to reflect on evidence from individual learners and groups to consider the extent and quality of progress made. A key consideration in assessment for independent learning would be to build the learners' capabilities as assessors of their own work and that of their classmates – *self and peer assessment*. Thus groups of learners would be encouraged to reflect on their own work and the work of their peers using the criteria as a basis for discussions. Having children build their expertise in looking at other children's work is a firm basis for their developing the critical skills necessary for them to reflect on their own work and to become more independent as learners. The skills of self and peer assessment, like other skills, have to be learned and practised. Learners need to understand the importance of paying attention to both learning and other learners, encouraging motivation as well as offering feedback on what to do next.

Interpreting and using evidence to provide high quality *feedback* is a further important aspect of the assessment for learning process. The collection of evidence and the feedback arising from an analysis of that evidence both relate to criteria – the standard against which pupils can compare their own work. Feedback may be offered as learners are engaged in tasks, or after tasks have been completed. A crucial factor in providing high quality feedback is interpreting evidence to make sure that the learners' thinking has been understood. Engaging learners in dialogue, asking open questions and listening carefully to their responses are important features of encouraging pupils to explore their ideas, understanding and reasoning. The teacher responding to Cara's answer of '5' to the arithmetic task '11+12' might have thought she had just picked the number 5 at random, had she not asked her how she had gone about the sum. Cara's explanation, 'I added 2 and 1 and got 3 then I added the 1 and the 1 to make 5', both clarified that she had been thinking – in terms of what she knew – but that there was need to work on place value.

Feedback must always pay attention to the learning and to the learner. High quality feedback is always constructive and is likely to be most effective in dialogue/ conversation. The conversations with learners need to be more than 'You did that well'; they should describe and discuss success, growth points (for example, what the pupil attempted without complete success) and next steps. It is crucial that learners are encouraged to believe that improvement is possible by focusing on particular next steps. Conversations should also help to explore the learners' understandings of both which next steps to take and how best to make progress. Again, involving learners in deciding on these processes is a sound strategy to build motivation and to find out more about what is likely to work most effectively with different individuals.

There is very clear and consistent evidence to suggest that grading of pupils' work should be undertaken with great care and used as infrequently as possible (Black and Wiliam, 1998b). As soon as a grade is allocated to a piece of work it will dominate both the pupil's and the teacher's thinking. If the grade is low it is likely to have a negative effect on a learner's perception of their ability to make good progress. This is particularly true for those who find learning hard.

All of these assessment for learning activities need to be integral to a rich understanding of curriculum and learning and teaching approaches (pedagogy). Assessment for independent learning seeks to engage learners throughout the process. A key recurring element is *dialogue* (pupil-teacher and pupil-pupil). It is a crucial means of challenging learners to reflect on their own thinking and to make unconscious learning processes overt, so that they can be considered, discussed and improved. This is what Marshall and Drummond (2006) refer to as the spirit of assessment for learning.

What about 'assessment for learning techniques'?

There are other approaches to assessment for learning in education systems. Particular 'assessment for learning techniques', such as 'traffic lights', 'wait time', 'fat (that is, open) questions' or WALT (We Are Learning Today ...), are sometimes presented as if they were assessment for learning. In themselves, they are not. They may be means of engaging pupils in aspects of the necessary thinking, but they are not of themselves assessment for learning. Indeed, they can be counter-productive if they are perceived as just teaching 'tips' or as techniques that inevitably improve learning. What is needed is really effective learning/teaching of what matters in the curriculum, incorporating all kinds of activity that cause thinking, reflection and collaboration and so enable both pupil and teacher to evaluate what is happening as pupils work. If a teacher decides that s/he would like pupils to think before they respond to a question, then wait time may be a helpful strategy to enable that process. Or if a teacher is concerned that the same few hands always go up in response to questions and wishes to find ways of engaging all learners, then a no-hands-up approach or using lollipop sticks may be helpful. However, the strategy comes in response to an identified issue – it is not an end in itself.

View from practice

Energy

This exemplar shows how the processes of sharing learning aims and identifying success criteria were very effectively developed by engaging the pupils actively in both.

Four weeks before the beginning of a new block of work the teacher explained that the class would be moving on to group projects on energy and that in two weeks the class would agree on the key things it would be important to learn. She asked the children to begin to collect information about energy, for example from television programmes, from the internet, from books, from the resource table set up in the classroom. She left blank sheets of paper on her desk and invited the children to add ideas over the two-week period. She herself also added ideas. Two weeks before the start of the energy project the teacher photocopied the completed sheets of paper and gave them to the class groups, asking them to look at the range of ideas listed, to cluster them into topics that different groups might investigate and to report back their findings to the class. Each group reported back and the teacher took notes. From these notes she developed the learning plan, which she shared with the children to ensure that she had represented their collective thoughts accurately. The class discussed the plan, agreed it and discussed the kinds of task that might best support learning in each of the topics identified.

They also discussed and noted what each group would need to show in the presentation of their project to demonstrate that they had successfully learned the topic or topics allocated to them – success criteria.

View from practice

History

This work featured self and peer evaluation of group presentations on researched topics. The research activities, using carefully identified library and internet resources, and the preparation for presentations constituted about 50 per cent of the classwork; pupils received direct teaching of subject content and skills in the other 50 per cent, in the classroom. The teacher justified this approach on the grounds that the process of learning was as valuable as the subject content and that practical application of history skills in the research/presentations deepened understanding of the ideas and evidence and developed not only interest in history but personal confidence and collaborative learning skills.

The research topics were controversial and therefore stimulating: for example, 'The Romans did not really create a civilised society in Britain. What is the evidence for and against this statement?'; 'William Wallace (a great Scottish hero) deserved to be executed by the English. How far do you agree?' Each group was expected to include in the presentation an introduction and background information, evidence to support the case for the argument, evidence against it and a reasoned conclusion. Before undertaking the research work the class spent a good deal of time discussing and agreeing with the teacher the criteria for an effective presentation. They agreed on three possible levels of success: a very successful argument with full evidential support; a capable but not complete argument, with some appropriate evidential support; and an argument that needed boosting in various ways. As each group made its presentation, the rest of the class made individual evaluations of its argument and evidence and then took part in group discussion to reach consensus on the criteria which had been met.

The teacher managed the feedback session after each presentation very effectively. He began with an open-ended class discussion, asking the class to consider the strong and weak points of the presentation and emphasising the need to provide evidence for the evaluation. This strategy kept open the possibility that pupils might come up with insightful comment on the work of each group without the help of the relatively pre-determined 3-level criteria statements (which the teacher nevertheless considered important as 'scaffolding' for pupils who were not yet used to making evaluative comments on one another's work). He encouraged the class to agree or take issue with statements made by individual pupils in this open discussion. After it the pupils individually and then in groups confirmed or revised the initial evaluations they had made as they listened to the presentation.

One significant aspect of the arrangements was designed to ensure that all the pupils benefited from working through the challenges presented by the research and presentation tasks. The groups were carefully selected as mixed-ability and there was a requirement for each individual member to undertake some of the research work and contribute in the presentation. Since the pupils knew their presentation was going to be judged by the whole class, much supportive teamwork developed in the groups, with pupils helping others to access and understand their particular aspects of the research topic and ensuring they could contribute effectively to the presentation.

(Adapted from Sliwka and Spencer, 2005)

Summary

Assessment for learning means finding out what has been learned, by any and every means that provides good evidence about this, and using the information to decide on next steps in learning and what needs to be done to help learners take these steps successfully.

It involves clear understanding of what learning *is* and how it is best developed. Part of this understanding is thorough grasp of what matters in the learning and progression specified in the formal curriculum. It also includes understanding of how learning/teaching activities, including assessment for learning, can develop pupils' capacities as independent learners. Intellectual challenge, thinking and collaborative working are key factors in the continuous process of developing independent learning.

This understanding of learning is crucial to identifying learning goals, designing learning activities and obtaining evidence about what is being learned. Curriculum, learning/teaching and assessment for learning thus form a complex whole.

Assessment for independent learning involves three recurring activities: stimulating learners to think about the topic, the learning goal(s); finding out, often through dialogue, what and how they are thinking; on the basis of this evidence, identifying with them next steps for more effective thinking and fuller, more certain grasp of what is being learned. Assessment for learning is thus itself a means of learning – assessment *as learning*. Key characteristics necessary to make it effective include:

- clarifying and sharing learning intentions and criteria for success;
- engineering effective classroom discussions and other learning tasks that provide evidence of understanding;

- providing feedback that moves learners forward;
- involving pupils in dialogue and in self and peer assessment that clarify and reinforce their own learning and help others to learn.

Reflective questions

- Think about a topic that you have recently taught or are about to teach. What do you intend that children will learn as a result of being involved in this topic?

  Reflect on the learning you have identified. Have you included aspects of knowledge and understanding, skills and attitudes? Does the learning identified relate to one area of the curriculum or to a number of areas? Are there other things you have identified as important?

  What kinds of evidence might you collect to ensure that you are able to reflect on progress in all the important learning you have identified?

- How have the ideas of intellectual challenge, thinking and collaborative working featured in the recent work you have planned for pupils?

  How might you have planned differently to ensure all three were central to the learning activities?

  (Or: How will you plan for them and put the plan into practical action in a forthcoming piece of work with pupils?)

- In recent work with pupils think about the quality of:

  o the steps taken to clarify and share learning intentions and criteria for success;
  o classroom learning tasks, discussions, questioning and any tasks designed to assess learning; and the evidence they provided of pupils' understanding;
  o feedback, and its usefulness to next steps in learning;
  o the engagement of pupils in helping one another to learn;
  o the action taken to help pupils be aware of how and what they are learning.

How might each have been improved?

Further reading

Black, P., Harrison, C., Lee, C., Marshall, B. and Wiliam, D. (2002) *Working Inside the Black Box: Assessment for Learning in the Classroom*. London: GL Assessment.

Black, P., Harrison, C., Lee, C., Marshall, B. and Wiliam, D. (2003) *Assessment for Learning: Putting it into Practice*. Buckingham: Open University Press.

Gardner, J., Harlen, W., Hayward, L. and Stobart, G., with Montgomery, M. (2010) *Developing Teacher Assessment*. Maidenhead/New York: Open University Press/ McGraw-Hill.

Hayward, L. and Spencer, E. (2010) 'The complexities of change: formative assessment in Scotland', *Curriculum Journal*, 21(2), 161–77.

CHAPTER 13

EDUCATION FOR GLOBAL CITIZENSHIP AND SUSTAINABLE DEVELOPMENT

Alan Britton

Key ideas

This chapter explores:

- education for global citizenship and sustainable development (EGCSD) as an important dimension in educational policy and practice;
- the themes that make up EGCSD and how they can be delivered as discrete subjects or in an inter-disciplinary way;
- pedagogical approaches and good practice for teaching EGCSD, and the positive effects these may bring;
- reflective planning and whole-school approaches for EGCSD.

Introduction

This chapter provides an introduction to education for global citizenship and sustainable development (EGCSD).[1] Its aim is to help you begin to plan relevant learning experiences in the primary school. In order to address these themes effectively the teacher has to do more than plan and deliver aspects of content knowledge; considerable professional reflection on the part of the primary practitioner is required, as well as strategic institutional engagement on the part of school leaders and other colleagues. It requires a whole-school approach.

There are different policy arrangements and guidance regarding these themes across different countries and jurisdictions. Every country has a distinctive political, social and educational history that inevitably leads to policy differences. As a result, when it comes to creating a 'citizenship curriculum' there is no 'one-size-fits-all' approach. Some countries emphasise the more patriotic and perhaps nationalistic dimensions of citizenship, while others promote a more cosmopolitan understanding of citizenship; some teach it in an abstract manner while others emphasise the active and critical components of citizenship. Similarly, it may be that in your context, education for sustainability is less prominent, or it might be labelled differently (perhaps with reference to environmental education).

What is meant by education for global citizenship and sustainable development?

If you are relatively unfamiliar with these terms it might be useful to define them before we go any further. It is not easy to pin down what is meant by *education for global citizenship*. Debate on what constitutes citizenship itself has gone on for centuries. The status or idea of the 'citizen' has varied enormously from place to place and over time: from ancient Greece to the present day, and in dictatorships and democracies. In simple terms, however, citizenship can be understood as a status involving a set of rights and (often reciprocal) responsibilities. For example, the right to vote is seen as a cornerstone of democratic citizenship, although this right may be rescinded if an individual commits a crime resulting in imprisonment. By breaking the rules or laws of society, the individual loses an element of their citizenship rights.

An example of the way in which our understanding of citizenship has been gradually moulded and re-envisaged over time can be seen if we trace the gradual historic extension of the franchise (the right to vote) in the UK from initially only the rich landowning classes, the aristocracy and some clergy (in the fifteenth to nineteenth centuries); to the general male working population (mid-nineteenth to early twentieth centuries); to women (1918, 1928), and more recently to younger people between 18 and 21 (1969).

A broader but related historical process, identified by Marshall (1950), was the progressive extension in many countries of three forms of citizenship rights: firstly the *civic* (relating to the autonomy of the individual, the establishment of government and the rule of law); then the *political* (including the right to vote); and latterly, to *social* rights such as the welfare state, health services and free education for all. Marshall's view was that you could only fully be a citizen if you had access to all three categories.

These examples suggest that in order to educate for citizenship, young people may have to learn about how society operates, how decisions are made, and how a nation assigns rights and responsibilities. Later on we will explore how such apparently complex ideas can be translated into learning opportunities in the primary school.

The more recent emphasis on the idea of global citizenship appears to have been prompted by a number of critical factors, including the rapid pace of change in contemporary society, the impact of globalisation, new technologies and changing patterns of population and migration. These social, political and economic trends are changing the way we live and work radically and rapidly, and the way we educate young people ought to acknowledge and reflect these changes. It is no longer enough to envisage citizenship as a concept defined and confined by the particular borders and boundaries of one country. Young people have to understand more about the global dynamics and processes that are shaping our lives in the present time, and into the future.

Sustainable development can be a problematic term, for different reasons. If we understand development to be the process by which societies are able to expand their economic capacity over time we have to understand how this growth is achieved. Major historic spurts in growth have tended to coincide with the application of new technologies or scientific discoveries, or with the exploitation of a newly accessible natural resource, for example the industrial revolution driven by steam engines and fuelled by coal, alongside other social, cultural and political factors.

Some argue that such development comes at a cost as it results in the over-exploitation of finite resources (such as forests, coal, or oil), the destruction or degradation of the natural environment, and increased social and economic inequality within and between countries.

It is estimated that if current rates of global consumption and economic development were to be sustainable we would need to live on a planet that was one and a half times more abundant in natural resources than Earth actually possesses. From this perspective, economic development is inherently unsustainable. A more optimistic view is that development can be achieved without imperilling the Earth's resources by, for example, making improvements in technology and promoting more sustainable practices such as recycling, and acknowledging that a vibrant consumer society is a key requisite for economic wellbeing.

Educating about sustainable development therefore requires teachers' and pupils' engagement with these issues and to acknowledge the contrasting and nuanced views that might be held on them. By addressing these issues in a pedagogical context of global citizenship it is possible to promote critical thinking and the exploration of values, attitudes and actions.

When it comes to teaching and learning, global citizenship and sustainable development can in fact be understood and applied in relatively straightforward terms, and can be embedded in primary schools very effectively. Furthermore, effective global citizenship education serves as the foundation of effective teaching and learning in more general terms. A really good school will tend to take global citizenship seriously. This will be evident in teaching and learning, but also in the quality of relationships between staff and pupils, in the role of the school in the local community, the sense of partnership with parents and carers, and the ways in which the children are encouraged and empowered to take actions to address issues of local or global concern.

This latter feature of global citizenship education is crucial in helping us to see it as about more than knowledge and skills development.

The concerns and goals of education for global citizenship and sustainable development

It is important to be clear about what EGCSD is trying to achieve. These themes reflect wider educational, social and economic ambitions for the future, as well as concerns around the nature of contemporary society, the attitudes and behaviours of young people, and the quality and sustainability of our natural environment. There is no doubt that some elements of the educational frameworks described in this chapter are directed towards changing the behaviours and attitudes of young people; however, there is clearly a wider agenda at play incorporating a range of other concerns. These are summarised in Figure 13.1 below. Immediately afterwards, Figure 13.2 lists some of the goals and intended outcomes of the EGCSD framework.

- **Political**: including the apparent disinterest of young people in traditional party politics, in voting, and other forms of civic engagement.
- **Social**: including the apparent rise in anti-social behaviour, the desire for greater community cohesion; greater equality and social justice.
- **Ethical**: linked to the social category above; including the idea that some young people are apparently unable to balance their rights with concomitant responsibilities, or, in crude terms, understand right from wrong. Also, a desire for fairer and more just social and economic practices locally, nationally and globally.
- **Economic**: including the employability of young people in a context of globalisation, post-industrial employment patterns and increased international competition; the promotion of enterprise and entrepreneurial attitudes, and fairer global economic relations.
- **Environmental**: including concerns about sustainability, biodiversity, habitat loss, and the possible impact of global warming.

Figure 13.1   What issues does EGCSD seek to address?

In general terms, EGCSD policies tend to promote some or all of the following attributes among young people:

- To be better informed, with greater awareness of the world, current global issues and the environment.
- To be more respectful.
- To be more democratically active.
- To be more politically literate.
- To be more active participants in local, national and global society.
- To develop enhanced critical thinking skills.
- To be more effective advocates and activists with regard to local, national or global issues.
- To show greater empathy and consideration towards the needs, values and cultures of others.
- To build more effective cooperation and collaboration with others.
- To develop entrepreneurial instincts and problem-solving abilities.
- To promote 'moral courage': the ability to do the right thing in the face of peer or other pressure.
- To exhibit more responsible behaviours, actions, attitudes and choices, including relating to sustainable practices such as recycling.
- To exert greater choice and influence over their own learning and aspects of their wider educational experience.

Figure 13.2   The goals of EGCSD

When presented as lists (which are not themselves exhaustive), these themes, goals and intended outcomes represent a challenging and ambitious vision of the child being led on the journey towards effective global citizenship. It is not a vision that is morally neutral: an underlying vision and discourse of what a good society ought to be like becomes apparent on closer reading.

Thinking point

- Imagine you are introducing an EGCSD topic to a class of older pupils in a primary school. What broad learning intentions might you share with the pupils in order to frame the topic and your lessons?

How should EGCSD be taught?

This section addresses two key points: how should EGCSD be approached in the primary school?; and is it preferable to approach these themes in a subject-specific or interdisciplinary fashion?

While many countries have embarked on developing EGCSD within their curricula, different countries continue to implement EGCSD in different ways. Even across the United Kingdom and Ireland there is considerable divergence in practice.

In England, citizenship became a statutory subject within the National Curriculum from 2002 and its position has been assured through the recent review. Elements of citizenship, pupil voice and sustainability are also evident in many wider school practices that are likely to be promoted within schools governed by the National Curriculum, as well as those institutions such as academies and free schools that might have greater curriculum autonomy.

Northern Ireland has curriculum strands on personal development and mutual understanding, and learning for life and work. Within these strands there are a number of key elements of local and global citizenship.

In the Republic of Ireland, the primary subject areas of social, personal and health education (SPHE) and social, environmental and scientific education (SESE) include elements of active and responsible citizenship, from local, national and global perspectives.

In Scotland, education for citizenship is a non-statutory element of the curriculum although schools are encouraged to incorporate it in a cross-curricular and whole-school fashion. Significant elements of citizenship can also be found in *A Curriculum for Excellence*, which is the main curriculum framework from 3–18. The term *learning for sustainability* has recently been adopted at a national policy level to encompass EGCSD.

In Wales there is a statutory requirement for the provision of personal and social education which incorporates active citizenship and education for sustainable development and global citizenship.

Although EGCSD is evident in the various curricula, each country addresses it in quite different ways. There appears to be no consensus on whether these themes are best addressed through a subject-specific and timetabled focus, or through interdisciplinary approaches. Arguments for and against both approaches are summarised below.

Table 13.1 Advantages and disadvantages of different policy approaches to citizenship education

Approach to Citizenship	Advantages	Disadvantages
Statutory	All schools likely to teach it. Seen as an entitlement.	Compulsion doesn't always work in education; teachers may find ways to resist or subvert policy they don't like.
Non-statutory	Provision likely to be led by enthusiasts; seen as a good/right thing to do, rather than being forced into it.	Provision might be sporadic or absent. Limited responsibility and accountability.
Discrete subject	Clarity around who delivers; opportunity for specialist teachers/teacher training.	Citizenship may be defined quite narrowly; conflicting or incoherent approaches might emerge across a school.
Permeates the curriculum	Broad definition and more coherent approaches transcending the subjects. Pupil voice may be a whole school priority.	Some provision may be ineffective, limited expertise; responsibilities may be avoided; competing in a crowded curriculum with other priorities.
Assessed	Can provide benchmarks and measure progress of pupils; schools more likely to take seriously and resource accordingly.	Children may be labelled as 'failing' citizens; also hard to assess some of the 'softer' citizenship skills and values.
Inspected	Increases accountability and consistency across the system; teachers will feel they have to address citizenship thoroughly. School management likely to prioritise citizenship.	Hard to inspect some of the 'hidden curriculum' dimensions to citizenship; imposes 'authoritarian' regime on an inherently democratic goal. Might 'deprofessionalise' teachers.

In a cross-curricular or interdisciplinary approach, a range of subject areas and topics lend themselves to the incorporation of citizenship. Some are especially relevant and potentially fruitful, including:

- social studies, including history, geography, and the study of people in society;
- environmental studies, including ecology, biodiversity and climate;
- religious, moral and philosophical studies;
- science; and
- technology.

Other areas also open up possible contexts for citizenship learning, possibly combined with some of the subjects above, including:

- creative subjects, including art, design and music; and
- foreign languages.

A third group of subjects includes those which can be explored in an explicit fashion relating to citizenship, or that can be seen as supporting the development of certain core skills that any effective citizen might need, including:

- English language and literature, and functional aspects of literacy such as oral communication, interpretation and written argument;
- mathematics and functional numeracy, including interpretation of statistics and data, and problem solving.

The broad range of subject-based opportunities and combinations highlighted hints that almost any subject can, with sufficient creativity and imagination, be incorporated into citizenship learning. It can be interpreted and conceptualised in so many different ways and 'delivered' through so many subject contexts that it risks becoming incoherent, lacking in purpose or clearly-defined goals. Given this danger, the value of effective planning becomes paramount. When planned effectively, an interdisciplinary approach can support the development of truly enriching learning experiences for EGCSD.

Thinking point

- Do you think that EGCSD should be a statutory subject in the curriculum?
- Should EGCSD be assessed, either in the classroom or through national exams?

The role of pupil voice and pupil participation

The United Nations Declaration on the Rights of the Child, established in 1989 and ratified across the UK in 1991 and in the Republic of Ireland in 1992, includes a range of clauses that seek to promote the protection, wellbeing and flourishing of young people across the world. All teachers should take time to reflect on the implications for their practice of the various articles contained in the declaration. Article 12 has an especially significant bearing on education as it states that young people have the right to contribute to decision-making processes that are likely to affect them, and to have their views taken into account.

It is often argued that citizenship education can only be meaningful to young people if such concepts and principles are actually evident in their lived experiences in the school and in wider society. Young people are very adept at identifying double standards and hypocrisy and they might become disillusioned if a school speaks the language of participation and democracy while ignoring the views of pupils on issues that matter to them, or by consulting them only in ways that are perceived to be cursory or tokenistic.

The following summary of one school's approach to pupil participation illustrates the very positive impact such approaches can have, but it is important to emphasise that such success requires commitment from the whole school community, and effective staff development, as well as positive and inspirational leadership.

View from practice

A head teacher was appointed to lead a school that was widely viewed as 'failing', and populated by pupils who were seen as 'unteachable'.[ii] In order to challenge the deep-seated problems in the school she sought to change the culture of the school, by creating a 'listening school' in which everyone (pupils, parents, staff) had a voice. This entailed going further than the usual recognised participatory structures, such as class and pupil councils, and instead involved the creation of whole-school all ages meeting groups where minor or major issues could be raised, discussed, and action points could be agreed.

Another significant change involved devolving greater control over learning both to individual teachers and to the pupils themselves. While teachers still prepare lesson plans, pupils are empowered to make choices about their own next steps. For many teachers this might seem a high risk strategy, but in this instance it appears to have been very successful, with a whole range of positive outcomes emerging from this approach; including improved attainment, attendance, behaviour and motivation. The external perception of the school has also shifted radically, in the eyes of parents and inspectors alike.

While the example above involved a whole school changing its culture under the leadership of a committed head teacher, there are ways in which any primary teacher can develop the participation of pupils in their own learning and decision-making, including: offering choice in relation to activities, texts or investigations; discussion and negotiation around classroom values and standards of conduct; negotiated target-setting with teachers; and involvement in the planning process (both short term and long term). Some primary schools extend the principle of pupil involvement into the evaluation of teaching and learning (pupils providing feedback on lessons), and even the recruitment process for new teaching appointments. These latter examples might feel quite challenging for some teachers. However, if they are authentic and supported by relevant training for pupils in, for example, the provision of effective formative feedback, they contribute to a culture and climate that recognises and values the pupils as citizens within the school community.

Thinking point

- In what ways might pupils in your class participate in decision making?
- Should pupils have a say in the review of lessons, courses or teaching?

Developing a global perspective among pupils

At the heart of the drive towards an understanding of the global dimension is the concept of globalisation: the process by which communications and the movement of goods, services, people, and culture around the world has become more rapid, fluid and dynamic. Globalisation can be exemplified in many different ways, including the fresh fruit and vegetables in your local supermarket that are imported from across the planet, the ubiquity of global fast food brands, the growth in travel, tourism and labour market mobility and the ease of global communications and access to information and commerce via the internet and mobile technologies.

While many young people appear confident in navigating and accessing certain aspects of this globalised culture, they may not understand it at a deeper or more critical level. If they notice that most of their clothing is manufactured in developing countries, can they unpick the social, political and economic conditions that lead to this reality, or the possible ethical implications (such as the relative pay and safety of the people who produce the clothes)?

While it would seem unreasonable to expect a primary school to promote a fully comprehensive global knowledge and understanding, it is possible to explore a range of ways in which you can develop the specific transferable concepts, skills, values, attitudes and pedagogies to frame a global approach. Oxfam's *Curriculum for Global Citizenship* (see web resources at the end of this chapter) provides a helpful framework for teachers. It notes that as well as learning about some of these issues and developing skills and values, it is vital that young people learn about their capacity for taking action as global citizens. This might include actions such as setting up a fair trade tuck shop in the school, or writing letters, emails or petitions on issues that they have identified as priorities for change. Carefully planned partnership and exchange programmes with schools in other countries provide considerable opportunities for authentic intercultural engagement.

Another factor that many schools and teachers may have to address is that their own school community might itself represent a microcosm of increased diversity and multicultural complexity. This is often viewed as a challenge; but it can also provide opportunities for enriched learning, as well as more effective and sensitive approaches to the integration of a broader range of cultures, values and identities in the classroom. The view from practice below illustrates how one school in this situation has responded.

View from practice

An urban primary school has a pupil population substantially made up of children for whom English is not their first language. As well as children from the local population of second and third generation migrants, in the last few years the school has also welcomed large numbers of new arrival children whose families come primarily from Eastern Europe, as well as some refugees and asylum seekers from Africa and the Middle East. There is often a rapid turnover in the school population, with some pupils staying only for a short period of time. A larger than average percentage of pupils is in receipt of free school meals, suggesting relatively high levels of poverty.

Although there is some excellent support from specialists in English as an Additional Language, the classroom teachers nonetheless have to be very adept at taking flexible and sensitive approaches to teaching and learning that meet the needs of this diverse group of children, while also ensuring stability and maintaining high expectations for all pupils. Global citizenship is seen as a key priority that helps the school to respond to these needs. This includes regular celebrations of the different nations and cultures represented in the school, viewing this diversity as a strength and an educational resource in its own right, finding a place for the use of 'mother language' in the classroom and whole school environment, planning learning experiences that tackle themes of diversity, equality, and discrimination, and maintaining strong partnerships with parents, carers and the local community.

This example highlights one of the key points from this chapter: effective global citizenship education is really about effective approaches to education in general. In other words, these are things that all schools should be thinking about, whether defined as global citizenship or not.

Planning versus opportunism in EGCSD

There are a number of ways in which you can plan for the provision of effective learning experiences in global citizenship. These might be organised as a series of short connected 'lessons' that are explicitly 'citizenship' focused; or they may be half-day or whole-day investigations or projects on a particular topic or concept; or it may be that you incorporate elements of citizenship into a short-, medium- or long-term programme of work that appears at first sight to be about something else entirely.

Alongside long-term and structured planning there are opportunities within EGCSD to be more flexible and reactive, and to be willing to (at least metaphorically) tear up your planned lessons for the day to address an unexpected or urgent citizenship-related theme or event. For example, a student teacher was on placement in a primary school when she encountered tensions and upset in the class around name calling and verbal bullying that had occurred over a lunchtime break. She was confident enough to devote the afternoon session to an improvised lesson around the concept of respect, without a plan or resources in place. With the approval and support of the school, she then devoted a number of subsequent lessons (involving a great deal of evening preparation) over the following week to address and resolve the pastoral issue that had arisen, mainly by utilising the conceptual frameworks offered by citizenship.

A more ambitious variant on this approach is often encountered in schools in response to a particular event or natural disaster, such as an earthquake, tsunami, conflict or famine. In such cases, the children might come into class the day after the news has broken and they turn quite naturally to their teacher for explanation and understanding.

After the 2011 earthquake and tsunami in Japan, some primary and secondary schools reacted swiftly by developing topic-based responses. These incorporated elements of geography, geology, Japanese culture, the role of government and NGOs in disaster relief; and in some cases, debates about the advantages and disadvantages of nuclear power (linked to the Fukushima power plant affected by the tsunami). Some schools also linked the formal learning to fundraising activities led by the pupils themselves. While primary schools had to factor in the considerations highlighted previously about age-appropriateness, they were nonetheless able to enhance the understanding of their pupils of a real world globally significant event.

Such an approach places the teacher in the role of 'curator' of knowledge, rather than as the principal source of knowledge; in other words, when information can be accessed so readily through technology, the teacher's role becomes one of facilitating the interpretation and critical appraisal of that information by pupils, as well as helping them to consider different responses.

A focus on sustainability and outdoor learning

Education for sustainable development is often regarded as complementary to, or even an integral component of, global citizenship. Children can learn about both the local and global aspects of sustainability; they can take part in recycling, tree planting, energy conservation and tidying up campaigns that have a positive local-ised impact, while also learning about (and supporting) more sustainable global approaches to the same issues. Playground greenhouses can be constructed from recycled plastic bottles, and orchards in the school grounds or on the rooftop can be linked to science topics, healthier diets and lifestyle, and enterprise activities.

The idea of 'outdoor learning' is increasingly being associated with both sustain-able development and global citizenship. This approach is based on the idea that young people should be encouraged to spend as much time learning outside the conventional classroom as possible. Evidence suggests that our increasingly risk-averse society fosters young people with limited appreciation of true risk thus cur-tailing their ability to assess danger in other contexts. Schools in urban as well as rural settings can plan outdoor learning experiences and take steps to improve the natural spaces in their grounds, playing fields and communities. School grounds can be stocked with 'natural apparatus' such as felled trees, mounds, tunnels, and some areas of grass left uncut for extended periods of time to enhance the environmental diversity of the landscape and to provide opportunities for open-ended and imagi-native play for children.

Summary

This chapter acknowledges the potential complexity of some of the underlying concepts and pedagogical implications of EGCSD, while trying to balance this with some recommendations that ought to help in the planning and delivery of effective learning in this area. When global citizenship is taught successfully, the impact on young people can be substantial, with positive effects on their knowledge, skills, values, attitudes and behaviours. Wherever you teach, and whatever the official policy on citizenship education or EGCSD is in your school or national system, it is important to recognise that to be a good teacher you have to be a citizenship teacher, whether consciously or implicitly.

In an ideal world, the whole school community should demonstrate a commit-ment to these themes, and leadership is really important, but you may find that you begin as a lone enthusiast for EGCSD within your school. If that is the case, you don't need to do everything discussed in this chapter. It would be impossible to do it all, and would in all probability just lead to a diluted or incoherent approach. Instead, take on board a few ideas, themes and teaching strategies, and incorporate them over a weekly, termly and annual planning cycle, while remaining open to the opportunistic approach described above.

Set yourself some targets and goals relating to authentic pupil participation in the learning process, and try to extend the principle of collaboration to colleagues, parents and the wider community. Listen to your pupils; find out about the issues, local or global, that concern them, and develop learning opportunities and actions around these. Above all, recognise that the children in your class are citizens of today as well as the citizens of the future, and your role is to help them to flourish and to contribute responsibly, ethically, actively and critically to the world that they are part of.

Reflective questions

- Why do different countries have different policy approaches to EGCSD?
- Is EGCSD likely to achieve its goals?
- What does a sustainable school look like?
- Should EGCSD be assessed? Should it be inspected?
- What are the limits to pupil participation in the life and work of a primary school?

Further reading

Britton, A. (2012) 'The citizenship teacher and controversial issues', in J. Brown, H. Ross, and P. Munn (eds), *Democratic Citizenship in Schools: Teaching Controversial Issues, Traditions and Accountability*. Edinburgh: Dunedin Academic Press. pp. 60–73.

McKeown, R. and Hopkins, C. (2010) 'Global citizenship and sustainable development: Transformation in the initial education of teachers', in T.L.K. Wisely, I.M. Barr, A. Britton, and B. King (eds), *Education in a Global Space*. Edinburgh: Scotdec/IDEAS. pp. 9–17.

Marshall, T. H. (1950) *Citizenship and Social Class and Other Essays*. Cambridge: Cambridge University Press.

Peacock, A. (2012) 'Developing outward-facing schools where citizenship is a lived experience', in J. Brown, H. Ross, and P. Munn (eds), *Democratic Citizenship in Schools: Teaching Controversial Issues, Traditions and Accountability*. Edinburgh: Dunedin Academic Press. pp. 120–32.

Web resources

5 Nations Citizenship Network. Brings together curriculum information and small-scale research on citizenship and values from across England, Northern Ireland, the Republic of Ireland, Scotland and Wales: http://www.fivenations.net/index.html

England:

Association for Citizenship Teaching (ACT): http://www.teachingcitizenship.org.uk/
CitizEd: http://www.citized.info/?strand=0

Northern Ireland:

Curriculum Information: http://www.nicurriculum.org.uk/key_stages_1_and_2/areas_of_learning/pdmu/

Republic of Ireland:

General curriculum information on citizenship: http://www.fivenations.net/ireland html

Scotland:

http://www.educationscotland.gov.uk/learningteachingandassessment/learning acrossthecurriculum/themesacrosslearning/globalcitizenship/index.asp

Wales:

General curriculum information on citizenship: http://www.fivenations.net/wales. html

Oxfam's Curriculum for Global Citizenship: http://www.oxfam.org.uk/education/global-citizenship

UN Declaration on the Rights of the Child (UNICEF site): http://www.unicef.org.uk/UNICEFs-Work/Our-mission/UN-Convention/

Notes

1. This abbreviation is used as a convenient label in this chapter for the combination of citizenship learning and sustainable development/environmental understanding that I describe and discuss, it might be called something else where you teach, but the concepts and ideas captured by EGCSD will hopefully be relevant to you.
2. This short section is based on the experiences described by Peacock (2012). See reference above in Further Reading.

CHAPTER 14

SPIRITUAL DEVELOPMENT

Leonardo Franchi and Leon Robinson

Key ideas

This chapter explores:

- what is spiritual development?
- how does spiritual development relate to what philosophers call the 'good life', that is, a life well-lived?
- what can and should teachers do to promote spiritual development?

Introduction

Spiritual development in education cannot be confined to one subject. In an extract from subsidiary guidelines issued to school inspectors by the Office for Standards in Education for England and Wales (Ofsted, 2012), we find the following:

> Pupils' spiritual development is shown by their: beliefs, religious or otherwise, which inform their perspective on life and their interest in and respect for different people's feelings and values; sense of enjoyment and fascination in learning about themselves, others and the world around them, including the intangible; use of imagination and creativity in their learning, and their willingness to reflect on their experiences.

We recognise that 'spiritual development' is a problematic term owing to a) the broad range of definitions of its root terms: *spirituality*, *spiritual* and *spirit*, and b) the ongoing debate over the nature of the relationship between spiritual development and religious education. In this chapter we do not propose to explore these debates in depth, but we will focus on spiritual development as related to the attributes which emerge from a good education: a sense of human flourishing, a recognition that what is of value is not measured in purely performative terms, a sense of 'wonder and awe' at the world, the potential of the human person to do good and an urge to discover and take delight in the search for meaning and purpose in life.

We begin by exploring what is meant by the term 'the good life'. Following this we will look at the challenges which arise when we seek to define 'spiritual development'. Finally, we will offer three examples of how these issues are applied in contemporary education.

The 'good life'

What is the 'good life'? When we ask people what they think about when they hear the term 'the good life' we will get quite different answers. Some will mention material prosperity and a life of fruitful leisure; others will mention peace of mind and contentment in personal and family life. Others may consider the good life to be one of social or political engagement, in order to make the world a better place for all.

In the context of philosophy (which means 'love of wisdom') the term 'good life' refers to a life which is 'good' and therefore we need to consider how we define what goodness is. A helpful (although not exhaustive) definition is that a good life is one which is lived for others and shows appreciation for concepts like *truth* and *beauty*. Indeed the linking of *truth, beauty* and *goodness* is essential to any understanding of the nature of education, as these concepts form the traditional bedrock of a civilised and mature society (Gardner, 2011). There is much to say on this subject and we acknowledge that the concepts of *truth, beauty* and *goodness* as objective values are challenged vigorously by those who claim that such alleged universal concepts are no more than personal or societal constructions of reality rooted in a particular culture.

In the contemporary field of positive psychology, psychologists seek 'to find and nurture genius and talent' and 'to make normal life more fulfilling' (Compton, 2005). Three distinct ideas of the 'good life' are outlined:

- *a pleasant life*, which involves good feelings about the past, present, and future, may be very agreeable, but ultimately it will be unsatisfying, as there is there is more to life than pleasure;
- *the engaged life* is associated with positive traits such as strength of character, bravery, integrity, citizenship, humility, prudence, gratitude, and hope. It may still have aspects which are unfulfilling, however, as the truly good life also requires a sense of purpose;
- *the meaningful life* is characterised by service, and may involve taking active roles in positive organisations. Examples of positive organisations might include family, workplace, social groups, and society in general. Membership of such groups fosters positive feelings of wellbeing, while also promoting character strengths, as seen in the engaged life (Compton, 2005).

Ideas about the relationship between the 'good life' and education have been explored by ancient and modern philosophers and continue to offer much scope for reflection, debate and study today. Future teachers need to be aware of the broad contours of this very rich debate.

Thinking point

- What is the purpose of education?
- What is goodness and how do we know that what is described as good is actually good?
- What, if anything, is the meaning, purpose and final goal of life?

The many different religious and philosophical traditions across the world and throughout history have agreed that the 'good life' is not equivalent to a life devoted solely to the pursuit of pleasure, a comfortable existence and plentiful material goods. Rather, the good life offers opportunities to do good to others and to appreciate what is good in others. While there are different philosophical and religious perspectives on what constitutes the human person, there is some degree of common ground within and across these traditions on what constitutes the 'good life' and a 'good education'.

Thinkers in the ancient east from China to India saw through the temptations of fame and riches, to a more fulfilling life of goodness. In ancient Greece, the philosopher Aristotle envisioned the 'good life' as consisting of the cultivation of virtues, leading to a 'happiness of the spirit' referred to as *eudaimonia*. From this classical world of ancient Greece, we receive a summary of qualities desirable for living the good life. These are the 'cardinal virtues' – so called as they are the hinges (the Latin *cardo* means 'hinge') by which the door of the good life is opened:

- *Prudence*: the ability to judge between options as to what are appropriate actions at a given time.
- *Justice*: the never-ending, constant will to give to each person what is rightly due to them.
- *Temperance* (or *restraint*): the practice of self-control, moderation of one's appetites.
- *Fortitude* (or *courage*): the capacity for endurance, and the ability to confront fear, uncertainty and intimidation.

The Christian church took up similar themes over the centuries, adding to the 'cardinal virtues' a further three 'theological virtues':

- *Faith*: belief in God, and in the truth of His revelation as well as obedience to Him (see St Paul's *Letter to the Romans* 1:5 and 16:26).
- *Hope*: the expectation of and desire of receiving; refraining from despair; never giving up.
- *Charity*: selfless, unconditional, and voluntary loving-kindness such as helping one's neighbours in their need.

In the current state of affairs, where most pupils are likely not to have been brought up in religious households, there is no need to abandon the idea of virtues altogether. Indeed, within positive psychology much attention has been given to virtues as signs of mental wellbeing. Peterson and Seligman (2004) distil the virtues into six areas, expanding these to outline a number of strengths suggested to be associated with such virtues:

- *Wisdom and knowledge*: creativity, curiosity, open-mindedness, love of learning, perspective, innovation.
- *Courage*: bravery, persistence, integrity, vitality.
- *Humanity*: love, kindness, social intelligence.

- *Justice*: citizenship, fairness, leadership.
- *Temperance*: forgiveness, mercy, humility, prudence, self control.
- *Transcendence*: appreciation of beauty and excellence, gratitude, hope, humour and 'spirituality'.

Related emerging concepts include self-efficacy, personal effectiveness, flow and mindfulness:

- *Self-efficacy* refers to a belief that one's ability to accomplish a task is a function of personal effort.
- *Low self-efficacy*, or a disconnect between ability and personal effort, is associated with depression.
- *High self-efficacy* is associated with positive change, including overcoming abuse, overcoming eating disorders, and maintaining a healthy lifestyle. It has positive benefits for one's immune system, aids in stress management, and decreases pain. (Bandura, 1977). The related concept, personal effectiveness, is primarily concerned with planning and the implementation of methods of accomplishment.

It is easy to see how it would be desirable to foster these virtues and their related strengths in young people. The study of positive human qualities has broadened the scope of psychological research to include mental wellness. Indeed, the leaders of the positive psychology movement are challenging moral relativism by suggesting that people are 'evolutionarily predisposed' toward certain virtues, and that virtue has a biological basis (Hauser, 2008).

The golden rule

Behind all these virtues lies a simple, clear guide, shared in one form or another amongst all of the great religious and philosophical traditions of the world: *the golden rule* (Blackburn, 2002: 117). The golden rule as stated by Jesus in the Gospel of Matthew (7:12) is: 'Do unto others as you would have them do unto you'. This simple, direct instruction is open to many different interpretations, however, and a proper understanding of *love* is needed, rooted in the wisdom of the ages and applied to life in contemporary society. Later in the New Testament, in the first Letter of John (4:18) we find, 'There is no fear in love; but perfect love casts out fear: because fear has to do with punishment and he who fears is not perfected in love.' Love requires knowledge and understanding; we would be hard pressed to love anything, or act in a truly loving way towards it, if we did not understand what it was, and what it needed. Think of trying to care for an animal, without knowing what sort of things it ate. Vegetarian lions do not flourish.

We have to give pupils what they really need, in order for them to flourish. There is no absolute distinction between physical, mental, emotional and spiritual flourishing. Advances in the cognitive sciences, aided in part by new imaging techniques, have added an objective dimension to what was once limited to subjective reports of mental states.

The good life cannot be lived in an abstract way. Activity and diet are both important to the good life. From the time of the earliest Greek philosophers, a healthy mind and a healthy body have been seen as the essentials of a good life. The effects of sugars, carbohydrates, psychoactive substances from caffeine and chocolate to opiates and artificial constructs such as LSD are better understood now. The insights are clear. It is not all a matter of opinion. Some things really are better for us than others.

In addition to this, children's senses are saturated by an almost inescapable barrage of advertisements for things that they can eat, drink or occupy their time with, which, while not quite being 'bad' in and of themselves, (to the point where they might be banned by law, or at least restricted), nevertheless contribute to a lifestyle which is undermining the possibility of children flourishing (Palmer, 2007).

Thinking point

- Chocolate chip cookies might be delicious, but they are no substitute for a balanced meal. Some children, left to their own devices, make this sort of substitution, to the detriment of their health and their happiness. Are guidelines enough? What is a proper balance for those in positions of responsibility to take?
- Should there really be opportunities provided for children, in the form of unsupervised vending machines and free access to junk food sellers, to indulge their damaging habits?

Taking the responsibility seriously for the spiritual wellbeing of children in our care needs to extend to a concern for what they eat, and for how they spend their leisure time. Encouragement, opportunity and guidance all have their place. Without opportunities for flourishing, no amount of encouragement and guidance will help.

School life offers opportunities for the living of the virtues. The pupil must be led to the often hidden wells of our cultural sources and draw from them the values and attitudes which allow him/her to live a good life. This immersion in the cultural and philosophical traditions is not an anachronistic return to an imagined 'golden' historical period but reflects the shared educational journey uniting past, present and future which a good education requires.

Thinking point

Some examples to consider in relation to truth and beauty:

Ideas of beauty vary widely from one culture to another, not only about the physical appearances of people and objects, but about the proper way to do things. Manners, for example, vary between cultures, and are concerned with the proper, pleasing way of doing things. Can the same variety be found in ideas about what is true?

Language plays an important role: a battle can be accurately described both as a great victory and as a terrible defeat, depending on which side it is viewed from. Is every situation, even every thing subject to such shifting views, or is there an objective viewpoint to be had (a 'God's eye view')? Is truth only a matter of perspective?

Some people use cosmetic surgery. Is there an important difference between the use of cosmetic surgery to restore the features of a disfigured victim of an accident, and a procedure undertaken purely for the vain pursuit of an imagined ideal look?

Spiritual development: ways of being and seeing

Although we may think that our experiences are reasonably objective, all experiencing is subjective, coloured by our individual temperaments and circumstances. For example, if it is raining how is this experienced? Is this a good thing, a bad thing, a stroke of luck, an inconvenience or a catastrophe? How determined are our responses by context, and how much by conditioning? Being in the moment, being mindful, allows the experience to be appreciated for what it is, in all its richness. We must beware of the 'Pollyanna' response, however, thinking that everything is wonderful. If we take this view, we may blind ourselves to the real suffering and injustice around us.

The lives of our pupils might be purposeful or chaotic, meaningful or meaningless, hopeful or despairing. Their dispositions might be anxious or carefree, depressed or cheerful, aggressive or peaceable, angry or calm, frustrated or fulfilled, bored or interested and engaged, despairing or hopeful. It is up to us as teachers to be clear about which dispositions we encourage, and which we seek to change.

In developing character we are assisting in the development of the spirit. Sometimes it will be necessary to emphasise the importance of self-control in building resilience (Funder and Block 1989). Too great an emphasis on delaying gratification, however, might lead an individual to become unable to take pleasure in life, seize opportunities, or remain flexible. A balance has to be struck, as both Aristotle and Siddhartha Gautama (the Buddha) saw clearly. The Middle Way between extremes is the path towards contentment.

To conclude this section, we suggest that while spiritual and moral development does not operate in isolation from the wider workings of the educational world, it offers another perspective of what is of value. While it is important that graduates in education become good people and effective professionals, their professionalism must be grounded in a full and engaging interest in the value of education as a process of learning for its own sake and not simply as a training ground where knowledge and skills are acquired and then offered in exchange for monetary rewards in the labour market.

Spiritual development: A rich field of definitions

This section resists any attempt to define such a rich term as 'spiritual development' as a glossary-style set of definitions would fail to capture the philosophical, religious and cultural nuances inherent in them. Nonetheless, there is some scope to explore the parameters of these terms in order to locate them in the field of educational thought.

What do we mean by 'spirituality'?

> Spirituality I take to be concerned with those qualities of the human spirit – such as love and compassion, patience, tolerance, forgiveness, contentment, a sense of responsibility, a sense of harmony – which bring happiness to both self and others (Dalai Lama, 1999: 22–3).

The term 'spirituality' cannot be fully understood without reference to religion and religiously-inspired ways of thinking. In presupposing this we have to pay heed to the challenging relationship between spirituality and religion. First we will set out why 'spirituality' is hard to define in a way which satisfies multiple audiences. The following examples illustrate the complexity of this situation.

Those concerned with the development and nurture of spirituality must pay attention to the work started by Alister Hardy (The Religious Experience Research Unit – *The Spiritual Nature of Man*, Hardy 1979) and continued with a focus primarily on the spiritual lives of children by Edward Robinson (*The Original Vision: A Study of Religious Experience in Childhood*, Robinson 1997), David Hay (*The Children's Spirituality Project*, Hay 2006) and Clive Erricker (*The Children and Worldviews Project* – see Further Reading for web link).

A shift in focus is evident from the names of the projects themselves, away from religion, into spirituality and then away even from the explicit mention of the 'spiritual' in the title of Erricker's study.

It is a question of ontology: what is the nature of being, particularly the nature of the human being. All words associated with 'spirit' and 'spirituality' are likely to provoke responses ranging from the sceptical to the hostile in those critical of religious traditions and ideas. Our challenge is to articulate an understanding of spiritual education which is acceptable to religious devotees of various traditions, non-believers, those who believe 'without belonging' and those who believe they belong to religious traditional groups without believing in any of their teachings. It must be made clear that any 'inclusive' articulation of a sense of 'spirituality' will never reflect the nuances and particular understandings of all these diverse groups and individuals. What is important is to try to find a shared understanding that is something more than a banal 'lowest common denominator'.

In order to attempt this, a broadly secular understanding of 'spirituality' might serve better as a starting place from which the terms of religious traditions might be explored and understood, not in reductive ways (for example, dismissing religious experiences as some form of psychological immaturity), but in such a way as to enrich the secular vocabularies employed without capitulating to the particular world views of religious traditions. Terms such as 'sacred', 'holy' and 'saintly' may or may not be useful towards enhancing a vocabulary for all. It may be that such terms carry too much cultural baggage to be universally useful.

Andrew Wright has offered a broad definition of spirituality as a 'concern for the ultimate meaning and purpose of life' (Wright, 2000: 7). There is no overt attempt at linking spirituality and spiritual development with any particular religious tradition. It could be argued that this approach is a strength as it removes the limitations which religion, allegedly, places on genuine human development.

It is not unreasonable to claim that a person of (undefined) religious faith would give limited assent to Wright's definition and would prefer a form of words which recognises the contribution of religion and religious ways of thinking to spiritual development and human flourishing. Marian de Souza (2009), for example, sees spirituality as a critical component of human development with a particular emphasis on the context of relationality. This means in essence that the human person and human life is most fruitful when lived for others in recognition of the ultimate meaning of existence. This understanding of 'spirituality' has had a significant influence on contemporary curriculum documentation.

Brendan Hyde (2008) takes a special interest in children's spirituality. He offers a tripartite understanding of 'spirituality' as a) an essential human trait or natural human predisposition; b) a movement towards 'Ultimate Unity' (admittedly a complex idea); and c) a given expression of a sense of unity which can be expressed in religious traditions (Hyde, 2008: 43–4).

How far can these positions be reconciled with each other? It would be a helpful for you to note your own understanding of 'spirituality', comparing and contrasting it to the limited examples above. When you have done this, evaluate the strengths and limitations of each example. If we cannot agree on a precise definition and universally accepted definition of 'spirituality' we might explore the implications of the following two positions:

- 'spirituality' is such a rich expression that its meaning cannot be exhausted by one religious tradition;
- 'spirituality' is a term which has been used to refer to so many different things that it is either vague and practically meaningless, or refers to nothing at all.

Promoting spiritual development in school

If the term 'spirituality' is hard to define, as we have seen above, how much harder it is to pin down the meaning of 'spiritual development' in the context of the modern school (Wright 2000: 1). What is the relationship between spiritual development and the subject of religious education in the modern school? The Scottish philosopher, John Haldane (2003) criticises those who regard an appreciation of art and music as a part of 'spiritual development', yet this association survives and thrives in the advice given to school inspectors. For example, 'spiritual, moral, social and cultural' development are routinely considered together, and religious education, art and music are seen as 'obvious examples' of where such development can be promoted (Ofsted, 2012).

If Haldane is correct in his claim that religion and spirituality are essential partners, them how do we deal with the spiritual development of pupils who have no stated religious faith?

Thinking point

- Consider those who self identify as members of faith groups, be they Christian, Muslim, Hindu or any other. Are these people necessarily 'spiritual'? What standards would we use to judge this?
- Has religious identity any bearing on the issue of spirituality at all?
- Amongst the faithful and faithless alike, we will find cruel and kind people, prejudiced and open-minded people, the cynical and those who seek to find the best in others. Is there any evidence that one group of people is more or less likely to display particular characteristics and qualities than another?

We need to explore whether it is possible to place spiritual development alongside what are understood as cognitive and affective development. Writing from within the Catholic Christian religious tradition, Buchanan and Hyde (2008) have suggested that a good educational process has to go beyond superficial learning and facilitate integral development by locating all teaching and learning within the following frameworks:

- learning and thinking about knowledge (cognitive development);
- reactions and feeling of the learner (affective development);
- inward reflection by the learner on the transformative aspects of learning (spiritual development).

We also need to consider whether spiritual development is best understood as an internal, personal matter, as outlined by Buchanan and Hyde (in which case, how might one determine the extent of such a development?), or as relational, and manifest in desirable behaviours, as outlined by de Souza (2009) above. It is clear that the education authorities come down firmly on the side of the relational dimension as they cannot concern themselves with individual, internal, personal matters. This should be a cause for concern for those genuinely interested in spiritual development, however, as to ignore the personal, invisible dimension may be to miss that which is essential. Howard Gardner has suggested that all learning is performative – in other words, if you cannot see evidence of it, it isn't there (Gardner, 2006; Munday, 2013). This willfully, perhaps perversely, ignores what some believe to be the most important, defining features of their lives: the inner experiences of beauty, joy, value, meaning and purpose.

Exploring good practice

Issues surrounding spiritual development are highlighted when official policy documents from state educational agencies declare that spiritual development is a key part of education. To take but one example, the Education Act (HMSO, 2002) for England and Wales states:

> The curriculum for a maintained school or maintained nursery school satisfies the requirements of this section if it is a balanced and broadly based curriculum which – (a) promotes the spiritual, moral, cultural, mental and physical development of pupils at the school and of society. (HMSO 2002: Provision 78 (1a))

We note the order of words: the curriculum is required first to promote the 'spiritual' development of its pupils. What is missing is guidance on how this could be done and it is left to the reader to decipher the intentions behind the wording of this Act of Parliament. It is not implied that the specific subject of religious education will be the principal vehicle for this. Rather, the broader life of the school, the 'taught' curriculum and the so-called 'hidden' curriculum, will contribute towards development in all the aspects suggested and hence offer an integrated education.

Despite the need to decouple spiritual development from the specifically religious dimensions of religious education, as spirituality is not the exclusive concern of religions, religious education is nevertheless uniquely placed and well equipped to introduce some aspects of spiritual development into the school curriculum. Religious education is the subject which, at best, makes sense of all the others, providing meanings, values and purpose not only to subjects studied in class, but to all the activities of the school, from lessons to playtime, extra-curricular activities and meal times.

View from practice

The first example regards a state secondary school of no religious affiliation which sought to raise the profile of religious education as part of a wider drive to improve the learning experiences of the pupils. Integral to this was a shift in perception of religion as an important cultural force in people's lives and in the local community. It is clear that this school was not trying to impose a particular religious view on its pupils but it was proposing that an understanding of the impact of religion on people's lives was essential to a good rounded education. Although the focus of this initiative was rooted in a particular subject an implicit aim was to raise awareness of the spiritual, moral and cultural life of the pupils. It was an academic exploration which went beyond the teaching of facts and data but began to open doors into a wider world of learning and meaning.

The focus here is on celebrating diversity: the pupils are learning that differences do not necessarily require judgment about which is better or worse. Care must be taken, however, about what values the school is teaching, otherwise such celebrations of diversity can slip into moral relativism, with its incapacity to discriminate between the desirable and the abhorrent.

Questions for example one

- How does this model of teaching and learning facilitate the spiritual development of the pupils?
- What are the strengths and limitations of this model of teaching and learning for pupils who have come from families with strong religious traditions?

View from practice

Example two refers to a state primary school which is affiliated to the Church of England. This school's approach to curriculum development was driven by 'Philosophy for Children' within religious education. In brief, this allowed for learning in religious education to be centred on a teacher-facilitated discussion of complex issues designed to promote the skill of enquiry and the construction of personal worldview. The methodology is composed of the following cycle of learning: communicate – apply – enquire – contextualize – evaluate. Each lesson has a set format: the key concept is introduced by way of a story or video, followed by a vote on which question should be used for the philosophical enquiry. There follows the discussion on the chosen concept. It is interesting to note that the school claims that children are now using this approach to solve playground disputes. Again, this approach appears to be inclusive, but is the school clear about its values?

Questions for example two

- Explore how the 'Philosophy for Children' approach to religious education meets the needs of all pupils in schools.
- What are the challenges of asking young children to involve themselves in this type of activity?

View from practice

'This is Our Faith' is the title of a syllabus for religious education for Catholic schools in Scotland. It is a part of the wider 'Curriculum for Excellence' initiative which covers all schools in Scotland. 'This is Our Faith' claims to assist young people to:

- develop their knowledge and understanding of Catholic faith;
- nurture respect for other Christian traditions and world faiths;
- experience opportunities for spiritual growth;
- acquire the skills of reflection, discernment and moral decision-making;
- commit to beliefs, values and actions in a positive response to God's invitation to faith.

(Continued)

(Continued)

This model of teaching and learning stands in contrast to the previous examples. While there is due recognition paid to generic religious education skills of 'reflection, discernment and moral decision-making' this is firmly shaped by Catholic Christianity and its associated worldview.

In the context of a Catholic school, the position is clear, but the extent to which the school values other, different world views will depend on how they interpret the Church's teachings on other faiths (see, for example, Second Vatican Council, 1965).

Questions for example three

- In what way is the distinctiveness of Catholic religious education beneficial to the spiritual development of the Catholic pupil at the Catholic school?
- How will the non-Catholic pupil who attends a Catholic school find opportunities for 'spiritual development'?

Summary

This chapter has highlighted some of the key areas related to the important matter of spiritual development in schools. We have mapped out some of the key questions which are likely to arise in the experience of teachers and student teachers with regard to defining 'spirituality'. We have also explored the links between the deep-rooted religious and philosophical traditions and the insights of contemporary psychology finding considerable common ground.

    Reflective questions

- Is the language of spiritual development of value to atheists?
- To what extent are the aims of theist spiritual development the same as the aims of positive psychology?
- How free are children to lead good lives?
- How do teachers balance respect for individuals' desire for freedom with the needs of the classroom, the school and other pupils?

Further reading

Books

Layard, R. and Dunn, J. (2009) *A Good Childhood: Searching for Values in a Competitive Age*. London: Penguin.

Palmer, S, (2007) *Toxic Childhood: How The Modern World Is Damaging Our Children And What We Can Do About It*. London: Orion.

Roehlkepartain, E. King, P. Wagener, P. Benson, P. (eds) (2005) *The Handbook of Spiritual Development in Childhood and Adolescence*. London: SAGE.

Online resources

Mason, M. (2000) *'Spirituality' – What on Earth is it?* Paper given at the International Conference of Children's Spirituality at Roehampton Institute, Summer 2000, by the former Education Officer of the British Humanist Association http://humanism.org.uk/wp-content/uploads/SpiritualitywhatonEarthisit.pdf

Kent Children's Trust (2009) *Shaping the Spirit: Policy and Practice for Promoting Spiritual Development in Schools* http://www.kenttrustweb.org.uk/UserFiles/ASK8/File/Whole_School_Issues/spiritual_development/Appendix_7_and_8_a_b_c_d_-_Aids_to_Development.pdf

Philosophy for Children (P4C) http://p4c.com/

Spirituality for children with special needs http://www.open.edu/openlearn/body-mind/childhood-youth/childhood-and-youth-studies/childhood/child-spirituality

The Children and Worldviews Project is an electronic resource, available at http://www.childrenspirituality.org/support/projects/childrenandworldviews/

CHAPTER 15

TEACHING FOR CREATIVITY AND CREATIVE TEACHING

Moyra Boland, Margaret Jago and Jan Macdonald

Key ideas

This chapter explores:

- what we mean by creativity and the historical context of the 'creativity' debate;
- why it is considered important to encourage creativity in education;
- how teachers can nurture a creative environment;
- how a creative environment would look, feel and sound.

Introduction

The language of creativity features prominently on today's educational landscape. As teachers, we are constantly being encouraged both to engage young people in the creative process and to teach creatively. The majority of newly qualified teachers in the UK would likely include creativity if asked to list desired pedagogical characteristics for teachers today, and *Teaching Scotland's Future* (Donaldson, 2011), the recent review of teacher education in Scotland, reported that teachers cited 'creativity' as one of the key characteristics of a twenty-first century teacher. But what exactly do we mean by *creativity* and why should it feature so prominently in current educational discourses? As importantly, what does this preoccupation with creativity mean for us as educators and how can creative teaching and learning manifest itself in the classroom and beyond?

This chapter begins by offering a brief examination of the historical and current understandings and definitions of creativity in education. We attend here to policies that have carved out a path for creativity and led it to such prominence in education and will then explore why creativity should be such a significant aspect of the educational framework. Finally, we ask what a creative learning environment might mean in practice.

What do we mean by *creativity*? The historical context

Given its ubiquity on the educational agenda, we need to establish an understanding of the concept of *creativity*. As Maisuria (2005: 142) observes, creativity has long been considered a 'multifaceted term, having various definitions in different disciplines'. Pope (2009) notes that the first recorded use of 'creativity' in the English language was as recent as 1875 but that cognate forms, such as 'creation', 'creator' and 'create', were around much earlier, initially with reference to the religious and then to the artistic. Indeed, between 1450 and 1600, the Renaissance saw 'the most extraordinary flowering of achievement on all fronts' (Robinson, 2001: 168) with Da Vinci, Michelangelo, Raphael, Galileo, Copernicus and Shakespeare amongst those flourishing in that era and leaving a prolific legacy of 'high creativity'. The new ideas, historically speaking, of the Renaissance might be categorised, following Boden (2004), as H(istorical) creativity, with concepts new to the individual labelled P(sychological) creativity. Anna Craft (2003) has proposed a distinction between 'extraordinary creativity' by people who 'change domains of knowledge, or create new ones' and 'everyday creativity', whilst Pope suggests that, through the ages, creativity has been perceived and interpreted in numerous ways by varying groups. For example, Pope (2009: 38) alludes to the otherworldly nature of creativity in seventeenth century Britain as 'something that could only properly be done by people with divine support and otherwise had better not be done at all'. But Curtis and Pettigrew (2009: 25) point out that it was with the birth of the Enlightenment that the 'blind faith' in religion and tradition was replaced 'with rational and methodical reasoning' and the idea that we would no longer need to rely upon interpretations of religious teachings or folklore for our explanations of the world. Robinson (2001: 70) concurs, suggesting that the 'medieval worldview had relied too much on uncritical sensory data and on religious dogma'.

The dawn of the industrial revolution combined with the domination of science in the late eighteenth and early nineteenth centuries worked to consolidate the view that religion was not a pre-requisite for creativity. But one recurring characteristic, common to old and new understandings of creativity, is that of *originality,* 'from the beginning' and 'fresh, new, novel, unexpected' (Pope, 2009: 57). Claiming that 'creativity is in(ter)ventive', Pope (2009: 62) argues that invention is rarely completely original and that there is actually an intervention occurring. This is reassuring; it would seem that we do not need to reach the dizzy heights of an artistic genius such as Leonardo Da Vinci or to make new astronomical discoveries such as Galileo's to be considered creative. Indeed, Howard Gardner (1993) suggests that whilst the type of creativity demonstrated by such a genius might be referred to as 'Big C' creativity, we can all be creative. Such 'everyday creativity' Gardner calls 'small c' creativity, suggesting that this is similar to the resourcefulness that everyone uses to solve problems or produce work. Arguably the extent to which an individual is considered creative may vary according to the value placed upon their discoveries by colleagues with a vested interest in upholding the intellectual integrity of their discipline; consequently the use of term 'creative' is subject to scrutiny within a specific area of activity as it is connected to the idea of placing a 'value' on the outcomes from human endeavour.

Policies for creativity in education

In the 1960s, the Plowden Report ignited a heightened interest in creative approaches to learning. Thirty years later, *All Our Futures: Creativity, Culture and Education* (NACCCE, 1999) stimulated the emergence of a number of curriculum-based initiatives that placed a strong emphasis on the promotion of creative teaching and learning. The latter report proposed that the capacity to think or behave 'imaginatively' is the first stage in the creative process: 'a first definition of creativity could therefore be imaginative processes with outcomes in the public world' (Robinson, 2001: 115). Creative thinking would secure outcomes that would be 'of value as well as original' (NACCCE, 1999: 29). More recently, educational policy has demonstrated significant backing for the creativity agenda. In 2005, the then Qualifications and Curriculum Authority published *Creativity: Find it, Promote It* (QCA, 2004), a report intended to encourage creative practice amongst teachers. In Scotland, the Roberts Report, *Nurturing Creativity in Young*

People, published in 2006, proposed an agenda for the development of creativity for young learners through mainstream education that would promote access to the creative industries. The Scottish perspective encapsulates both originality and imagination in its hopes for creativity in education: 'creativity should involve thinking or behaving imaginatively in a purposeful manner and should generate something original and of value' (Roberts, 2006: 12). It is not surprising then that curriculum guidelines in the UK make explicit reference to creativity. In particular, Scotland's *Curriculum for Excellence* advocates that learners should 'think creatively and independently' (Education Scotland, online-c).

Thinking point

- Do you think that creativity is a gift or a disposition?
- How would you define creativity?

Why should we encourage creativity in education?

Creativity is emerging as 'part of a universalized discourse' (Craft, 2003: 113). In a world in which economic competition is fierce, the demand for innovation and creativity in the practice and produce of the workforce is significant. Indeed, 'the economy demands creativity, and a healthy economy is necessary to a wealthy society which then produces assets for general consumption; better public amenities and services' (Craft, 2003: 114). Similarly, Bohm and Land (2009: 79) note the general assumption in Britain is that we exist 'in a knowledge economy where creativity and innovation are the engines of productivity and economic growth'. Moreover, Craft (2003) points to Maslow's belief that 'the creative individual is a fulfilled one'. A creative individual can problem solve and innovate with consistency and regularity. A need to nurture 'everyday creativity' in all individuals is recognized by Lambeir (2005: 354-5) who asks if an education offering respect premised on qualifications and certificates adequately encourages the autonomous, worthwhile individual. He considers such a society 'disturbing', contending that creativity should involve 'being captivated and interested, with joy and with being content, with taking time for oneself and for the other' (Lambeir, 2005: 355). For many, this is the crux of the tension in the creativity debate. If creativity is to do with nurturing autonomy and the encouragement of imagination and originality in the individual, how do we reconcile these desirable qualities with a requirement to produce someone or something that will boost the economy by tapping into human capital?

This tension might be traced back to the education speech of the then Prime Minister, James Callaghan, at Ruskin College in 1976 in which Callaghan outlined a vocationalisation of the school curriculum as a means of responding to the unskilled workforce that was a predominant feature of society at the time. In the ensuing years, education was bound to a tight curricular framework that was prescriptive and rigid in nature. As noted by Maisuria (2005: 142), this framework resulted in 'squeezing the principles of creativity and autonomy out of teaching and learning'. If the primary purpose of education should be to 'free the pupil's mind to conceive creatively as many ideas as possible, which in turn opens up more possibilities' then restrictions on pupils' learning experiences were 'undermining cognitive emancipation and empowerment by limiting horizons' (Maisuria, 2005: 144).

The late 1990s saw a resurgence of the promotion of creativity across the UK; it returned to prominence on the educational agenda and in curricula. This welcome revival can best be described using the analogy of a photographic lens: 'the lens that the child uses to engage with the world gets bigger and deeper through a creative education and, in this paradigm of enlightenment ... is able to conceive more and more complex perspectives' (Maisuria, 2005: 147). What results is an educational setting that unapologetically fosters creativity in the curriculum to achieve the highest level of learning.

What might be involved in teachers nurturing a creative environment?

Whatever the tensions in the debate on whether creativity be deemed a socio-economic commodity or personal quality, today creativity features strongly in both the Curriculum for Excellence in Scotland and The National Curriculum in England. Currently, in Scotland, the overriding aim of the Curriculum for Excellence (CfE) is:

> ...to ensure that all children and young people in Scotland develop the knowledge, skills and attributes they will need if they are to flourish in life, learning and work, now and in the future... (Education Scotland, online-c)

CfE encapsulates four core capacities which reflect the drive to address society's need for economic security and global competitiveness. Alongside fiscal objectives, the determination to enable individual wellbeing is strong. Creativity is deemed worth developing, both as a national economical necessity and as a life-enhancing personal quality. Similarly, the National Curriculum in England Framework document for 2014 promotes these expectations setting out a curriculum that aims to introduce 'pupils to the best that has been thought and said; and helps engender an appreciation of human creativity and achievement' (DfE 2013c: 5).

All teachers, therefore, are expected to nurture creativity in the classroom. In thinking of *how* to nurture such a creative environment, ideas gleaned from past and present research into what constitutes creativity may be helpful.

Because of the ongoing nature of the debate around nurturing creativity, there is a plethora of research into various components of creativity; that research inevitably reflects various emphases and foci in keeping with the nature of the debate prevailing in society at the time. In the 1950s, 'originality' featured strongly and was often 'measured', frequently by test responses (Guildford, 1950). Later, in the 1980s, dispositions, predispositions and learning preferences associated with very highly talented people became an important theme. From the 1990s, the actual creative process came under scrutiny. Considered in isolation no one of these aspects provided the whole answer to what was required to develop creativity. Yet each aspect does still offer something of relevance for today's teacher. In addressing the challenge of establishing a creativity-friendly environment, it may be worth bearing in mind that, cumulatively, these recurring debates on creativity, if addressed, could amount to more than the sum of the parts.

Originality and range of ideas

Guildford's (1950) initial tests for originality sought respondents' multiple suggestions for the uses of objects such as drawing pins or paper clips. Taking this approach a step further he discovered that divergent (lateral) thinkers were more likely to be creative than convergent (logical) thinkers. Originality remains a feature of creativity. But what has to be kept in mind is that what is familiar to older children and adults may be completely novel and original for a child in primary school. Children can often be rewarded for producing the 'right' answer and Claxton and Lucas (2007) suggest that, since they want to please, they can suffer from being conditioned to give the right answer, as if only one 'right' response is possible in all situations. It follows that children become conditioned to thinking that questions demand convergent thinking. If teachers are to promote divergent thinking, in support of creativity, then more open-ended tasks and an acceptance of multiple responses will be required.

Predispositions and learning preferences associated with very highly talented people

Creative people tend to have the confidence to trust the fruits of their imaginations, including 'intuition' and 'hunches' (Bowers et al., 1990). As Robinson (2001: 141) put it, '(i)magination is the ability to bring to mind things that are not available to the senses'. Intuitive responses may be the result of unconscious thought based on pre-existing deep learning and knowledge, that is, they emerge from information and experience gained previously and this is quite distinct in form to formal knowledge. Another means of teachers encouraging pupils' creativity might, therefore, be to set tasks based in the real, material world or in an imagined world, that encourage the use of intuition and the development of hunches in problem solving.

As well as acting upon intuitive responses, when considering a problem or puzzle, highly creative people enjoy satisfying their curiosity and they have a capacity to persevere, tenaciously, in seeking solutions. When the imagination is fully operational, a welter of possibilities may emerge inducing high levels of uncertainty and confusion (Argyris and Schön, 1995). Creative individuals are comfortable letting this 'messy buzz' rest and incubate. They understand that the fermenting messiness simply represents part of the creative process (see below) and that out of the muddle a clear line of thought will eventually emerge. Faced with this scenario, convergent thinkers could feel distressed and, at this point of discomfort, may abandon the task, not for want of their ability to deal with the problem but because they are unable to cope with the resulting anxiety and panic. Csikszentmihalyi (1997) discusses attitudes and behaviours associated with creative activities, pointing to risk-taking, the ability to tolerate high levels of uncertainty and disorder with creative activity. The message for teachers here is that they need to provide safe environments, fun and reassurance, to counteract any task-generated anxiety and to be sensitive to any pupil anxiety.

Another consideration for teachers keen to promote creativity concerns the use of time. Howe (1999) has shown that 'practice makes perfect', stating that those who become highly skilled in science, sport, mathematics, language, literature or the arts share one common characteristic. Those who excel, in any field, will spend endless hours in practise, while those whose contributions are so original and so highly valued as to be considered to have changed the course of history will have immersed themselves to a much greater extent. While curriculum demands limit the amount of time children can spend on tasks to which they apply knowledge and skills, perhaps more 'practise' time could be introduced.

Csikszentmihalyi (1997: 95–6) provides another argument for more generous time allowances for learners to become fully immersed in creative activities. He describes immersion as 'flow', that is a state of high concentration in which individuals are immersed, totally involved in, original, inventive activity. He stresses that 'flow' needs time and that being in a 'flow' state represents experiencing the ideal conditions for creativity. Again, curriculum constraints provide a challenge to the teacher but the trend towards integrating the curriculum may provide a means of addressing this time challenge.

View from practice: Transition from primary to secondary

Stephen was a teacher in an inner-city primary school. His class comprised of 33 pupils aged 11 years. The pupils were in their final term at primary school and were looking forward to the move to secondary school. The main focus of the term's work was the transition to high school and the preparation that the children needed to make to ensure they were emotionally resilient for the challenges that might face them in secondary school.

The school had very few resources to support learning in this area. Stephen was faced with the challenge: how could he prepare his pupils to feel confident for the move to secondary school using only the pens and paper he had in the class? In his struggle to plan for learning, Stephen felt he was restricted because there were no resources to support the children. Eventually he explained to the pupils that they would need to start the topic without resources and the first step would be to define as a group what their worst fears were about going to secondary school. From this simple beginning grew a list of fears and anxieties connected to the move. From this list the pupils were invited to make a counter list that explored the best things that could happen in secondary school. Stephen set the two lists side by side with a physical space between them and asked the children to imagine the space being the transition between their worst fears and the best things that secondary school could offer. The pupils were invited to give suggestions about what they could do to help them move across this space, to move from fear to enjoyment. The responses from the pupils revealed a wide variety of ideas and activities which became the basis for the topic throughout the term.

Thinking point

- In what ways could you identify Stephen's approach as being 'creative'?
- What links can you make between 'creative teaching' and 'encouraging creative responses'?

The creative process

In education, creative thinking is often aligned to problem solving (Greene and Noice, 1988) because, like problem solving, it involves making creative responses to a stimulus or problem to find solutions. Within set limitations or boundaries, activities which encourage creative responses are fundamentally open-ended. Robinson (2001) claimed 'creative and cultural education are not subjects in the curriculum, they are general functions of education.' So teaching for creativity involves a process in which teaching and learning are not driven by outcomes and grades but by the need to engage fully, to be immersed, in that process. The creative process is commonly understood in stages. Using Dewulf and Baillie's (1999) categories, we can identify six such stages, as follows:

- preparation – defining the problem;
- consideration of possibilities – experimentation – moving beyond habitual ways of thinking, thought-showering;
- incubation – uncertainty (illumination – the Eureka moment);
- verification – analysis of ideas followed by planning and action;
- implementation – production;
- evaluation.

Society has moved on from the idea that creative talent is a gift of the gods. So, creativity is not a subject to be taught but rather a staged process, and certain dispositions, pre-dispositions, contexts and conditions can help its development. Having started to unpack these dispositions and conditions, we now consider how teachers might best create and incorporate these in their teaching environments and so inspire young people to be creative.

How might a creative environment look, feel and sound within the system?

Desirable conditions for creativity are unlikely just to happen. Indeed, as noted above, it is almost 15 years since the influential report on *Creativity: 'All Our Futures'* (NACCCE, 1999) called for systematic change regarding the establishment's attitudes to teaching and learning for creativity. In Scotland, part of the policy response to that call is realised in Curriculum for Excellence. As outlined above, and in relation to the core capacities, clear links exist between what is expected of this curriculum and the conditions required for the development of creativity in learners. CfE also places demands on Scotland's teachers, which will be addressed below, in terms of teaching both creatively and for creativity.

In common with many educational policies, the English and Scottish education systems encourage life-long learning, recognising that some individuals who eventually become highly creative do not necessarily show great promise as children at school. Such individuals will continue to learn and develop throughout their lives.

In relation to the pre-dispositions above, if teachers can encourage the dispositions we have outlined in today's children then tomorrow's adults may be more motivated, enterprising and creative. They may be better able to communicate in different ways and in different settings, better able to apply critical thinking to new contexts and more able to demonstrate an enterprising attitude.

However, the changes envisioned by governments in both Westminster and Edinburgh cannot happen without appropriate resources, including the more flexible use of space and time. Required of the system, in addition to inspiration and ideas, is support in the forms of continuing professional education about new approaches to teaching and learning, time to prepare new courses and time and finance in order to put new resources into place. Like children, teachers can benefit greatly in learning about theory and practice through sharing their experiences, progress and challenges. Each school, of course, has its own distinctive profile and 'personality' and, providing the system allows for flexibility, schools could develop creative learning and teaching and creativity amongst their pupils through very different projects. Ideals and practices that benefit children might simultaneously benefit teachers by, for example, affording opportunities for teachers to work outside the classroom and school and by engaging them in partnerships with outside agencies. However, there remain certain overarching requirements of schools and personnel which, more than a set of policy guidelines (however well-intentioned and worthy), require the determination and collective will of staff to ensure that development in creativity gets off to a good start and can be sustained.

How might a creative environment look, feel and sound in schools?

For creativity to flourish in schools there has to be a shared ethos, understanding and acceptance that, within and beyond the classroom environment, creativity can be nurtured: it is a real possibility. The ethos must value creativity, acknowledge the possibility of change at all ages and stages and so ensure that a wide range of contexts for learning provide opportunities for teachers and pupils to be creative.

Teachers' values and beliefs are the most powerful generator encouraging the establishment and sustainability of inclusion in the classroom according to Head (2007). The same, we suggest, will apply to the generation of an environment in which children's creativity can flourish. In any classroom, it is the teacher's disposition, values and attitudes that determine whether the self-esteem of children is nourished, whether the 'flow' required for creativity in any field is possible and whether assessment is carried out in such a way as to motivate and challenge rather than to discourage. At the heart of it all lies the teacher's awareness of the learners' learning needs and her understanding of how best to meet and address these.

How might a creative environment look, feel and sound in the classroom? The expectations on teachers

Respectful relationships between teachers and learners are essential if creativity is to flourish but the behaviours of some 'creative' learners in classrooms can be seen as 'challenging' (Cropley, 1992). Teachers may have to respond to creative individuals who might be 'flexible, curious, and comfortable with using and living in their imaginations' (Joubert, 2001). Are such children regarded as problems or do pupils who tend to challenge assumptions and to be 'persevering, resilient, divergent thinkers, risk takers who are also able to see new ways of doing things and to see problems as opportunities' (Joubert, 2001) benefit from encouragement as they demonstrate what we know to be some of the qualities and attributes so necessary for creativity? In contemporary inclusive classrooms, children are empowered, in part at least, to have a voice in their own learning agenda. If we can empower pupils through sensitive planning that is attuned to individual needs, motivations and ways of learning then we may be able to open up learning possibilities less likely to inhibit and frustrate a 'creatively behaving' child.

Additionally, creativity may be facilitated by working outside the school. Of course, partnership engagement with outside agencies is not new; ensuring opportunities for peer collaboration and a flexible use of space and time have been aspects of good practice in Scotland since 1982 and the introduction of the previous National Curriculum Guidelines 5–14. 'Playful' or 'games-based' approaches with a degree of learning autonomy marked a change in style and focus introduced three decades previously.

The concept of autonomy also applies to teachers in relation to pedagogy and curriculum planning and, so, from Eric Booth's 'Habits of mind for creative engagement' (Booth, online), a relatively autonomous teacher seeking to provide opportunities for creativity might design and implement tasks deploying and encouraging 'creative skills' such as the following:

- generating multiple ideas and solutions;
- trusting one's own judgements;
- formulating good questions and problems;
- improvising;
- finding humour;
- enquiring skillfully;
- persisting;
- self-assessing;
- thinking analogically;
- observing intentionally;
- trying on multiple points of view;
- working with others – collaboration.

Thinking point

- What experiences do teachers need to become more creative?
- What dispositions do teachers need to be creative?

Challenges

To teach creatively and encourage creativity in learners will necessitate a change in the hearts and minds of some teachers and, for all teachers, will be a challenging endeavour. However, Claxton and Lucas (2007: 10) remind us that habits of mind can be changed and so, with that in our minds, we turn now to an outline of the challenges of educating creatively for creativity.

Despite policies that encourage creativity, governments' prevailing demands for what many regard as conflicting imperatives may not bode well. Accountability and constant improvement agendas, a narrow, largely academic, assessment regime and rigid curricula that leave teachers little time for anything that is not assessed, may all work against the fluidity and imaginative teaching that might encourage creativity amongst learners.

Secondly, if disposition and pre-disposition play such an integral part in creativity, in any field, where does that leave those whose dispositions are contradictory to the types of features outlined above? How does the teacher accommodate those children who panic at the lack of a single 'right answer' and those pupils who, sometimes like their teachers, fear a loss of control, or fear being given responsibility for their learning? To enhance the development of creativity and to encourage convergent thinkers and sensitive learners to become more creative, teachers need to create conducive environments and conditions; that may be a challenging task. Imagine Da Vinci's teacher reprimanding him, 'Leonardo, if you continue with this daydreaming and doodling you will not get full marks on Friday's test!'

View from practice – The sports team

Fiona was a peripatetic PE teacher in a rural primary school. She coached the children in Pop Lacrosse. The team was very successful and won their way to the National Finals. Eight teams gathered for the final, which was a full-day event. The morning consisted of a mini-league in which each team played a

(Continued)

(Continued)

10-minute game with all seven other teams. At the end of the morning the top two teams were given a bye to the semi final in the afternoon while the other teams took part in a play off to reach the semi finals.

At the end of the morning, Fiona's team was last in the league. Over their packed lunch Fiona talked to the pupils and acknowledged that they had failed but assured the team that they would learn from this failure and use the new learning in the afternoon to win their place in a semi final. They did exactly that in the afternoon. The team went on to win their semi-final and were set to play the final for the National Pop Lacrosse Championships.

Before they played, Fiona took the team to a quiet spot in the stadium. She asked them to close their eyes, to listen to her question and wait for a minute before answering her. Fiona asked the children to think of sporting strategies they could use beyond those they had practised. The team sat in silence with their eyes closed for well over a minute. The silence was broken by a team member suggesting that when play commenced they would play almost entirely in silence because they knew their routines so well. The whole team readily agreed because they had already played their upcoming opponents in the morning and the children had noted that the opposition shouted a lot and hugged in an exaggerated way after scoring a goal. The team decided to focus on speed, concentration, minimum talking and resetting quickly once a goal was scored. These strategies unnerved the opposition and Fiona's team went on to win the National Final.

Thinking point

- What creative features were present in Fiona's coaching of these pupils?

Summary

In this chapter, we have outlined what might be meant by creativity and the historical context of the debate surrounding it. We considered why, in the early twenty-first century, it is important to encourage creativity in education and how teachers can nurture a creative environment. We also considered the desired learning conditions that allow the majority to develop creativity as a means of stimulating and creating a vibrant environment in which relationships are alive and interactive. We have considered how that creative environment might look, feel and sound in and beyond schools and classrooms. So that we do not become so concerned with challenges to creativity that we decide it is too difficult, we might recall Einstein's view.

> Imagination is more important than knowledge, for knowledge is limited, whereas imagination embraces the entire world, stimulating progress, giving birth to evolution. It is, strictly speaking, a real factor in scientific research. (Einstein, 1931: 97)

Creativity is a habit of mind potentially accessible to all. Teachers can nurture and develop this habit through acknowledging the value of creativity and it is the responsibility of all teachers to commit to it in their practice.

Reflective questions

- How has this chapter challenged your understanding of what is meant by 'creativity'?
- In what ways can you ensure that your pupils have time and opportunity to respond creatively to learning experiences?
- How do we, as teachers, become and remain creative in our teaching?

Further reading

Education Scotland http://creativityportal.org.uk/

Education Scotland's website offers support on Curriculum for Excellence. This particular portal is a valuable resource for exploring what is creativity. Useful examples of creative practice in Scottish schools make interesting reading.

Creative Partnerships Programme http://www.publications.parliament.uk/pa/cm200607/cmselect/cmeduski/1034/103406.htm

This is the report from a Select Committee evaluating the effectiveness of the Creative Partnerships Programme.

British Council http://creativeconomy.britishcouncil.org/Policy_Development/policy-environment/

In outlining the major policy initiatives relating to creativity and the creative industries in the UK, Europe and the wider world, this site provides a good overview of how policies have an impact on practice.

CHAPTER 16

DIGITAL LEARNING

Stephen Boyle and David McKinstry

Key ideas

This chapter explores:

- the centrality of information and communications technology (ICT) in the primary school for meeting the holistic needs of children;
- interdisciplinarity in learning and teaching;
- children's understanding of and influence over themselves, others and their environment.

Introduction

There is little doubt that technology underpins the wealth, health and freedoms extant across the world. ICT, in particular, now suffuses and connects personal, public and professional spaces. As a matter of societal concern, primary teachers and their pupils are entitled to support with ICT. This chapter will contribute to that support.

ICT is a unique tool in enabling interdisciplinary pedagogy, whereby pupils are supported in making connections within and across a range of knowledge fields whilst developing their social, emotional and thinking skills through solving purposeful and engaging problems.

This chapter shows how creating, exploring and critiquing knowledge mediated through ICT can be a force for 'good' in education. 'Good' here is defined as children being not only 'taught' but cared for within contexts which place their wellbeing at the heart of effective teaching and learning; with this wellbeing including the use of strategies which progress children's aspirations, self-efficacy and knowledge of self, others and society (UNICEF, online; SG, 2008c).

This chapter will support your understanding of and engagement with ICT, enabling you and your pupils to develop a useful level of ICT capability. Commentary, blending views from practice with theory, standards and curricula, will enable you to apply, analyse and evaluate your use of ICT and to create effective interdisciplinary lessons that effectively utilise aspects of ICT.

You will also be encouraged through the inclusion of thinking points and end of chapter questions to engage critically with the validity of utilising ICT in relation to values and aspirations (including your own) associated with primary education.

ICT as pedagogy: an overview

The Scottish Curriculum for Excellence Technologies Principles and Practice document (SG, 2009d) and the Computing National Curriculum for England (Department for Education, online) highlight the value of ICT in helping children explore, analyse and contribute to their world.

Such frameworks stress that in addition to being a curricular area in itself, ICT offers equally a set of resources to enhance teaching in all areas. Examples presented by the Department for Education (2013b) in their report *Digital Technology in Schools* show that ICT can enhance assessment, increase pupil motivation and provide access to a wide range of interdisciplinary teaching strategies within the classroom through the use of devices such as electronic voting systems or applications that allow the creation and dissemination of multimodal texts.

Therefore, ICT as a pedagogical approach in primary education should not be about fetishising information (Poster, 1993) but rather the significance of ICT as pedagogy is its potential to motivate children and to act as a vehicle for interdisciplinary teaching.

ICT and the teacher

The role of the teacher in embedding ICT within the teaching and learning cycle is important. Unfortunately, as is reported from school inspections in England, ICT can become mired within mediocre teaching where children are subjected to boring didactic 'lessons' involving 'copying and pasting' within word processors and spreadsheets (Ofsted, 2011). We encountered similar findings from beginning teachers in Scotland who reported no or ineffectual use of electronic interactive whiteboards in primary classrooms. These experiences do not meet children's needs nor do they inspire beginning teachers.

However, we know from involvement with primary school teachers that effective strategies *are* being utilised that rely on effective uses of ICT. These are successful because they have been carefully reflected upon and crafted by the practitioners involved to meet the needs and raise the aspirations of pupils. It is beyond the scope of this chapter to demonstrate the transformative power of the entire range of ICT available in primary schools. However, the views from practice will be used to demonstrate how this transformative power, which could be termed the genius of ICT, can provide a pedagogy which enables teachers to meet the needs of children; needs which encompass cognition (for example, developing literacy in a technologically advanced society) and the personal, social and emotional aspects of children's development including a sense of belonging and of being valued.

We dispute the view currently held by some that ICT as a pedagogy in primary schools should be supplanted by a 'computing studies' model from high schools to meet an employability agenda. We would argue emphatically for ICT in primary school to be more closely aligned with the identity of teachers in meeting needs of children as active citizens whose voices should be heard.

 View from practice

Authoring multimodal texts – healing emotional wounds through digital storytelling

This vignette describes the centrality of the knowledgeable, enthusiastic and committed teacher to the effective use of ICT. It illustrates how teaching through ICT can facilitate a range of processes necessarily associated with effective pedagogy referred to in other chapters of this book.

Patricia is a primary teacher working with 7–8-year-old-children. David, her pupil, requires additional support in communicating verbally and through written text. This is exacerbated by David's personal circumstances as his

---

parents are going through a turbulent separation; both are seeking to be his legal guardian. Presently, David lives with his grandmother along with his mother. David has been in court hearings when, asked his views about whom he would like to stay with, he found it difficult to respond; despite the good intentions of court staff, David feels overawed by the court proceedings. The court had expressed concern over David's ability to communicate his wishes.

Through a multi-professional approach involving social work and speech and language therapy and with the consent of both parents and David, Patricia volunteered to collaborate with David in finding a strategy that would ensure his views are understood.

Patricia was keen to support David as his advocate so negotiated time to work with him while the additional support for learning co-ordinator taught the rest of Patricia's class.

Having attended an e-learning course as part of an early years' diploma, Patricia had become enthused about PhotoStory3; a free piece of intuitive software. PhotoStory3 allows a film to be authored using a blend of still images, narration, on-screen text and music. Patricia realised that it could be a useful resource for motivating David to express his views. She was keen to scaffold David's use of PhotoStory3 as an interdisciplinary learning and teaching process that would meet a range of his needs.

David, after viewing PhotoStory3 exemplars, was keen to use it to communicate his wishes in court. A lot of exploratory talk (Mercer and Hodgkinson, 2008) was generated, with David offering reasons why PhotoStory3 could be useful to him. Patricia supported him in self-assessing the progress of his endeavours.

One specific conversation centred upon an 'emotions tree' that David had drawn. David included that in his PhotoStory3 using a scanner. He suggested including a favourite piece of music and a photo of himself with the emotions tree in the film. Patricia saw this as a breakthrough as David had tended to shy away from projecting himself to an audience.

Using PhotoStory3, David realised that, using features such as the transition effect, he could influence the involvement of the audience by, for example, transiting from a long-shot to a close-up of an image to evoke a deeper emotional response.

David showed his film in court. It had a profound impact, communicating both the depth and range of his emotions as well as clearly indicating the rationale and strength of his wishes.

Patricia later used PhotoStory3 with the rest of her class. One idea, related to science, involved groups creating films arguing for or against hydroelectric power. David took a productive role in his group with Patricia observing him to be more confident and articulate during group discussions.

Analysing view from practice

ICT capability and interdisciplinary learning

Patricia's support for David was based upon her responsive evaluation of his needs coupled to a high level of teacher ICT capability, whilst effectively integrating ICT throughout the teaching and learning cycle. The 'view from practice' box above can be defined as interdisciplinary because, to Patricia, such a concept meant developing cognition and metacognition, relationships and dispositions because of the influence each element exerts over the others in learners. Patricia realised that David's challenges in communicating were restricting his personal, intellectual and social development and undermining his self-worth. She realised that the features of PhotoStory3, including its capability to combine a range of media, provided a non-directive and non-threatening approach for David that allowed him a significant level of autonomy in authoring his film. This raised his self-esteem and celebrated his levels of knowledge as well as challenging his thinking (for example, about what communication is and his ability to communicate effectively). With Patricia, and later with his peers, his confidence grew and he was keen to demonstrate this through contributing to positive relationships in class, at home and even in the daunting surroundings of a courtroom.

Patricia's ability to apply ICT effectively to meet the needs of her pupils was crucial. Allen et al. (2011: 211) describe teachers' ICT capability as the development of a set of skills such as being able to access information from the Internet or being able to touch type. We believe that teachers' ICT capability is more profound than that. Patricia demonstrated a high level of ICT capability by being prepared to undertake CPD to raise her level of ICT capability and being able to match the needs of David to learning events that encompassed appropriate use of ICT.

Patricia set out to help raise David's aspirations through his use of PhotoStory3 with the goals of:

- improving his overall communication skills;
- building his self-esteem;
- celebrating his interests and beliefs;
- challenging his thinking;
- providing personal resources. (Price, online)

So whilst we agree with Allen et al. (2011) that teachers have to possess at least a satisfactory knowledge of a range of ICT, we believe that is not sufficient. Patricia's actions showed a cogent and cohesive response, utilizing ICT, to meet David's needs, based upon the crucial principle that 'not knowledge but self-realization is the goal [of education]' (Dewey, 1902 cited in Kelly, 2009: 85). If a teacher does not adhere to that principle then the 'genius of ICT' as pedagogy in the primary school is severely compromised. Therefore we offer our definition of a teacher's ICT capability as their level of effectiveness in utilising ICT to facilitate interdisciplinary learning.

Thinking point

- 'Children nowadays know more about ICT than we do and they can teach us. We, as teachers, therefore don't need a high level of ICT capability.' Do you agree or disagree with this view? Why?
- Patricia wants to be in a position to use her ICT capability to meet the range of her pupils' needs. To what extent and why do you think Patricia's view of the purpose of education influences her ICT capability?
- Find out more about PhotoStory3. What features of PhotoStory3 could engage David and why?

ICT and effective planning

Patricia's teaching incorporated SMART (specific, measurable, achievable, realistic and time constrained) elements (Doran, 1981). An example of this is the learning intentions Patricia associated with David's needs and, in turn, with David's engagement with PhotoStory3. Here are two of them (there were others, bearing in mind that David created his film over several hours):

- David will be able confidently to present a film to adults concerned about his welfare that clearly communicates his wishes with regard to his guardianship.
- David will be able to develop his ideas using ICT tools to amend and refine his work and enhance its quality and accuracy.

Patricia does not structure the learning as 'subjects' to be transmitted into the empty vessel of David's brain. Rather, the focus is on David and how he can purposefully utilise ICT. Patricia is concerned that David's knowledge of himself, including his desire to ensure his voice is heard, is enhanced in a non-threatening manner. She encourages him to be resilient and resourceful by planning opportunities for David to develop his task and self-knowledge (Anderson and Krathwohl, 2001). She also plans, utilising PhotoStory3 as a storytelling device, to enable David, who is experiencing trauma on a number of fronts, to reconcile the past with the present and the future, thereby taking control of a situation and, in effect, to self-heal (Perry, 2008). Patricia has therefore planned David's use of PhotoStory3 partly as therapy. Later, she recognises that she can use PhotoStory3 to further enhance David's development in terms of raising his self-esteem when he is happy to engage with his peers collaboratively creating a film about hydroelectric power.

Thinking point

- Other aspects of Patricia's planning had to be carefully considered. What could they be and why were they important?

ICT and assessment as learning

Patricia realised that the set of features (automatic functionality, capacity, range, interactivity, speed and provisionality, which are easily recalled using the mnemonic 'A CRISP') delineated by Allen et al. (2011: 8–10) associated with any ICT were particularly advantageous within PhotoStory3 and would provide both the means and the contexts for enabling reflection by and amongst pupils (assessment as

Figure 16.1   Image manipulation in PhotoStory3

learning). An example was the ease with which the children could add, delete or change the position of images within the timeline in PhotoStory3 by clicking on a single button or dragging and dropping within the software (Figure 16.1). This was particularly effective used with the electronic interactive whiteboard as the children could use their fingers as the computer mouse, facilitating real time inclusion and collaboration. Even Patricia was pleasantly surprised by the amount of exploratory talk (Barnes, 2008) this provisionality and interactivity generated.

The children were able to try out a range of suggestions whilst simultaneously analysing and evaluating the results. Justifications (thinking skills in the form of predictions, inferences, generalising and hypothesising) were offered for suggestions, and the children developed social skills through asking for clarification, offering encouragement and seeking consensus whilst planning, drafting and completing their film. Thus the use of PhotoStory3 helped pupils to build effective relationships that contributed significantly to their ability to interrelate and reinterpret knowledge to 'understand new experiences and ideas' (Barnes, 2008: 2).

In using such rich pedagogy, Patricia was integrating the development of thinking skills and social skills with the acquisition, exploration and creation of knowledge (Fogarty, 2009) through real time assessment for learning.

Thinking point

Considering David in particular...

- Why would integrating crucial aspects of teaching and learning be more efficacious utilising ICT such as PhotoStory3?
- Offer reasons why you think ICT is or is not unique as pedagogy in being able to facilitate such a rich opportunity for interdisciplinarity.

View from practice

Mobile devices and interactive voting – A primary/secondary transition project

This shows how teachers, working collaboratively, can enable opportunities for self-regulated learning (Fazey and Fazey, 2001) using free software and pupils' own mobile devices, such as smartphones and touchpads.

(Continued)

(Continued)

Two years on from being David's teacher, Patricia is now working with pupils in their final year of primary school. She is collaborating with Philip, a history teacher from the associated secondary school, on a primary/secondary liaison initiative...

Philip: Patricia, I know your reputation as an effective user of ICT in your school and realise that you will have your own ideas about enabling a coherent transition for your primary seven pupils to the secondary school, whether that involves ICT or not; however, I have to admit that I'm really fired up about this idea but feel free to point out any downsides that I haven't considered...

Patricia: I did have some ideas and so did my pupils but I'm really keen to hear what you have to say. Fire away; I'll take a good idea from anyone!

Philip: Thanks for that! I've been reading more about self-regulated learning. It's based upon teachers supporting pupils to become more intrinsically motivated, to increase their perceived level of competence and to enable higher levels of pupil control. It indicates that it is not our job to abdicate our involvement but rather to scaffold the children's learning through interaction between everyone in the class.

The idea would be for my third year class [Year 9 in England and Wales] to create a quiz for your primary class using free voting software. Your pupils would use their mobile devices to respond; they don't need to use any of the old-fashioned clicker devices; all they need is Internet access which both schools have through their wireless networks. I've already spoken to my class about the idea. They liked it and also suggested that I test their knowledge on whatever topic we decided to focus on so that they would do a good job of helping your children out; and then one of them suggested WW1 as a topic as they do that in primary seven. The girl who had the idea said that our class had probably forgotten most of it and that this would be a good chance to revise their knowledge and maybe even learn more about it...

Patricia: That's correct. This class always 'do' WW1. We haven't done it yet so we could do something for the transition to secondary school. I'm a fan of thematic work but sometimes it can be used to 'tick a box'. Talking of boxes, what's inside the WW1 topic box in our school hasn't been updated for a while. This could be a way to use ICT to engage the children more.

Philip: We've also been having issues with mobile devices in our school recently. Some teachers really dislike smartphones. Some pupils use them inappropriately during class, texting when they're meant to be involved with the lesson, and some have been put on behaviour management cards for taking photos in class with them.

Patricia: They are banned in our school but some children do bring them in.

Philip: ... So I thought, why not make the problem an opportunity? With this free voting software not only can teachers create a range of questions but the kids can do it themselves. This would be a chance to use their mobile devices with purpose; a chance to take responsibility for their behaviour and a chance to support your pupils' engagement with the WW1 topic, which is quite a responsibility! The third years would need to plan the quiz but in such a way as to make it challenging – not predictable.

Patricia: I'm really starting to like this... I could ask my pupils what they already know about WW1 and what they would like to know and why and how they will find out about it. Your pupils could visit us and explain the quiz idea. They would talk to us about what it is we are going to research and then base the quiz on that. We would not know what questions were going to come up so we would have to work together; we could work in teams and be allowed to answer in teams. We would have to predict and individuals in the team could specialise in an area such as the home front or the causes of the war...

Philip: Well then, do you want to try the idea?

Patricia: Absolutely! I'll have to chat to my class to get their views about it and I'll need to ask my head teacher to temporarily lift the ban...

Philip: Yes, and we'll need to check on the facilities your school has for children who require additional support. One of my pupils has cerebral palsy and uses a wheelchair. There are two with challenging behaviour; I'm hoping taking on some responsibility for the quiz and being allowed to use their devices productively could motivate them more...

Patricia: If you come over after school we can cover the idea with my head teacher.

Analysing the view from practice

Epilogue

Both teachers returned to school to discuss the idea with pupils. Philip realised that three pupils in his class did not have a mobile device but could be supplied with touch-pads by the school. After consultation with the local resource centre the pupil with cerebral palsy was supplied with a head switch for his wheelchair allowing him to respond to the questions.

The WW1 quiz showed gaps in the secondary school pupils' knowledge. Through the voting software all the children could make responses to Philip's questions without the stigmatisation of a 'hands-up' scenario. Philip could also track the responses of children within his class with complete confidentiality. Philip was intrigued when his class suggested to him that they work in teams to frame questions and verify answers for the primary class. He set aside time to meet with groups to discuss what they wanted to study and why. This involved a visit to Patricia's class where Philip's pupils asked the children what they were studying and from where they were finding out information so that the quiz would be fair and challenging.

Philip's class suggested carrying out trial runs of the quiz. This allowed them to iron out any snags and to make sure their own knowledge was more than sufficient.

The final quiz on WW1 was a huge success. The collective aspiration to respond successfully within the primary class was palpable. The satisfaction among the secondary class in implementing a successful lesson was measurable, with all pupils completing an evaluation via their mobile devices and the voting software that showed their enthusiasm for using such devices in school.

The idea was adopted by colleagues at assemblies to gauge pupils' opinions about matters where normally some might feel intimidated by others and either not vote or vote contrary to their true opinion. The following year, Patricia's school, along with other primary schools and Philip's school 'participated' in a local election using the mobile devices to cast votes; a councillor stated that the children were ahead of local government in using the 'voting devices of the future to encourage participation in the democratic process'.

Thinking point

- List five advantages the transition project could have over more traditional modes of classroom interaction such as a hands-up scenario, explaining those benefits.
- Can you think of another context where using the resources and strategies associated with the transition project could meet the needs of a specific group of pupils?

ICT and the flipped classroom

Patricia and Philip's initiative was designed as an opportunity for both classes to take control of their learning. This taking control was crucial to the validity of the initiative, as was the use of the tools for mediating learning. The tools were not alien to the children. The children used such resources regularly (often for social networking) as something enmeshed with their individual and collective identity, their culture.

Both teachers realised from their reading, combined with reflecting on practice, that schools at a micro-level and society at the macro-level (see commentators such as Palmer, 2006) were demonising mobile devices. Some pupils were reacting to their culture being labelled negatively by 'acting out' associated with the labelling.

Patricia and Philip 'flipped' (Bergman and Sams, 2012) their classrooms, giving the pupils control that was significantly enhanced through the pupils' use of tools that they valued. Part of this strategy included the teachers sourcing online video content on the topic of WW1 that the children were to watch at home. These were then used as the basis for classroom activities associated with the transition project. The didactic part of teaching was still used via the videos, delivered by experts on the subject, but class time was freed up for experiential work focused on the children analysing and evaluating their knowledge of WW1 and configuring strategies (with the aid of their teachers and peers) to progress self-knowledge (what do I know and what do I need to know?) and task knowledge (how am I going to find out?) related to the transition project (Anderson and Krathwohl, 2001).

Patricia and Philip understood that the ICT scaffolded learning (Margaryan, 2006). This can be associated with Vygotsky's (1978) theory whereby tools mediate learning between individuals. Those tools scaffold such a dialectic process so that an individual's Zone of Proximal Development is extended (Vygotsky, 1986); the ZPD refers to the difference between what a learner can achieve on her own and what she can achieve with the assistance of a more capable person (the other pupils, and Patricia and Philip). Patricia and Philip were also aware of the work of Laurillard (1993) who argued that media (tools) have a range of affordances:

- narrative (tells the learner something);
- interactive (gives the learner feedback);
- communicative (encourages discussion between learners);
- adaptive (responds to the learner);
- productive (helps the learner to create something).

Laurillard (1993) showed that multimedia that can mediate all of the above for learners is the most efficient tool for progressing knowledge acquisition. For the transition project the mobile devices transmitted information to learners (narrative) and facilitated self-knowledge (Anderson and Krathwohl, 2001) based on the set of responses allowing the learners to engage in metacognition (interactive). The results (the feedback) of the voting stimulated dialogue between the learners focused upon not only their present state of knowledge but what that state of knowledge needed to be and could be (for example, in order for the secondary pupils in turn to scaffold the learning of the primary pupils). The results of the quizzes created by pupils changed in relation to the knowledge acquisition of the learners (adaptive); it became a symbol of their learning.

Thinking point

- How does 'flipping' a classroom challenge some views of the teacher's role, especially related to their identity?
- Has this section changed your views on teaching resources (for example their importance)? If so, how and why?

ICT and the motivated classroom

The transition project can be associated with McLean's (2004) 'motivating classroom' because both teachers were at a point in their professional development where their identity as teachers was firmly grounded upon a democratic view of pedagogical quality as opposed to a traditional view of quality based upon competition (Pfeffer and Coote, 1996).

Figure 16.2 shows how McLean (2004) defines the ideal classroom in terms of motivation associated with relationships. McLean argues that teachers can raise pupil aspirations and thus knowledge acquisition through scaffolding that affirms and empowers pupils as opposed to rejecting and trying to control them via authoritarian methods.

The transition project:

- engaged pupils through aspects of their culture being valued and being given responsibility for their own improvement (and that of others);
- provided a structure that scaffolded autonomy and trust through clear objectives, expectations and ownership;
- stimulated creativity within pupils by setting them a purposeful problem to solve that was responsive to the needs of both classes;
- provided formative opportunities for feedback in terms of the pupils' knowledge acquisition related to implementing a successful WW1 quiz for a specific audience (McLean, 2004).

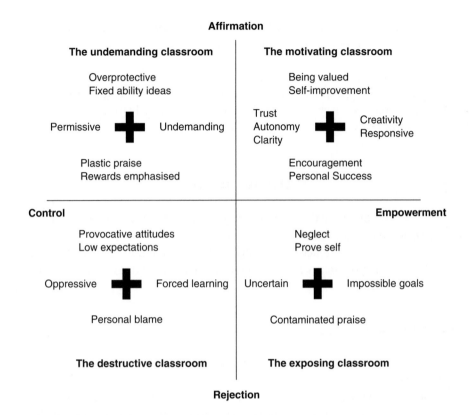

Figure 16.2 Classroom environments (from McLean, 2004: 16, 24)

Thinking point

- Why would the transition project be as or not as effective under the leadership of a teacher who, for example, engendered an 'undemanding classroom' climate, or would it even have been utilised?
- Using the A CRISP acronym from 'View from practice 1' explain how the tools involved in the transition project would be effective mediators of learning.

Summary

ICT can be used most effectively in primary school as a pedagogical strategy through the teacher's reflective consideration of ICT across the teaching and learning cycle. This requires teachers to possess at least a satisfactory level of ICT capability enabling them to scaffold lessons that integrate:

- evaluations of children's needs with…
- the selection of appropriate ICT that motivates children to learn through…
- the considered use of ICT as contexts for self-regulated learning utilising…
- the A CRISP features of ICT for formative assessment

Reflective questions

- How would you argue the case for using ICT as pedagogy in primary school as opposed to treating it as a discrete subject area?
- How can beginning teachers be supported in developing their ICT capability?
- Is the teaching of literacy across curricula redundant if it does not consider ICT?

Further reading

Bruff, D. (2009) *Teaching with Classroom Response Systems Creating Active Learning Environments*. San Francisco: Jossey-Bass.

Goodison, T. (2003) 'Integrating ICT in the classroom: A case study of two contrasting lessons', *British Journal of Educational Technology*, 34(5), 54–6.

Poore, M. (2012) *Using Social Media in the Classroom: A Best Practice Guide*. London: SAGE.

Salmon, G. (2006) *E-tivities: The Key to Active Online Learning*. London: Routledge Falmer.

CHAPTER 17

TRANSITIONS

George MacBride and Margaret McCulloch

Key ideas

This chapter explores:

- transition in and out of primary education;
- established good practice in transition;
- sharing information about learning;
- the learner's role in transition;
- transition and inclusion.

Introduction

This chapter focuses on the processes of transition from nursery or other early years provision to primary school and from primary to secondary or middle school. The word 'transition' is used rather than 'transfer' which suggests only a change of location while 'transition' implies that there is some form of development, change of status or adoption of a new culture as well as change of location (Chedzoy and Burden, 2005).

There are three levels of factors influencing continuity and progression in learning across transitions: systemic, school and classroom. The first includes curriculum specification, national assessment arrangements and enrolment systems. Each of the four UK nations has its own laws, curricular structures, assessment policies and systems of schools organisation which affect transition from one sector to the next. The second level includes relationships and practice within a schools cluster or learning community, internal school structures and school improvement plans. The level of school autonomy differs among these four countries but within each there exist considerable differences in policy and practice among schools. We do not consider these often shifting systemic and school level factors in any detail.

This chapter focuses on the third of these levels, the classroom, where all teachers can contribute to effective transitions for the learners. We outline key findings, identified from research and practice, which you will be able to use in your own contexts to ensure that your practice supports learners at transition.

Transition as a contested area

There are several widely accepted, apparently simple, markers of successful transitions (Ashton, 2008; Capel et al., 2007; Chedzoy and Burden, 2005; Wilson, 2011):

- Children settle without major problems into their new school, adopt its routines and make new friends; they maintain and improve their self-esteem and confidence.
- Children make steady progress in their learning.
- Parents are happy with the process and outcomes.
- The process is manageable for teachers and schools and does not have perverse effects on teaching and learning before or after transition.
- Learners are active and valued partners.

Transition, however, has been an issue of concern internationally over a long period of time. This has especially been the case as learners move from primary to secondary school but similar points are made about the move from nursery to primary school. At both these major transition stages, a range of interested parties may have differing, possibly conflicting, concerns and priorities:

- *Local authorities* look for transition procedures which will enhance pupil progress and achievement. Their main concerns arise from the common perception, albeit based on evidence largely derived from a small number of curricular areas, using a limited range of forms of assessment, that learners' attainment and motivation tend to dip in the early years of secondary education (Evangelou et al., 2008; Wilson, 2011). They have a particular interest in the progress of children identified as vulnerable and for whom detailed information is collected, for example, pupils with specific disabilities, or those who are looked after. Local authorities may disseminate good practice and facilitate working across clusters of schools.

- *School management teams* have a responsibility to ensure continuity and progression in learning and positive social and emotional outcomes for the young people concerned. They have to develop effective and efficient procedures which balance the expectation of improvement in pupil achievement with the cost of staff time necessary for gathering and sharing information. There is evidence that the sharing of 'pastoral' information is often more effective than the sharing of 'learning' information.

- *Teachers* who are passing information onto colleagues in another sector may have different concerns from the recipients. There may be tensions around the volume, focus and format of the information provided or expected. There may be fundamental differences in the philosophical beliefs about whether the transition should be conceptualised as a gentle progression or as a move to a new context with different, usually more demanding, expectations. Evidence, both anecdotal and from research (McCullagh and Jarman, 2009), suggests distinctive cultures in different sectors. Secondary teachers are accused of testing pupils on entry because they do not trust primary teachers' well-founded judgements. Some secondary teachers do not use evidence of prior achievement but provide pupils with a 'fresh start'. Similarly, early years workers often feel that early stages teachers undervalue or even ignore information gathered about children's learning prior to their transition to school.

- *Other school staff,* for example, pupil support assistants working with potentially vulnerable children, may have detailed knowledge about individual children's learning and ways to support them. They may have concerns about how support arrangements and strategies which encourage effective learning and support the children emotionally will be continued after transition.

- *Parents and carers* are concerned about how their child will deal with transition. Evidence suggests that parents consider social aspects of transition at the primary-secondary stage as more important than issues relating to learning (Zeedyk et al., 2003). They may have additional anxieties around their child being able to access the school of their choice, either through selection or availability of places (Evangelou et al., 2008). Similarly, the limited evidence around nursery-primary transition suggests that if there are concerns, these tend to be around socio-behavioural skills such as following directions or sitting still for extended periods (Wildenger and McIntyre, 2011).

- *Children,* like parents, have their own individual concerns (Topping, 2011). Research, in the UK and beyond, indicates that at transfer to secondary, these are more likely to be related to coping with the new environment and dealing with peer relationships, including bullying, than to academic concerns. Research (Jindal-Snape and Miller, 2008; Lucey and Reay, 2002; Osborn et al., 2006) has highlighted that some children experience high levels of anxiety at transition to secondary, although generally children regard transition positively (Evangelou et al., 2008; Graham and Hill, 2003). A major re-negotiation of personal identity may be required, and gender, as an aspect of identity, may take on even greater significance, particularly as the move to puberty often occurs concurrently with transition to secondary school.
- *Other professionals,* for example, social workers, educational psychologists or health services workers may be involved in children's lives and thus concerned to sustain progress and engagement with learning at times of transition. Transition procedures must ensure that their knowledge and perspectives relevant to learning are shared with teachers.

In addition to the different stakeholders involved in transition processes, there are significant structural differences amongst educational contexts which may impact on both the arrangements and the experiences for pupils:

- In early years establishments, while individual children are likely to have a key worker, several early years workers will have in-depth knowledge of the learning and social development of each child and will provide detailed information to be passed on to the first primary teacher. At the primary level, teachers working with pupils preparing for transition will have a thorough, holistic knowledge of each pupil which they will wish to communicate effectively to secondary staff, some of whom may teach each pupil only once or twice a week for an hour. There are implications here for the type of information and the format in which it is provided.
- As children progress, establishments normally become larger and more complex. This has implications both for pupils as they deal with the transition and for the sharing of information. Discussions of children's progress which occur regularly in early years establishments become less frequent as children grow older; time pressures mean that information about secondary pupils is often transferred on paper. Secondary schools are usually organised round subjects but information about academic progress is often presented principally in relation to literacy and numeracy, with less detail provided in other areas.
- In secondary schools, pastoral care has traditionally been carried out by specific teachers; supporting transition is generally part of this role. This can lead to other teachers seeing transmission and sharing of information as outside their responsibilities. Recent developments (Education Scotland, online-e) in which all teachers take the role of 'key adult' for a group of young people may address this bottleneck.

These concerns are exacerbated by systemic pressures. Supportive friends may be separated due to parental choice. Selective systems, formal or informal, impose intense pressures on teachers and young people at transition. Performance systems based on measuring narrow aspects of learning prevent teachers from promoting depth and breadth of learning before, across and after transitions. The growing tendency to measure progress at times of transition may lead to 'potentially limiting assumptions' (Vogler et al., 2008: v) being made about children. The use of the concept of 'value-added' when comparing schools' 'performance' leads to schools searching for a 'baseline' against which to measure progress from the earliest stages. Baseline testing may be used to stream or set pupils, rather than plan learning, particularly when there is a lack of opportunity for professionals in different contexts to develop a shared understanding of 'standards'.

Apart from some aspects of pastoral support, there is little evidence of children being given more than a token role in managing transitions and, in particular, for ensuring progression and continuity in their learning. This is perhaps surprising, given the commitment of all jurisdictions in the UK to recognising the rights of children and given that children have immediate knowledge both of their own learning and of the contexts in which that learning takes place.

Some research into transition has been criticised on methodological grounds: very small samples have been used, evidence from one school may not be generalisable to others, attainment measures are restricted to a few curricular areas and use a limited range of forms of assessment. Difficulties may be greater in prospect than they are in reality. Because transfer involves a change in status (going to 'big school'), pupils may expect to experience a degree of discontinuity (Davies and McMahon, 2004). Children who are negative about school may want to make a fresh start. Nevertheless the evidence is sufficiently robust as to require teachers to consider how they can contribute to their pupils enjoying a successful transition process.

 ### Thinking point

'I like to be given as much information as possible about children's attainments and requirements for additional support before they come into my class.'
  'I like to find out about my pupils for myself rather than be influenced by other people's judgements about them.'

- What would be the advantages and disadvantages, for children and teachers, of each of these approaches to practice at transition?

Established good practice

Many teachers have been working to ensure successful and enjoyable transitions for all children.

- Schools have invested staff time and expertise in developing administrative and pastoral arrangements so that children feel at home in new schools and key information is readily available to all staff who need it.
- Electronic management systems ensure more effective access to valuable data (regrettably sometimes also to data of doubtful worth).
- Induction days for pupils before they enter their new school, shared social events and buddying arrangements contribute to the settling-in process.
- Schools make use of national curriculum frameworks and share their curricular plans.
- The growing emphasis on early intervention and on target-setting in primary schools has increased awareness of the importance of effective transition for children moving between early years establishments and primary schools.
- Flexible approaches to curriculum organisation take account of the range of developmental stages likely to be found in any one cohort.
- Special arrangements provide support to certain groups of pupils.
- Key professionals outside school contribute much to such arrangements.
- Schools are developing the use of profiles and portfolios.
- Schools are creating opportunities for professional dialogue across sector boundaries, including joint classroom planning and moderation of assessment.

Such practice has proved crucial to pupils' wellbeing and supports the effective sharing of information to ensure progression in learning.

Sharing information about learning

Teachers and schools are increasingly recognising, in line with research, that good practice at transition must go beyond sharing pastoral information, essential though this is to ensuring that children are known and secure in their new school and that they and their parents perceive this. We must go beyond references to official national curricular frameworks (Gorwood, 1991); even where the intended curriculum is prescribed in some detail (and this is not the case in all areas of the UK) the enacted curriculum in classrooms will vary considerably and the curriculum experienced by learners even more so. Nor is sharing pupil records is sufficient, however detailed these are; even where supported by such devices as an electronic management system or a summary profile, these cannot give a full picture of either the learner or the context of their learning.

The traditional separation of curriculum, pedagogy and assessment is no longer tenable (West et al., 2010). Sharing information about learning involves sharing and discussing information about all aspects of practice:

- curriculum specification;
- curriculum plans;
- classroom organisation;
- learner responsibilities;
- teaching methodologies;
- assessment methodologies;
- examples of pupils' work.

Research identifies several conditions if sharing this information is to lead to changes which promote continuity and progression for individual learners.

- Teachers must trust one another's judgements; research is clear that good relationships developed through collaboration are crucial to this.
- Dialogue should afford opportunities to develop knowledge about the culture and workings of the other sector.
- Successful dialogue is supported by looking at learning plans, by sharing expectations of pupil outcomes and moderation of pupil work, by spending time in each other's classrooms and by asking questions about practice observed.
- Teachers' trust in one another's judgements about pupils' achievements is more likely where the purpose of assessment is formative, designed to support progression in learning.
- The system must support teachers, focusing on the transfer of information which teachers consider valuable and eliminating practical difficulties about dissemination of information (Hayward et al., 2012).
- Schools and teachers make use of a number of strategies to transfer information to support learning across transition.

Standardised assessments

Standardised assessments (for example, SATs in England, tests of verbal ability) have often been developed primarily to monitor school success and at best give some general indication of an individual learner's achievements (see Chapter 11). Many doubt their value at transition because they may not be closely related to curricular specifications and because they cover limited aspects of learning. Because they are used to hold schools and teachers accountable, they are likely to encourage 'teaching to the test' which lowers expectations and leads to limited breadth and depth of learning, before, across and after transition.

Curriculum standards and levels of achievement

Pupil progress is often defined in terms of curriculum levels and standards which may be summarised as a letter or a number; in some cases these are broken down into sub-levels, officially or otherwise. If we are to use standards to support progress across transition we must go beyond marks or grades or simply reading published descriptors. Standards statements only become meaningful when they are interpreted by the teachers directly involved, making professional judgements on the evidence of work which they consider as illustrating progression towards the desirable knowledge and skills. The achievement of key learning can be validly evidenced only when supported by a significant body, rather than a single piece, of work. The phrase 'best fit' is applied to this use of a body of work to provide evidence of learning. In addition to class work it may be necessary, in some curricular areas, to design specific tasks which provide opportunities for learners to demonstrate breadth and depth of learning and application of knowledge and skills. Discussion should develop teachers' understanding of the relationship between immediate 'next steps' and the 'big picture' of progression through school in terms of key learning in a curricular area.

Planned discussions

Teachers can develop their understanding of how pupils can progress through using time spent in one another's classrooms to inform discussion of the curriculum, consideration of samples of pupil work from across the curriculum, and the sharing of information on the teaching and learning processes which led to this work. School clusters can set time aside for this purpose; ICT can support sharing of materials and teacher dialogue; teachers can create communities of interest, online or offline. Involving pupils can contribute to the understanding of all adults involved of what it is like to learn in a particular school or classroom.

Bridging projects

A number of schools have found that a bridging project, where the first part of a topic is taught in the last months of primary school and the remainder at the start of secondary schooling, can support effective transition (Braund, 2007; Davies and McMahon, 2004). A well-planned bridging unit can provide opportunities for teachers to develop their understanding of the range of the curriculum covered in the other sector and of pupils' achievement in the relevant knowledge and skills. This information can inform planning so that pupils experience greater continuity across the transition.

View from practice

A bridging project

All pupils in their final year in the eight primary schools associated with a particular secondary school used KODU software to develop computer games. Each school organised the preparation and development of the games in ways that suited their situation best. Each class then selected one of the games created to take to the transition days in the secondary school.

These pupils attended the secondary school for seven days in May and June, in the classes of which they would be members in August. On these days, the games selected by the pupils were the focus for learning in a number of departments (English, mathematics and ICT). Learning crossed the boundaries between primary and secondary: primary staff worked with secondary colleagues in their classrooms and there were considerable opportunities for dialogue, informal in classrooms and formal in timetabled meetings. Pupils also had sessions during these days devoted to school values, citizenship, buddying and respecting rights. The induction days ended with an exhibition for parents of the work done.

The project was repeated the next year with one difference: the pupils who had participated in this first year acted as mentors to the new primary teachers involved and supported them in developing their ICT skills.

Thinking point

- What might be some of the benefits for the pupils of a project like this?
- What might be some of the challenges for teachers in both sectors?

The learner's role in transition

Based on the commitment of the UK government and of the devolved governments to the United Nations Convention on the Rights of the Child, children have legal and moral rights to being involved in planning their education (see Chapter 13). Children's involvement in transition processes is valuable because they have immediate expert knowledge and understanding of their learning, of the education system and what is needed to develop their learning (Ashton, 2008; Perry and Dockett, 2011). The involvement of children in the transition process is not an add-on to the 'real' planning and reflects the ways in which children have become more directly involved in their own learning through the use of pedagogies based on principles of socio-cultural learning and on constructivist principles (Thurston et al., 2010). Self and peer assessment, personal learning planning and profiling all exemplify how learners contribute to planning the learning process.

Traditionally, pupils have contributed to transition processes by being asked to identify possible concerns; these have often focused on the social and environmental aspects of moving school. Reflecting this, schools have gone on to involve pupils in mutual support at transition. Schools use pastoral information and children's preferences to place friends together, use induction days to allow familiarisation with school routines and use buddy systems to develop understanding of school culture and build confidence (Thurston et al., 2010). ICT can supplement school visits, through e-mail, on-line meetings or videos of school life; this can be especially useful where children are not accompanying the majority of their peers to a particular secondary school. There is strong evidence that successful learners are those who feel attachment to their school, have a sense of autonomy in taking decisions about their learning and can rightly regard themselves as active agents in their learning (McLean, 2004).

At a very practical level, this approach to learner responsibility can be developed to address the criticism made of approaches like bridging projects that pupils who transfer from schools where the project work has not been undertaken will be disadvantaged. ICT allows individual pupils to participate to some extent even if their own school is not involved and peers can support non-participating pupils on entry to the secondary school.

Transitions require learners to be able to transfer previous learning (knowledge and understanding, skills and attributes and capabilities) in all areas of the curriculum into very different new contexts. Learners must be able to understand the purposes of their learning, to have the capacity to reflect on and articulate their learning, and to assess what and how they have learned. Pedagogies such as cooperative group work support this self-knowledge, requiring learners to make explicit their learning. Engaging learners requires the development of their understanding of the goals of their learning, the criteria by which it is assessed and their ability to assess their own work. Such pedagogies also support the development of positive social relationships before, across and after transition which can then underpin post-transition achievement.

Teachers and learners need to be able to summarise evidence to allow them effectively to share this information on progression in learning. Schools are developing portfolios which provide evidence of learning accompanied by commentary on what makes this successful and on how it can be taken forward. Learners can be supported to take responsibility for gathering and updating the evidence of their latest and best learning which demonstrates a 'best fit' with high-level learning intentions across the curriculum. A portfolio may include classwork, specific assessment tasks designed to demonstrate breadth, depth and application of learning, and evidence gathered from learning outside school. The creation and maintenance of such a portfolio with annotations and plans builds on the practice of personal learning planning and need not be onerous in terms of time.

Such a portfolio can at a minimum be used as a reference point by staff to inform discussions between teachers in the two establishments and their planning; at best it forms the basis of learning conversations between the learner and teachers in the new school. Teachers and learners can together reflect on, understand and discuss what matters to enable pupils to achieve the intended learning and transfer this into new contexts. Learning conversations involve teachers in making connections between previous learning and the curriculum, linking both backwards and forwards, so that pupils can appreciate what they have done before and will do in the future. They can together plan tasks which enable all pupils to show breadth of learning, challenge within learning and application of knowledge and skills in new and unfamiliar situations. A key requirement is the use of 'rich' learning intentions and demanding success criteria rather than long checklists of detailed points, each of which has to be ticked off. Portfolios may be supplemented by profiles created by learners and teachers which provide further information on their interests and skills in learning.

Thinking point

- What do you think might be the main differences in the teacher's role between organising personal learning planning for the next few weeks within one classroom and encouraging evidence to be created for a portfolio designed to sustain and progress learning across a school transition?
- How can you help learners develop a 'big picture' of their learning as well as identifying immediate next steps in their learning?

Transition and inclusion

Transition processes must be inclusive and meet the needs of all pupils, including those who may in some way be vulnerable. The same aims and principles underpin any additional support at transition as underpin good transition procedures which support all children. Any particular support afforded to individuals should be a supplement planned within the regular transition procedures for all young people, not an alternative or substitute for these.

Groups who are considered likely to benefit from some form of additional support at transition include children with recognised additional support needs or special educational needs, children for whom English is an additional language or children who are looked after and accommodated (Brewin and Statham, 2011; Nash and Henderson, 2010). Sometimes more narrowly defined groups are identified, such as those with specific difficulties in literacy or numeracy or those affected by Asperger syndrome. Sometimes vulnerable groups are defined socially, such as those with a negative attitude towards school or those at risk of being bullied. Some consider ill-defined social groups as likely to have difficulties at transition, often making use of pejorative labels such as 'broken families' or 'poor parents'. Labelling children as vulnerable can lead us to think that they are different from an assumed 'normal' and are best dealt with outside the frameworks which support all young people. Intervention must meet the needs of the individual; not every member of any single group will need the same sort of support; some may need no additional support. Transition processes must recognise the importance to young people's self-image of not being made to feel different or singled out in front of their peers.

Additional support at transition has taken different formats. In some cases, effort has been devoted to ensuring that pastoral aspects of transition are enhanced. There may be a longer induction process to ensure that the child is familiar with and comfortable in the new school; buddying may play a bigger role; medical information may be shared with teachers; social background information may be known to key members of staff; meetings may be organised with other professionals. In other cases, very detailed information on learning achievements and difficulties is provided to staff in the new school, at least in some curricular areas. The role of professional dialogue amongst teachers in supporting this transfer of information is crucial and is often recognised in formal structures: it is important that class teachers as well as school managers are closely involved.

Good practice extends beyond this to considering the views of the learner and parents. Dialogue with other professionals (for example health services, psychological services, social work, youth justice) may contribute to ensuring progression in learning. Dialogue is, if anything, more important here than dialogue among teachers if we are to ensure that there is sharing of understanding of the aims of education and of basic educational principles. Paper reports may be essential but are unlikely to be sufficient to ensure insights into planning effectively for learning in the new environment. The role of the class teacher, as the person with greatest knowledge of the child's learning, in facilitating and informing, if not managing, this dialogue is significant. It is also clear that on legal, moral and practical grounds the child, wherever possible, should be an active participant in these discussions; it is likely to be the responsibility of the class teacher to ensure this.

A view from practice

Additional support needs?

One of the pupils entering a primary school reception class next session is J who has recently arrived in the UK from Poland with his family (father, mother, baby brother); the father is employed in a local factory; the family speaks very little English. The nursery school he attends informs the primary head that J's sight is limited, that he is physically active and socially skilled and that he has in his short time in nursery made friends with the other children in his group; he plays with some of them outside nursery. Transition for J will involve other professionals (and time must be found for this) but the schools decided that the fundamental issue is to build on J's strengths and ensure the continuing support of his peers. They support his group in creating a diary of their activities and learning in and out of school, including photos, drawings and pupil statements. J's mother contributes, with the support of an interpreter, information on the family; J is very attentive of his baby brother.

Thinking point

- If J was coming into your primary class from nursery, how could you use this information in a positive way to organise learning to support J's effective transition?

Summary

In this chapter we have identified some of the areas of debate around transition. We have argued that, while transition processes which are focused on ensuring that children feel physically and emotionally secure in their new surroundings should support them in making good progress in their learning, it is also vital to focus on the learning itself. Much discussion centres on what information is necessary and how it is gathered and used. We have suggested that effective transition requires meaningful discussions amongst staff from the different sectors involved and children themselves. These discussions should be based on evidence gathered from a range of sources which should allow children to demonstrate their abilities in a range of ways, and over a period of time, as opposed to a check-box approach to 'levels' in individual curricular areas. Shared understandings amongst staff of curriculum content and of pedagogical approaches which embed formative assessment practice into learning can also enhance transition experiences for children as well as enhancing professional confidence (Hayward et al., 2012). The support of school management and local authorities in making time available for conversations amongst staff from different sectors is essential. It is crucial that information gathered and passed on does not have the effect of limiting the expectations which the receiving teachers may have of a child or group of children; on the other hand, support strategies which have been found to be effective should be sustained as appropriate after transition.

While class teachers may not have any control over the level or amount of liaison with colleagues around transition, they clearly play a key role in supporting children to recognise and provide evidence of their own learning progress across a range of contexts. Individual discussion with teachers around progress is highly valued by children (Hayward et al., 2012). In addition to increasing children's sense of responsibility for their own learning, taking this more holistic approach to children's learning enhances teachers' own sense of efficacy in making judgements about children's progress.

 Reflective questions

- How might information from nursery colleagues impact on the way you organise learning in your classroom?
- What assumptions do you have about priorities and practices in the early years and secondary sectors which might influence children's experiences at transition?
- How might you ensure that information passed on to secondary colleagues does not negatively influence their expectations of children in your class?

Further reading

Evangelou, M., Taggart, B., Sylva, K., Melhuish, E., Sammons, P. and Siraj-Blatchford, I. (2008) *What Makes a Successful Transition from Primary to Secondary School?*

Effective Pre-school, Primary and Secondary Education 3–14 Project (EPPSE 3–14) London: Institute of Education, University of London. http://www.ioe.ac.uk/ Successful_transition_from_primary_to_secondary_report.pdf (accessed 28 June 2013).

Case study of a primary–secondary transition initiative http://www.educationscot-land.gov.uk/sharingpractice/s/supportingprimarysecondarytransition/introduction. asp (accessed 28 June 2013).

CHAPTER 18

WORKING WITH OTHER ADULTS

Mike Carroll

Key ideas

This chapter explores:

- the role of School Support Assistants (SSAs) in supporting inclusion;
- teachers' supervision of SSAs' work and training;
- creating a dialogic space to help prepare SSAs;
- avoiding exclusion by misguided good intentions.

Introduction

In schools there are a range of adults who work either as 'teachers' or 'support staff', including parent helpers. Support staff fall into five broad categories:

- learning support staff who work with teachers in the classroom, including classroom assistants, Additional Support Needs (ASN) assistants, peripatetic specialists (for subjects such as physical education, drama and music), English for Speakers of Other Languages (ESOL) teachers;
- specialist and technical staff, including librarians, information and communication technology (ICT)/audio visual (AV) technicians, science technicians, food technology technicians;
- pupil support/welfare staff, including youth workers (for example Active Break Workers), attendance officers, school nurse;
- administrative staff, including administration and finance assistants, clerical assistants, team leaders (office);
- facilities staff, including catering, janitorial, cleaning.

Support staff can either have direct or indirect contact with children. In this chapter I am primarily concerned with support staff who have direct contact with children in the primary classroom with the intention of supporting teaching and learning, particularly those whom classroom teachers are expected to supervise.

Classroom assistant (CA) is the most widespread term adopted in Scottish schools with paraprofessional being the preferred term in the US (Bedford et al., 2008). In England the terms 'teaching assistant' (TA) and 'higher level teaching assistant' (HLTA) are used to describe adults who are employed to work alongside teachers in classrooms, particularly providing support to children considered as having additional support needs (Howes et al., 2003); however, in this chapter I will use the term school support assistant (SSA) to describe those charged with supporting children's learning.

Changing classrooms

Workforce reform has prioritised the deployment of class teachers to concentrate on learning and teaching in an effort to improve standards by identifying activities, particularly administrative tasks, to be undertaken by SSAs, so freeing up teachers' time to teach. An increased number of SSAs have been appointed to support the realignment and transformation of the educational landscape with respect to the structure and philosophy of special education (Moran and Abbott, 2002), resulting in the inclusion of children with additional support needs (ASNs) in mainstream schools. Previously these children were effectively excluded from their local neighbourhood school by being educated in separate establishments, so-called 'special schools'. The move towards inclusive education represents a rejection of separation on the basis of perceived need, arguing that it is a form of 'educational apartheid'.

The simple but nevertheless powerful underlying assumption of inclusive education is that all children have the right to be educated in their neighbourhood school and to receive the same educational opportunities as every other child of their age (Angelides et al., 2009). The implication of this for schools is that they need to consider how they can provide equal opportunities through the adaptation of an inclusive pedagogy to meet diverse needs. The policy of inclusion leads directly to the perceived need for additional in-class adult support for children with ASNs (Muijs and Reynolds, 2003) in order to meet their learning (curricular and intrapersonal skills), physical (personal care and mobility) and social (behavioural, communication and interpersonal skills) needs (Takala, 2007).

Support from SSAs for children who require additional support for their learning is also seen as being crucial as we move towards constructing more collaborative, active and interdisciplinary learning experiences, with children taking responsibility for their own learning. Blatchford et al. (2009) argue that SSAs have become an essential component of practice with regard to the integration of children who have barriers to their learning in mainstream schools. The relief provided by an 'extra pair of hands' in the classroom should not be confused with effective education for children (Giangreco et al., 2005). If we are truly seeking inclusive education, with all children participating as members of the school community, then having an 'inadequately trained' adult by a child's side, for all or part of the school day, may only serve to exacerbate rather than ameliorate the child's sense of exclusion (Angelides et al., 2009).

The changing classroom topography requires you as a teacher to take responsibility for the supervision and ongoing mentoring of SSAs despite the fact that there has been scant recognition of the specific skills and personal aptitudes required by teachers for working with adults in the management of classroom support. Perversely, the addition of SSAs to create classroom teams can add to your responsibilities as you will be expected to supervise and support these other adults. Experienced teachers, previously accustomed to high levels of autonomy, have had to adjust to the demands of team-working in the support of children's learning. It has been largely left to staff to form new understandings of what it means to work cooperatively and collaboratively. Furthermore, as SSAs become increasingly skilled, the middle ground between the prescribed duties of SSAs and teachers provides a source of potential confusion and conflict (Calder and Grieve, 2004) as it is not always easy to delineate neatly between teaching and supporting.

SSAs originally took care of 'housekeeping' in and beyond the classroom by undertaking clerical work such as preparing materials for lessons, putting up displays, supervising non-teaching activities taking place outside the classroom, for example, playground duty, as well as assisting with personal care. More recently SSAs have begun to undertake more of a pedagogical role under the direction of the teacher (Burgess and Mayes, 2007). Indeed, HLTAs are intended to make a substantial contribution to the teaching and learning process and to support improved attainment. This can involve providing supervision in small-group settings, facilitating follow-up instruction, such as paired reading, practice of reading words and phonics, as well as supporting children in the development of their social skills focused on the development of positive relationships and behaviour. The National Association of Professional Teaching Assistants' (NAPTA) second newsletter (NAPTA, 2005) outlined four key areas of activity for most SSAs that included:

- support the curriculum by motivating children to work, encouraging independent learning and discussions;
- support children by working with individuals and groups, reinforcing behaviour strategies, providing pastoral care;
- support teachers by preparing resources, assisting with record keeping, setting up displays;
- support the school by working in line with school policy.

Working alongside a SSA you may find it difficult to negotiate the boundaries between teaching and non-teaching roles, giving rise to a zone of uncertainty (Moran and Abbott, 2002) with some SSAs drifting into a 'teaching role'. SSAs can work across several different members of staff, all of whom will have slightly different expectations with respect to the role of the SSA; clearly this will have an impact upon how you choose to define your role. In addition, some SSAs are employed to support individual children, usually someone with a significant barrier to their learning, whilst others function as general SSAs and can be used more flexibly in that they can support an individual child as well as moving between groups of children. The feature that they all have in common is that the primary purpose of their work is to assist and support children's engagement with the learning process in cooperation with the classroom teacher (Takala, 2007). However, this is not unproblematic as arguably the drift towards pedagogical engagement by SSAs can be construed as a threat to teachers' professional identity. This is broadly consistent with the concern expressed by Howes et al. (2003: 147) who suggest that assistants 'teaching' 'potentially threatens the distinctive role of the qualified teacher in schools'.

Thinking point

- In what ways could additional support within the classroom assist the children's learning?

Professional development

Generally appointed with little by way of training, qualifications or experience, SSAs usually learn on the job with knowledge being socially situated and constructed within communities of practice. Beyond the induction phase, SSAs often find their continuing professional development (CPD) needs are not adequately addressed (Rubie-Davies et al., 2010), apart from undertaking some short courses provided by Local Authorities targeted at generic aspects of the SSAs' work, such as supporting children with autism. School-based, on-the-job support is the dominant model of professional development with knowledge being constructed through observation and participation within the school. Furthermore, experience within and between schools can vary considerably with SSAs being allocated to more than one classroom, working alongside different teachers each with their own expectations and ways of working. The complexity of training is increased as SSAs also absorb a range of different administrative duties as well as supervision in the school's public spaces.

Angelides et al. (2009) indicate that there is little by way of pre-service or in-service training, for both teachers and SSAs, designed to support the inclusion of SSAs in the classroom. As a consequence, learning about the job can be somewhat haphazard with SSAs 'picking things up' through discussions with other SSAs and, when opportunities arise, from observing and talking to teachers. However, there is a growing body of evidence that SSAs are being trained prior to undertaking classroom duties. For example, Numeracy Support Assistants (NSAs) appointed in England to provide extra support for low-achieving children during and after mathematics lessons engaged in a variety of training activities, as part of the Gatsby Mathematics Enhancement Programme Primary. Muijs and Reynolds (2003: 223) describe how NSAs took part in an initial three-day training event that involved examining their role in the classroom, how to identify underachieving children, the purpose and practice of assessment, observing and discussing mathematics lessons, an introduction to the main calculating strategies, an examination of the National Numeracy Strategy, theories of learning, interactive teaching, the use of mathematical language and questioning techniques. This extensive range of training was supplemented by four follow-up meetings examining the range of problems encountered and identifying further training needs.

Although extensive, the MEPP framework nevertheless pales into insignificance when compared to the education of SSAs in Finland, who are expected to successfully complete 40 weeks of study, including 12 weeks of practice in schools, with one study week being equivalent to 40 hours of work (Takala, 2007). This culminates in an assessment of the skills of a classroom assistant with the programme being regulated by the National Board of Education (Takala, 2007).

The comparison with the UK is stark, as most SSAs enter the classroom to work alongside teachers with little by way of guidance as to their respective roles and responsibilities. The responsibility for developing SSAs tends to be allocated to the institutions in which they are placed requiring a whole-school, team-led approach aimed at providing support and training within schools (Burgess and Mayes, 2007). It remains debatable as to whether this should be the case if we are truly serious about realising the principles of inclusive education. In addition the supervision of other adults in the classroom needs to be addressed at all levels of teacher development, from initial teacher training onwards; however, currently there appears to be little by way of coordinated effort to achieve this.

For on-the-job orientation and training to have any meaningful impact it becomes necessary for you as the class teacher to take on the role of 'mentor' in order to facilitate understanding of duties and tasks to be undertaken as well as the development of basic 'teaching skills'. Therefore you effectively act as a 'more knowledgeable other' (MKO) to support a SSA's participation in real-life teaching contexts.

Sociocultural learning theory suggests that the more the SSA participates under guidance from the teacher the more they will come to understand. For learning to take place it is necessary for you to create a 'dialogic space' to support discussion, sharing of ideas and negotiation of practice. Notwithstanding the fact that organising support and training for both teachers and SSAs is not unproblematic, the mentoring role of the teacher is made difficult by the fact that although the work of SSAs may be under your supervision this does not mean that you are their line manager (Mistry et al., 2004). Line management of SSAs can be unclear in that they may interact with a number of classroom teachers as well as the school management team whilst taking direction from the Special Educational Needs Coordinator (SENCO) (Bedford et al., 2008). The issue here is not that the SSA interacts with several staff but rather that this is likely to lead to breakdowns in communication that will hinder attempts to provide staff development opportunities for SSAs.

Thinking point

- What would on-the-job orientation and training involve in order to facilitate effective co-operation between teachers and SSAs, as well as parent helpers?

Creating time to talk

Angelides et al. (2009: 85) describe an extreme situation where there was an absence of communication between a teacher and a SSA, so much so that not a single word was exchanged between them throughout the course of an entire lesson. Scheduling meetings, no matter how brief, provides space and time for communication between teachers and SSAs to take place. The nature of the talk that takes place will vary depending upon what needs to be accomplished but the acronym PAIRS helps describe five basic elements for you to consider:

- **P**lanning talk during which the learning intentions to be achieved are discussed.
- **A**ctivity talk focused on identifying the different teaching strategies that are available to achieve the desired objectives, for particular groups and individuals.
- **I**mplementation talk focused on agreeing roles and responsibilities of the teacher and SSA in order to implement the plan.
- **R**eview talk to discuss whether targets have been met and what adjustments to future plans need to take place.
- **S**ocial glue talk attending to the relational context of the classroom team in getting to know each other.

Finding opportunities to talk is a key concern as regular meetings are important to maintain rapport and communication and to discuss progress or problems; 'effective practices are associated with planning; all adults working with children need to understand the aims of, and their own role in, the educational process' (Takala, 2007: 55). The extra pair of 'hands, eyes and ears' provided by SSAs is often not put to best use as there is insufficient time set aside for teachers and SSAs to plan their work together. Time scheduled for discussion, let alone planning, remains rare with collaboration between teachers and SSAs being largely informal and dependent upon the teacher. Communication is critical not only to ensure productive learning experiences for children but also to help create and support a productive work environment constructed upon mutually reinforcing professional relationships. The issue will always be one of when to meet. For some this will mean scheduling specific times to meet such as at the start or end of the school day, assuming the SSA is available. The reality may be that communication involves flexibility, linked to the commitments of both the teacher and SSA. This may mean that all that is available are a few brief moments snatched prior to lessons, during activity transitions or during 'quiet moments' within a lesson when children are working independently. The point is that it is worthwhile to persevere in identifying opportunities to sit down and talk, otherwise SSAs will engage in roles for which they are not fully prepared.

Thinking point

- How and when could teachers facilitate dialogue with SSAs?

At a basic level scheduling opportunities to talk will serve to ensure that you and the SSA will understand your respective roles by considering what each of you will be doing with respect to individual and group interaction linked to the instructional set for a given classroom-based learning experience. As part of this talk it may be worthwhile to consider models of co-teaching. Co-teaching will provide you, working alongside SSAs, with an opportunity to be more creative in meeting the cognitive and socio-emotional needs of an increasingly diverse classroom population. Although primarily designed to co-ordinate the activities of two teachers working together these models are nevertheless applicable to SSAs as you can determine levels of involvement of the SSA in a way that is responsive to all of the children's needs. Four models of co-teaching are worth considering:

- one teach, one observe – SSA observes behaviours of particular children or groups in support of you as the teacher, such as time on task and pattern of interaction. This can also be used to support the professional development of SSAs through observation;
- small group, different material (station teaching) – this involves you and the SSA being actively involved in instruction with children rotating through pre-planned activity stations that cover different material;
- small group, same material (parallel teaching) – this involves you introducing the lesson to the whole class followed by the SSA working with one of the groups while you work with the rest of the class;
- one teach, one support – this can be used to provide general support with the SSA 'drifting' around and interacting as and when required or to target support at particular individuals and/or groups. This also tends to be the fall-back position for most unplanned teaching interactions (adapted from Friend and Cook, 2007).

Over time, as the SSA's understanding of teaching and learning develops, it may be possible to introduce an alternative teaching approach. This would involve groups of children being provided with different instructional sets. As you deliver a planned lesson to most of the class the SSA would deliver an alternative lesson, or the same lesson taught at a different level, to a small group. This approach enables support to be provided to children who require reinforcement or those who require further challenge.

View from practice

Professional development in one primary school consisted of teachers' and SSAs' training needs being met by a combination of separate and joint

(Continued)

(Continued)

workshops, often delivered by outside agencies, supported by in-house reinforcement. Training on 'peer mediation' as part of adopting 'restorative approaches' throughout the school was initially delivered separately as part of recognition of power imbalance between teachers and SSAs, the teacher as 'boss', and it was felt important to recognise the fact that children relate differently to teachers and SSAs. However, another reason for this was to enable the 'voice' of teachers, SSAs and the children to be heard separately to help inform collaborative efforts to create a restorative environment in which teachers, SSAs and the children would have complementary roles and responsibilities. Teachers were trained to know how to direct and organise the work of the SSAs they work with. The SSAs were trained to work with the children, particularly those children who acted as mediators. Training sought to bring about a cultural change affecting everyone in the school.

In the same school digital support training, using technology to support reading, was delivered jointly as this formed part of the SSAs' generic supporting role. Having training together helped clarify the role and responsibilities of SSAs and teachers. The SSAs took responsibility for developing interactive materials as and when required by teachers who in their turn coordinated their requests for support, so exercising a management function. This development helped support the inclusion of children with difficulties in accessing text whilst at the same time encouraging teachers and SSAs to think of themselves as part of a team through the development of classroom activities linked to planning and review. The school demonstrated a commitment to developing a team ethos by adopting a whole-school approach to training.

Through talk you can support a SSA's understanding of what is needed in meeting additional support plans, for those children who have them. Taking this further you can provide SSAs with knowledge as to the methods to be used to address particular aspects of learning as well as any modifications that may be required in terms of teaching and materials to be used. It is important not to assume that the SSA understands the conceptual framework that underpins teaching nor why you choose different strategies to teach different concepts. Providing the SSA with clear explanations is essential if you are both to become a classroom team so that the SSA can help you to effectively implement the teaching plan (Hauge and Barkie, 2006). Plans do not always work in the way they are intended, so incorporating review of classroom activity and children's work will enable the classroom team to identify and implement adaptations to the curricular plan for individuals, so personalising the learning experience. This will ensure that all members of the classroom team are aware of every child's progress to avoid demarcation of responsibility for particular children, especially those with barriers to their learning, being assigned to only one member of the team.

Planning does not always remove issues with respect to appropriate pedagogical and social interactions between SSAs and children. Periodically it may be necessary, as part of the process of review, to take time to provide the SSA with insights as to how to alter their interactional matrix in order to improve their effectiveness in bringing about positive outcomes for children. This may also be necessary to promote the development of positive relationships and behaviour, for example, SSAs being proactive in identifying 'tell-tale' warning signs of disengagement and taking steps to alter this using school/classroom protocols. It is crucial that the classroom team have an agreed protocol for intervention, particularly when impediments to learning are identified. Such protocols are critically important in order that a SSA does not 'lose face' in front of the children as this would only serve to undermine any future contribution that they have to make within the classroom. It is essential that you undertake any sensitive discussions, aimed at realigning a SSA's understanding of practice, in private rather than in front of children or other colleagues (Hauge and Barkie, 2006).

Avoiding exclusion in the classroom

Blatchford et al. (2007) indicate that teachers are generally positive about the contribution of SSAs in terms of:

- increased attention and support for learning (more one-to-one attention particularly for children with ASNs);
- increased teaching effectiveness in terms of productive group work, utilisation of practical activities; and
- effective classroom management.

The presence of another adult in the classroom will provide you with the possibility to hand over to the SSA children who are most demanding of your time, for example, lower-ability children, those designated with ASN, and those with emotional and behavioural difficulties, all of whom are likely to have complex needs; SSAs working with more able children is a less common scenario. Blatchford et al. (2009) state that this is another aspect of the changing educational landscape as prior to the growth in the number of SSAs, teachers would have provided support for all the children in their classroom. The advantage of giving the SSAs the 'neediest' children is that it will free you up to focus attention on the rest of the class in order to meet their needs. This can be easily rationalised as the most vulnerable children being provided with individual support (Giangreco et al., 2005). Increasingly, SSAs assigned to accompany children with specific barriers to their learning or to aid in a more general way are being asked not only to take on responsibility for meeting the disparate support needs of children but also to assume a pedagogical role (Blatchford et al., 2007). The inherent problem with this approach, however attractive it may appear to you as the teacher, is that the least qualified adult is assigned those children with the most complex learning needs. Yet it is the teacher who has the skill set to manage complex learning and behavioural needs. This may explain, in part, why the available evidence as to the impact of SSAs on academic attainment has been largely unconvincing (Blatchford et al., 2009).

The increased adult–child interaction provided for children with barriers to their learning is mostly from SSAs rather than teachers. In working to support children with ASNs and those with emotional and behavioural difficulties, SSAs make a positive contribution to classroom management. This means that you may spend less time on dealing with 'disruptions' within a lesson, giving you more time to spend providing individual attention to the rest of the class. However, a consequence of the proximity of SSAs is that a supported child can end up having less, rather than more, contact with you as their teacher. This can be exacerbated if SSAs periodically take children out of the classroom. Even when teachers and SSAs are working within the same classroom they may well be focusing their attention on different children and adopting, in the absence of coherent planning, different approaches to teaching and patterns of interaction. For instance, SSAs tend to be less mobile than teachers with a tendency to work in one location with their designated children, while teachers are more fluid in their pattern of interaction moving between whole class, group and individual interactions. There is an inherent problem here in that SSAs are not providing additional support but alternative support; consequently although the classroom may be inclusive due to the presence of diversity it can remain exclusive with respect to practice.

The proximity of SSAs can result in them becoming 'overprotective' towards children placed under their wings, albeit borne out of misguided good intentions, leading to separation from classmates, dependency on adults and loss of personal control (Causton-Theoharis and Malmgren, 2005). SSAs often form very close relationships with children, particularly when compared to the relationships that you may be able to develop, bearing in mind that you have to address all of the children's needs (Hauge and Barkie, 2006). Some children can be in constant contact with SSAs during the course of the school day, during lessons and at break times, so minimising the extent of contact with other children and yourself. As such the SSA can provide a 'connecting bridge' between the children they have responsibility for and the teacher (Mistry et al., 2004) so it is important for you to understand this relationship in order to detect the emergence of 'nannying' (Moran and Abbott, 2002) with children seeking assistance only from the SSAs rather than from their peers or you as the teacher (Takala, 2007).

An aspect of 'nannying' to be aware of is that the challenge of your planned learning experiences can be diminished if the SSA completes the task set rather than the child (Takala, 2007), even in the absence of any request for assistance from the child to do so. This is often rationalised in terms of enabling the child to 'keep up' with the rest of the class (Moran and Abbott, 2002). Another aspect of this is that children with barriers to their learning often have difficulty with social interaction, such as misunderstanding social cues and not following social conventions of taking turns in talking. There are a number of ways by which the development of social skills can be compromised, such as removing children from the classroom environment, particularly when they are perceived as being disruptive. Other common problematic practice includes working with a child away from other children so reducing opportunities for peer interaction as well as providing incentives that reinforce social isolation, for example, individual computer time. These fairly common practices serve to reduce the amount of time that children have available to interact with their peers in the classroom and they do nothing to alleviate any difficulties with social interaction these children may already have.

View from practice

SSAs are often deployed to work with children who have social, emotional and behavioural problems in order to contribute to the inclusion of these children through developing their intrapersonal and interpersonal skills. The role of the SSA can be a challenging one as they are required to function simultaneously as social workers and educators. One such instance involved a Primary 4 (7–8 years) teacher who worked in cooperation with an SSA to support a child who engaged in inappropriate touching with peers and adults. Part of the strategy implemented to develop the child's understanding of personal space included the use of Social Stories (Gray, online). The class teacher and subsequently the SSA were trained in developing social story cartoons that involved the child. The class teacher negotiated, with the headteacher's support, a weekly planning meeting with the SSA at which time they would talk through and develop a storyline for the forthcoming week. The SSA would then develop the

(Continued)

> *(Continued)*
>
> materials in close consultation with the teacher. The SSA, rather than the 'authoritative' figure of the class teacher, would work with child on daily basis as part of their designated duties to construct a social bridge between the child and their peers by establishing what constitutes appropriate behaviour and thus nurture good relationships between the child and their classmates. The direct involvement of the SSA was critical in developing positive relationships both within and outside the classroom, particularly as the SSA had playground duties. Another important aspect of this strategy was the involvement of the SSA alongside the class teacher in reviewing the goals and objectives set out in the Additional Support Plan so keeping a tight focus on addressing the child's needs. The positive adult–child relationship that developed facilitated discussion about other issues and dialogue about progress.

The practice, during paired work, of the SSA acting as the partner rather than supporting peer interaction can also reduce the possibility of social skill development as well as compromising the learning intentions underpinning collaborative work (Causton-Theoharis and Malmgren, 2005). Opportunities for peer interaction can also be subverted by the asymmetrical power relationship between the SSA and child as, during group work, all communication can go through the SSA leading to the supported child being sidelined. Independence with adult support can be seen as a goal of inclusion; in reality this may only exacerbate social isolation within an inclusive setting as arguably the real goal is one of interdependence with peers and adults (Causton-Theoharis and Malmgren, 2005). The trap to be avoided is in assuming that because a SSA is available to a child, due to there being an identified barrier to learning, this need for support defines the possibilities for that child. That the child needs to be supported is not in question but it is important for you to encourage them to contribute to decision-making about how supports can be enacted within the context they find themselves. This could involve making adjustments to the support provided by replacing some, or all, of the support from the SSA with that of support from peers. The SSA can be located outside the group whilst remaining available to intervene when needed so allowing the children to support each other.

Summary

Regular discussion should help you foster good working relationships, so when working with a SSA it is important that you take steps to meet in order to plan, discuss classroom activities and review progress as well as to develop strategies to deal with any emerging concerns. Including SSAs in regular discussion should achieve two key goals. Firstly it will provide necessary support in developing a SSA's understanding of the issues to be addressed in bringing about progress in children's learning. That the SSA is aware of the plan and what is involved in its implementation is likely to facilitate more effective engagement with the children's learning and avoid exclusive practice. Secondly, in addressing the relational context we signal that the relationship between all those charged with providing productive learning experiences for children is one of mutual respect. Without a sense of respect participants are likely to remain closed to each other and consequently it will prove difficult to work collaboratively as SSAs in particular may feel excluded from any sense of being part of a classroom team (Mistry et al., 2004).

  Reflective questions

- In what ways can the presence of a SSA promote the inclusion agenda?
- What are the implications (for you) in working with SSA(s) who may work across several different classrooms?
- What do you see as the opportunities and challenges in helping to support the professional development of any SSA(s) that you work with?
- Can you think of ways to engage in PAIRS talk with your SSA(s)?

Further reading

Kamen, T. (2011) *Teaching Assistant's Handbook: Level 3: Supporting Teaching and Learning in School.* London: Hodder Education.

This would be a useful as a means of supporting focused professional dialogue between teachers and SSAs.

Spooner, W. (2010) *The SEN Handbook for Trainee Teachers, NQTs and Teaching Assistants.* Abingdon: Routledge.

This text provides case studies and vignettes on issues relevant to trainee teachers and Higher Level Teaching Assistants.

Further information on themes explored in 'views from practice' can be found at the Education Scotland website: http://www.educationscotland.gov.uk/

Peer mediation: Pathway to resources – Supporting Learners → 'Positive Learning Environments' → 'Positive relationships and behaviour' → 'Approaches – Restorative Approaches' → 'Peer mediation'.

and

Digital support: Pathway to resources – 'Supporting Learners' → 'Additional Support Needs' → 'Resources – Books for All'.

CHAPTER 19

WORKING TOGETHER: IMPROVEMENT THROUGH PRACTITIONER INQUIRY

Beth Dickson and Irene McQueen

Key ideas

This chapter explores:

- Why do teachers at varying stages of their careers engage in inquiry?

    o The need to understand practice
    o The concept of the extended professional
    o The role of inquiry in professional learning and development
    o The impact on pupil learning and attainment of teachers engaging in inquiry

- How can teachers engage in inquiry?

    o Identifying issues for inquiry
    o Engaging with the literature
    o Considering sources of evidence
    o Ethical conduct of inquiry

Introduction

In constant attempts to improve education, the quality of teaching staff has been cited as the area which has the greatest potential to make a difference to improving educational outcomes for learners (Darling-Hammond and Bransford, 2005). There are various ways in which education systems tend to try to improve the quality of teachers' learning. Some rely on standards which set shared expectations of what a teacher should know and be able to do. Some systems rely on continuing professional development (CPD) comprising discrete courses which are often delivered in a location other than the school. While these can be effective in introducing new knowledge, they are less effective in changing teacher behaviour or pupil outcomes (Kennedy, 2005). Some rely on prescriptive curricula which teachers are expected to 'deliver' rather than 'teach'; there is little room for professional autonomy within a prescriptive curriculum.

However, much recent consideration has been given to the role of inquiry learning in teacher education. 'Inquiry learning' enables teachers to take forward their own learning interests, often in collaboration with other members of staff. Together teachers generate answerable questions, gather evidence of various kinds and make decisions on whether or how to modify practice in the light of what has been discovered. Teachers who are not only effective and reflective, but who inquire into their practice in order to be able to modify it or justify it are sometimes described as 'extended professionals' because they are taking responsibility for their own professional learning.

Although the attention given to inquiry learning has been growing recently, educationalists have long preached its virtues. With respect to curriculum change, in the mid-twentieth century, Lawrence Stenhouse argued that teachers were the only group which could change the curriculum meaningfully because they were the only ones who knew what was going on in classrooms. Stenhouse's (1985) definition of teacher inquiry as 'systematic' inquiry 'made public' is commonly used to define the activity. 'Practitioner inquiry' is a generic title given to inquiry processes undertaken in a variety of professional settings in order to understand practice in a more sophisticated way and is often related to the completion of a higher degree or professional study. Although similar to practitioner inquiry, 'action research', commonly seen as a problem-posing inquiry process, can be distinguished from the more generic term 'practitioner inquiry'. Action research may include investigators other than teachers and may have wider emancipatory aims (Carr and Kemmis, 1986). Practitioner inquiry may be constructed as an action research project or it may use a different methodology depending on what is being investigated.

While policy voices have often declared what teachers ought to know and have tried to ensure that this knowledge is transmitted to teachers through conventional CPD courses, there has always been a significant tradition which argues that teachers have within themselves, or, in collaboration with others, the capacity to improve their teaching. Such arguments find their way into government-commissioned reports. Although not discussing practitioner inquiry as such, in a general way, *Introducing the Cambridge Primary Review* (Hofkins and Northen, 2009: 34) argues that 'the seeds of open enquiry' should be sown in initial teacher education and specifically *Teaching Scotland's Future* (Donaldson, 2011: 42) argues that inquiry should be a significant strand in career-long teacher learning. Collaborative inquiry is often associated with a high view of teachers as competent, autonomous and trusted professionals.

Practitioner inquiry: what is it?

Practitioner inquiry is a form of professional inquiry and learning. In the teaching profession it is built on a knowledge base about processes of learning and how these emerge within a particular subject area. Practitioner inquiry differs from empirical sociological research in that it is undertaken by practitioners (rather than professional researchers) with a view to finding things out in order to improve outcomes for pupils. Although it is important to be open-minded, self-critical and systematic in procedures, the findings which result from the process will be used to understand and therefore improve learning. Improvement may take many forms: improvement in attitudes towards learning, in relationships amongst peers, in the quality of learning, or improvement through attainment as measured in test scores. It is sometimes argued that this bias toward improvement skews understanding of the issues being explored. However, most education systems have particular problems which they desire to improve – often related to under-attainment of children who lack literal or social capital. Most teachers regard these sorts of issues as social blights and are highly motivated to eradicate them. From this value-base, inquiry is a powerful tool to help teachers understand the context in which they work.

Inquiry is often set up collaboratively. This is important because much teacher learning takes place through dialogue. A group of teachers may come up with an area which they wish to find out more about and can work as a group, or in pairs, in order to establish an inquiry. A partner may be able to offer in-class support in observation or recording of data. The key point is that teachers discuss their findings with each other and understand them in the light of what is already known about the inquiry topic. Collaboration not only includes dialogue with other colleagues but can be broadened to include those who research education professionally. While inquiries are often undertaken by a pair or group of colleagues, they can be facilitated by educationalists who have an expert interest in the area of focus or in the techniques often associated with practitioner inquiry: journal keeping, observation, peer dialogue, feedback and recording of data.

The phrase 'inquiry as stance' was coined by Marilyn Cochran-Smith and Susan L. Lytle (1999). While the processes are common to many varieties of practitioner research, 'inquiry as stance' implies a set of emancipatory values:

> In our work, we offer the term inquiry as stance to describe the positions teachers and others who work together in inquiry communities take towards knowledge and its relationship to practice. We use the metaphor of stance to suggest both orientational and positional ideas, to carry allusions to the physical placing of the body as well as to intellectual and activities over time. In this sense, the metaphor is intended to capture the ways we stand, the ways we see and the lenses we see through. Teaching is a complex activity that occurs within webs of social, historical, cultural and political significance. (Cochran-Smith and Lytle, 1999: 288–9)

These sorts of values have been forged in order to improve educational outcomes for students from a diverse range of social backgrounds with the aim of creating 'the kind of schooling that can sustain a just and democratic society' in the US, which often conceives of teaching as an activity which is instrumental and the quality of which can be ensured by performative measurement (Cochran-Smith and Lytle, 2009: 152). Inquiry as stance is not only predicated on improvement but also on challenging the status quo in order to generate democratic debate about forces and beliefs which continue to exclude children who do not have a white middle-class background. It is here that practitioner research impinges on inclusion – one of the chief challenges of twenty-first century education. Inquiry learning provides a means by which teachers can interrogate their own values and beliefs with a view to examining the extent to which they develop or hinder learning (Baumfield et al., 2008).

Why would teachers engage with inquiry learning?

There are a number of benefits to practitioner inquiry. Teachers who engage in practitioner inquiry understand more clearly what is happening in the learning of their students. They also are able to communicate better with each other about teaching and learning. This is important given the tacit nature of much teacher learning. The ability of teachers to speak about learning means that they are able to communicate more effectively with parents and with other professionals. Inquiry learning has also been linked with sustaining motivation – very important across a career which can last for more than four decades – and for those who have been introduced to it after a period where teaching has become highly routinised, inquiry learning has even been linked to professional renewal.

Impact on pupil outcomes: two examples from literacy

Most descriptions of inquiry focus on why it is theoretically important and how it should be done to the point of disseminating the results of inquiry to broader communities of interest. However, in order to illustrate some of the debates around practitioner inquiry here are two practitioner inquiries which focus on pupil experiences and outcomes.

Inquiry 1

In 'Learning about Literacy: Children's versions of the Literacy Hour', Veronica Hanke (2011) describes an inquiry she undertook as a practising teacher in an action research project jointly undertaken by a group of primary school teachers and the University of Cambridge's School of Education. The inquiry examines the responses of 5-year-olds to the prescribed teaching of the Literacy Hour, then part of the English National Literacy Strategy, by asking them to annotate drawings of each quarter of the literacy hour. On the basis of 28 annotated A3 drawings she elicited a wide range of pupil responses. Some children enjoyed the reading of the text and the work that followed it. Others found the work hard and were anxious about displaying their work in the final plenary because they knew they often made mistakes. With her colleagues on the project Hanke was able to discuss how to interpret the children's drawings. Her findings led Hanke to question the prescribed pedagogy by comparing it with the work of Vivian Gussin Paley whose pedagogies were more open-ended. From this study Hanke cannot say whether such reactions will continue as pupils grow older or whether they are true of all 5-year-olds. Such questions of validity and generalisability are often used to point to limitations in inquiry learning as a research process when compared with empirical quantitative studies which can lay claim to generalisability. However, as Campbell et al. (2004) point out, 'this research tradition emphasises the context-specific nature of all stages of its methodology ... and tentative and highly provisional conclusions... [The contextualist] would not see this as a problem but rather an inevitable aspect of social inquiry' (Campbell et al., 2004: 8). The persona which emerges from this study is of a hard-working, intelligent, thoughtful and responsible teacher who is genuinely troubled by the constraints on her pedagogy. Inquiry is not a soft option nor need it be a mechanical process. Rather it tends to end in further questions rather than solutions and some of the emergent questions are very searching, going to the foundations of national policies and educational values. It is also apparent that inquiry develops the learning of the teacher as much as it opens up opportunities for improvement for pupils.

Inquiry 2

The issue of the impact on pupil outcomes is faced squarely in the work of Helen Timperley and her colleagues. In 'Promoting professional inquiry for improved outcomes for students in New Zealand', they argue that,

> Broadly speaking, approaches to professional development have either focused on developing better prescriptions for teaching practice or on collaborative reflective inquiry into practice. Neither approach has been particularly effective in achieving substantive improvement in student outcomes. (Timperley et al., 2009: 227)

In their project, practitioner inquiry was sited in a broader research context funded by government in order to find out whether practitioner inquiry which specifically focused on improved pupil outcomes could indeed lead to improved outcomes. External facilitators worked with teachers to identify *teacher learning needs* as a consequence of pupil learning needs. The project took place in 218 primary schools over two years and the focus for investigation was either reading comprehension or writing. Through initial interviews with students, teachers could identify where students found difficulty with writing. Teachers were surprised to find out that pupils were vague about what was being expected of them in writing but they (the teachers) then knew where they had to address their efforts. Teachers were facilitated to engage with written sources to develop their professional knowledge. Some senior teachers were trained in observation methods and in giving feedback because teachers were not sure that their current skills would enable them to enact in the classroom what they had come to understand that they needed to do and they indicated that they would benefit from feedback from other colleagues. As the process continued, teachers would check with pupils to see whether the actions that the teachers had taken had made a difference. Again modifications to practice would be undertaken in order to improve learning.

This project demonstrated an improvement in the reading and writing of students. Here are the writing results:

> The average effect size gain (Cohen, 1977) (relative to where the students started) on standardised assessments for schools that chose to focus on writing was 1.28 for the first cohort and 1.05 for the second cohort, equivalent to approximately twice the expected gain for all students in the country over the two years of the project. For the lowest 20% of students, the target group of students, the effect size was 2.05 for the first cohort and 2.53 for the second cohort, which is approximately four times the expected gain for all nationally students over the two years. (Timperley et al., 2009: 236)

This technical conclusion is quoted in full to demonstrate the type of basic statistical language in which teachers will become proficient as they deepen their familiarity with inquiry. As pupils showed improvements in learning and attainment, teachers also reported greater pleasure in teaching writing and in being in control of their own professional learning (Timperley et al., 2009: 239).

While the two inquiries contrast in scale and scope, with Hanke's inquiry being more typical of the genre and Timperley's a large-scale government-funded project which took place in a number of schools, there are also comparisons. Teachers are motivated to learn in order to enable their pupils to achieve better outcomes. Teacher learning in both studies was facilitated to a greater or lesser extent by externals, required engagement with the current literature, took place over an extended period and required 'checking' to see whether teacher actions had had any effect on learning. A key feature of both inquiries is the intensity and reciprocity of the relationship between the teacher and the student. When students can achieve what they are supposed to be learning, they are more motivated to learn; when teachers understand what students need to do to learn and take steps to ensure that they know how to respond to that, the improvement in student learning is deeply motivating and satisfying for them. It would appear that this focus on the teacher-student relationship, not on one partner or the other, is integral to the learning process and when the learning relationship becomes the object of improvement for both parties the outcomes of improvement, that is, satisfaction and pleasure, are seen. Such outcomes are rarely described in the literature on performativity.

Challenges

Establishing inquiry processes in schools can be challenging. The benefits of practitioner inquiry are not universally acknowledged for a number of reasons. Some argue that the inquiries are weak and skewed by the bias to improvement. Time is needed for teachers to come together and talk about their focus for inquiry. As teachers are busy professionals, the time needed to inquire systematically needs to be sanctioned and structured by school leaders or required by initial teacher education curricula. In this context, time is money and school leaders may wish to direct resource to other areas of work. Depending on where teachers have been educated or how recently they have been educated, relatively junior members of staff may have more formal knowledge than senior staff who will be able to draw on greater experience. Roles and identities can become tense in such situations and work needs to be undertaken from the outset in sharing purposes and values of inquiry. Undertaking an inquiry when you are on a student placement can prove difficult if the placement is short and you are concentrating on passing your assessment well, especially if the ethos of the school does not include a focus on inquiry. These difficulties surface in different forms in continuing practice. Adopting 'inquiry as stance' will, at least, mean being curious about how learning occurs.

How teachers can engage in inquiry

The impetus to conduct an inquiry will almost certainly stem from a situation, incident, or need that has presented itself in the classroom. As a beginning teacher, or an experienced practitioner, issues will continue to arise in the context of your professional life which require you to reconsider accepted practice, refresh your thinking on teaching and learning or find out how to improve relationships and interactions in order to impact positively on pupil learning.

While the view might be taken that only when you have been in the classroom for a period of time can you begin to inquire into practice, it is becoming more readily accepted that practitioner inquiry should be part of initial teacher development to embed the knowledge, skills and conceptual understanding of inquiry-based professional development from the earliest phase of teacher education. In *Teaching Scotland's Future*, the author recommends that '(e)xploration of theory through practice should be central to all placement experiences – emphasising effective professional practice, reflection, critical analysis and evidence-based decision making' (Donaldson, 2011: 42). The inclusion of evidence-based decision making in this statement is important as it provides the teacher with demonstrable affirmation of the impact of what they do in the classroom.

Taking an inquiry stance to teaching involves practitioners learning from investigating their own practice. But, unlike other forms of research, its approach is about improving rather than proving aspects of practice (Campbell, 2007). Practitioner inquiry is not anecdotal and not based on supposition. It should have substance and be the result of a conscious desire to improve practice for the benefit of learners.

According to Fletcher (online):

> Teachers' action research is on-going professional development for teachers, by teachers rather than being done to teachers by outside 'experts'. It is a form of systematic inquiry undertaken by individuals or groups who share a passion to improve their own and others' teaching and learning to support students in school.

Therefore it is important for teachers, at whatever stage of their career, to have space to engage in systematic thinking about their practice and to be able critically to review and debate the relationship between policy, practice, theory and research. An inquiry stance enables evaluation of teaching and learning through engagement with and engagement in research.

So how can teachers engage in practitioner inquiry? Dana and Yendol-Silva (2009: 7) suggest that '(t)eacher inquiry invites intentional, planned reflection, heightening your focus on problem posing'. This necessitates construction of a question or formulation of a focus for the inquiry. Once this is achieved the stages of the inquiry are to read around the topic, to plan how to gather evidence and then implement the strategy in the classroom in order to effect the change. The rest of this section will look at each of these stages in turn.

Formulating a focus for an inquiry

The types of potential inquiries will be many and varied. Every classroom is different because it is made up of different individuals (including the teacher and other support workers) with different intentions, learning needs and aspirations. Here are some of the questions students have posed which have arisen from their experiences:

- In what ways can ability grouping promote pupil motivation?
- What causes a student's motivation in school to deteriorate as they become older?
- Can co-operative learning raise attainment in mixed ability geography classes?
- I would like to learn more about the role of praise in motivating learners.
- Does providing a nurturing environment at school help to motivate learning?
- Do rewards have a positive impact on a child's behaviour in the classroom?

As can be seen from the range of questions, the areas of interest are extensive. These questions do not appear fully formed. They can have small beginnings which may be more akin to 'wonderings' (Dana and Yendol-Silva, 2009) or 'hunches' (Baumfield et al., 2008). So an idea or reflection in a classroom setting can develop from an initial thought, to identifying the issue, to the formulation of a question which is capable of investigation.

Thinking point

- Why not try identifying your own 'hunch' and developing your own question from it?

Literature

The next stage is to review the available literature on the topic of your inquiry. For students engaged in initial teacher education this is unproblematic as they will have access to their institution's library of research, theoretical textbooks and academic journals. The same is true for teachers engaged in further study through, for example, a university. However, for the practitioner in post accessing reading is sometimes not so straightforward. It is an issue for local authorities and senior management in schools to consider because without easy access to the educational literature and research, how can the integration of theory and practice be fused in the career-long development of teachers?

There is, of course, the world wide web which can make access to literature easier if you know how to search efficiently and effectively. Google Guide (http://www.googleguide.com/) will help give you tips on effective searching. Google Scholar (http://scholar.google.co.uk/) will retrieve scholarly literature. It is important to bear in mind the need to evaluate internet sources. The key questions to ask are:

- Do you think the information is accurate?
- Is it written by an authority on the subject?
- Is it objective or biased in some way?
- Is the information current?
- Is the coverage of the subject comprehensive enough?
- Is there contact information should you wish further information?

Thinking point

- What literature is available about your choice of inquiry? Try doing a search for current reading on the issue.

Sources of evidence

In order to investigate the topic, there needs to be a period of data collection. There is a plethora of educational research methods books on the market which will give ideas for data collection methods and outline the advantages and disadvantages of different tools (see, inter alia, Baumfield et al., 2008; Bell, 2010; Elton-Chalcraft et al., 2008). Significant sources of evidence for the practitioner are:

- observation;
- pupil voice;
- interviews and focus groups;
- inquiry diary;
- assessment evidence;
- focused study;
- documentary evidence.

The important questions to ask about gathering evidence are:

- Why are you collecting this evidence?
- What exactly are you collecting? (What different sources of evidence will allow you to learn best about your inquiry? How much evidence do you need to really learn about this topic?)
- Where are you going to collect the evidence and for how long? (Are there ways to build evidence-gathering into the normal activities of the classroom?)
- When are you going to collect the evidence and for how long? (Can you afford the time to gather and record evidence using the strategies you have selected?)
- Who is going to collect the evidence? (Is there evidence which can be generated by pupils? Is there a colleague who can observe in your classroom who can assist with evidence gathering?)

Thinking point

- What evidence could you gather to illuminate your inquiry?

Ethical conduct of practitioner inquiry

An aspect of practitioner inquiry which it might be easy to overlook is the effect of carrying out an inquiry on the participants in that inquiry. The participants might be the young people in the class, parents, or other professional colleagues. Practitioners engaged in inquiry:

> must consider the extent to which their own reflective research impinges on others, for example in the case of the dual role of teacher and researcher and the impact on students and colleagues. Dual roles may also introduce explicit tensions in areas such as confidentiality and must be addressed accordingly. (BERA, 2011: 5)

Campbell and Groundwater-Smith (2007: 5–6) suggest that in order to avoid ethical concerns during inquiry, teachers should:

- research 'with' rather than 'on' practitioners;
- find secure procedures for research with children, especially those who are vulnerable or have special educational needs.

Teachers' Standards (Department of Education, 2013a), *Code of Values and Professional Practice* (GTCNI, 2004), the *Standards for Registration* (GTCS, 2012) and the

Code of Professional Conduct and Practice for Registered Teachers (GTCW, 2010) lay out clearly the requirement for professional integrity which is the foundation of any form of classroom inquiry.

View from practice

Vignette 1

Ms Stewart teaches a class of nine-year-olds in inner city Glasgow with pupils from a range of different ethnic backgrounds including some refugee children. She is interested in using co-operative learning approaches in her classroom and wants to know about the views of her pupils on the advantages and disadvantages of working together in class. She decides to conduct an inquiry on this issue, beginning with a baseline questionnaire of what the pupils think before she tries some co-operative learning approaches and then a follow-up questionnaire at the end of term.

What ethical issues might arise and how should they be addressed?

Vignette 2

Mr Shah has been using video to record lessons whilst he has been experimenting with assertive discipline techniques with the 14-year-olds in his maths class. He has been asked to give a presentation about his experiences of using this approach to behaviour management to colleagues in his subject association at their next local meeting.

What does he need to have considered before agreeing to give the presentation?

Thinking point

- Are there any ethical considerations surrounding your choice of inquiry? What are they and how would you resolve them?

Summary

In this chapter we have considered the purposes, nature and content of practitioner inquiry as an aspect of developing teacher professionalism which inquires into practice in order to improve learning for pupils. We have discussed the advantages and disadvantages of inquiry and have given an overview of the stages commonly associated with inquiry. We have argued that the implementation of inquiry learning will increase teacher professionalism.

Reflective questions

- How would you define practitioner inquiry?
- What is the difference between practitioner inquiry and 'traditional' professional development of teachers?
- Do you agree there is a distinction between reflection and inquiry?

Further reading

Learning how to learn: http://www.learntolearn.ac.uk/
Schools of Ambition: http://www.scotland.gov.uk/Publications/2010/10/27132811/2
Teaching and Learning Research Programme: http://www.tlrp.org/index.html
Teacher Research: http://www.teacherresearch.net/

CHAPTER **20**

LEADERSHIP FOR LEARNING: THE EVOLVING ROLE OF THE PRIMARY TEACHER

Christine Forde and Margery McMahon

Key ideas

This chapter explores:

- pedagogic vision;
- visible learning;
- professional learning communities;
- career-long professional learning;
- leadership for learning for all.

Introduction

The idea of 'leadership for learning' has become a key theme in education. There is an increasing body of work investigating the educative variant of the more general concept of 'leadership' and the term 'leadership for learning' is used to characterise the important link between leadership and learning in education. The term, however, is often used loosely in policy and guidance materials for teachers with little precision in terms of its meaning and particularly with regard to the sets of practices that would constitute 'leadership for learning'. This idea of 'leadership for learning' is used variously to describe the responsibilities and activities of those in formal management roles in schools as well as the activities of teachers who have a predominantly pedagogic focus and a classroom remit. The focus of this chapter is on the latter, the form of leadership for learning exercised by teachers.

This book has explored a wide variety of areas related to the role of the primary teacher: child development, aspects of the curriculum and pedagogic approaches. This chapter seeks to build on the aspects discussed in earlier chapters by exploring the meaning and implications of characterising a primary teacher as a 'leader *for* learning'. Macbeath and Dempster (2009) identify five key principles of leadership for learning evident in different educational contexts:

- a focus on learning: learning is the central concern of everyone in a school and shapes the work and experiences of all members of the school's community;
- creating the conditions favourable to learning: the culture of the school encourages and provides the opportunities for learning and ensures that learning is celebrated;
- creating a learning dialogue: learning experiences are explored and shared by all involved in teaching and learning including teachers, support staff and pupils;
- the sharing of leadership: in the day-to-day life of schools drawing on the experience and expertise of all members of the community through collaboration and discussion is evident and everyone is encouraged to take a lead role in a range of tasks and activities to which they can contribute;
- shared accountability: all members of the school community engage regularly in self evaluation based on the evidence and values in order to improve learning.

Our intention in this chapter is to draw from these discussions of leadership for learning in order to challenge some of the policy rhetoric around the idea of leadership for learning. Here we highlight some of the tensions in this idea and then build a model of leadership for learning which reflects the changing expectations of primary teachers as teacher leaders (Murphy, 2005). We do this by exploring firstly, the underpinnings of a pedagogic vision upon which leadership for learning needs to be grounded. Secondly, we consider how this pedagogic vision of leadership for learning should shape 'leadership *of* learning', that is how this vision shapes the pedagogic practice of teachers working with learners. If this pedagogic vision is to be realised in sets of pedagogic practices that enhance the learning experiences of pupil then teachers' own professional learning is critical and so we explore the idea of 'leadership *by* learning' and consider the relationship between teacher learning and pupil learning. Here we suggest that if teachers are to exercise leadership for learning, fresh approaches to teachers' education and career-long development are necessary.

Leadership for learning: vision, values and purposes

There is an extensive literature related to leadership, including leadership in education, and across this wide ranging discussion the central idea is that of 'leadership as influence'. The focus is on 'transformational leadership' (Leithwood et al., 1999) where leaders influence others to achieve specific purposes. In this broad definition there is no determination of the quality and ethical nature of the specific purposes to be realised. Given recent historical experiences of examples of leadership that have inflicted immense harm on groups of people, and indeed on whole nations, there is a need to add greater substance to this idea of 'leadership as influence'. In an educational context an important focus is the role of leadership in building the culture to generate and work towards a shared vision and set of purposes (Bass and Riggio, 2006). Here 'vision' is a broad term used to characterise the sense of purpose and aims of a particular enterprise such as a school: a leader works with the members of the school to build a 'vision' of what the school and its community should be working towards collectively (Davies, 2011). The values are those principles upon which the strategies used by educators to work towards this vision must be based and assessed; these values are related to education and learning and to wider socio-political issues such as equality, fairness, sustainability and social justice.

While much is written about the importance of school leaders, especially headteachers, in building a shared vision and a common set of purposes, we need to consider the implications for primary teachers who work collaboratively to build a shared vision for the leadership for learning in their school and classroom. The idea of a shared vision underpinning the work of a primary school is crucial but there are significant tensions, particularly when there is increasing political direction around the purposes and outcomes of education. Educational policy is now part of a wider set of social and economic policies. Thus across the globe many countries are looking to education as the means of building greater social cohesion, especially in increasingly diverse societies. At the same time, education is the means of enhancing economic performance by producing a highly skilled workforce necessary for economic growth in a globalised economy (OECD, 2010; Barber and Mourshed, 2007).

Debates around what should be included in the school curriculum are an example of some of the tensions related to the development of a shared vision and sets of values in education. In England, the Secretary of State for Education's ambition to build a common set of values around the nature of 'Britishness' by specifying the purpose and content of areas of the curriculum has provoked considerable debate. In Scotland and in Wales we can see a similar political influence with the drive for a set of values related to national identity: placing Scottish literature and culture or Welsh language and culture as core elements in the curriculum.

The role of education as part of 'nation building' is evident in education in the UK and so the constructing of a shared vision and set of values lies not simply within the context of the school. Instead, schools have become the means by which a common set of values are engendered across different sections of society. The examples above illustrate education as a means of conserving social and cultural traditions. Education also has a role in achieving social change by not only enabling pupils from disadvantaged or minority groups to be able to progress through education into a range of occupations that might not previously been available to them but also by contributing to the nurturing of values related to social justice and equality among learners.

When we look at the exercise of leadership for learning by a primary teacher we can see the critical importance of vision and values as the basis for practice. In Scotland, for example, in a major reform programme of the curriculum for ages 3–18 years, a set of values underpins the purposes of the *Curriculum for Excellence* (SE, 2004b). The outcomes of the *Curriculum for Excellence* are the four capacities: successful learners, confident individuals, effective contributors and responsible citizens. Underpinning these capacities is firstly, a sense of the importance of effective learning both for the individual and for the wider society and secondly, there is also a clear stance in terms of an inclusive approach with all learners engaging in meaningful and productive learning experiences that enable them to achieve their potential. The values upon which the curriculum programme is based are complemented by the statement of values for the teaching profession set out in the professional standards for teachers in Scotland: social justice, trust and respect, integrity, professional commitment (GTCS, 2012).

Teachers need to be able to articulate their own values, argue for them and draw upon these in the daily life of classrooms. At the same time teachers need to recognise that values in education can be deeply contested. There are increasingly explicit statements about the purposes, outcomes and underpinning values in education. At one level these values seem uncontroversial and indeed there is a sense that any right-minded teacher would, of course, hold these values. However, there is a danger that these statements of values are part of the technologies of managerialism which seek to regulate and systematise professional practice and to contain the exercise of professional autonomy in decision making and practice. Tensions come to the fore when these values are tested in situations where there are limited opportunities, resources and support; decisions have to be made and actions taken that may advantage one group or individual over other individuals and groups. Murphy (2007) identifies such questions as ethical dilemmas – situations where not only is no simple solution but any solution you come to will disadvantage some group or individual. Murphy examines these dilemmas in terms of the role of a headteacher in school and the decisions he or she will have to make. This question of dealing with ethical dilemmas is equally applicable to the role of a primary teacher in the classroom. A primary teacher will be faced every day with situations where they will be called upon to make decisions about how much effort, time and resources should be spend on particular areas. In the high stakes accountability climate that schools and teachers work in currently, test results become the measure of effective education. In such circumstances does a teacher narrowly comply and choose 'to teach to the test', that is engage in a programme of rote learning whereby pupils are enabled to succeed at the test? Such an approach runs counter to sets of values related to the importance of deep learning and of pupil autonomy in learning. Further, in such pressurised situations does a teacher focus on those pupils who are likely to score better with a little extra support – at the cost of those pupils experiencing the types of difficulties that would make it unlikely that they would score well (Diamond and Spillane, 2004)? It is in examples such as these that we can see where external imperatives, which are often politically driven and lack any sense of educational purpose, clash with the values of the profession. There is no easy solution for the individual teacher and so ultimately the only way in which a course of action can be decided on is, as Murphy (2007) argues, the basis of values. For primary teachers 'leadership *for* learning' is about developing personal and professional codes (Shapiro and Stefkovich, 2011) and working consciously with others to build and sustain a sense of purpose and a vision to shape the work of the school or the department.

Thinking point

If effective learning for all, then, is the core value: what courses of action would you suggest a teacher takes in the circumstances outlined above?

Leadership of learning: developing pedagogy

Schools are situated in a context where there is rapid change, socially, economically and technologically and in these dynamic circumstances the limitations of top-down reform programmes are being gradually recognised. Against this backdrop another way of looking at leadership and learning is to examine the means by which a primary teacher 'leads learning': what approaches and activities does a teacher use to promote pupil learning and achievement. Here it could be argued that this idea of 'leadership *of* learning' is simply another way of describing teaching and by substituting the word 'leadership' for teaching there is a danger that we overlook the pivotal importance of teaching. This is a considerable concern but this idea of 'leadership of learning' helps to focus on the importance of seeing the success of teaching in terms of the learning outcomes achieved by pupils, and so this idea helps surface the relationship between teaching and learning and the importance of the pupil's agency.

The Teaching for Understanding Framework (TfUF) that was designed at Harvard University in the 1990s (Wiske, 1998) is in many ways an antecedent for current strategies that promote 'visible learning' (Hattie, 2009). The framework emphasises four key concepts: performances of understanding, generative topics, understanding goals and ongoing assessment. A core focus is on learners being able to demonstrably show or 'perform' their learning and understanding. Thus effectiveness in teaching is in terms of its impact on pupil learning. Hattie (2009) has taken the question of effectiveness in teaching further in his concept of 'visible learning'. Over a 20-year period Hattie has conducted a study of the impact of specific interventions or strategies teachers used to shape pupil learning by conducting over 800 meta analyses of specific approaches. In each of these meta analyses, Hattie has drawn together a wide range of studies conducted in different contexts with different groups of pupils to examine the effect that a particular strategy has on pupil achievement, for example, the use of feedback. Through these meta-analyses Hattie argues that most strategies have 'an effect' on pupil learning but the crucial issue is the size of this effect. By making pupil learning visible, teachers can assess the effectiveness of specific strategies.

While the outcomes of student learning are central to both approaches, Hattie (2012) has also highlighted the importance of the teacher. He proposes that the role of the teacher is 'to evaluate the effect I have on my students' (p. 19) and argues that we need 'powerful, passionate and accomplished teachers' (p. 19). Therefore 'leadership *of* learning' relates to the pedagogic expertise of the teacher who can determine what sets of strategies are appropriate for making learning visible for different groups of learners. Thus a teacher as a 'leader of learning' will be able to draw from a wide repertoire of strategies as well as from a strong values position.

The Teaching and Learning International Study (TALIS) report, *Teaching Practices and Pedagogical Innovation* (Vieluf et al., 2012) also found that it is a combination of different practices that is most promising for supporting both cognitive and non-cognitive student development. These include:

- enhanced activities including challenging tasks and content;
- student-oriented, supportive practices; and
- teacher-directed practices that provide structure and clarity (Vieluf et al., 2012: 118).

This recognises the highly complex and skilled dimensions of teachers' work. The study highlighted key features of teachers' professional practice based on research undertaken in 23 countries. These included:

- Teacher professional practices encompass both teaching practices in the classroom and broader professional practices that shape the school-learning environment.
- Instructional quality is complex. There is no single best way of teaching and teachers continually must adapt their practices to serve the needs of the specific context, class and students.
- A combination of a constructivist and of a more direct approach to instruction is needed.
- The concept of a school as a learning organisation is gaining popularity in education and considers teachers as part of a professional learning community with a high level of collaboration, coherent activities of professional development and shared practices.
- Cross-cultural research suggests that pedagogical traditions and national cultures have considerable influences on the use of teacher professional practices (Vieluf et al., 2012: 26).

Increasingly teachers are becoming involved in new sets of professional practices that require them to design, implement, assess and evaluate learning interventions and opportunities for a range of learners, including their teaching peers, in their classroom and schools. Capability to do this effectively is contingent upon their ongoing professional learning and development and the extent to which they exhibit leadership of their own learning as well.

 Thinking point

When you try out a new strategy in the classroom, how you do assess the success of this approach?

Leadership by learning: teachers working and learning together

Increasingly there is an awareness of the impact of the culture and ethos on pupils' attitudes to learning and so on their achievement. Sergiovanni (1994) highlighted the importance of conceiving a school as a community and part of this community is the educative process. Learning within this school community involves not just pupils but all members of the school and its extended community, including teachers and parents.

The influence of international benchmarking schemes such as the Programme for International Student Assessment (PISA) and governments' response to national performance in such tests, has also begun to exert considerable influence on learning and teaching in recent years. Research, such as TALIS, undertaken by supranational organisations like the Organisation for Economic Cooperation and Development (OECD), provides evidence across systems of the range of approaches to learning and teaching that are adopted and gives some measure of their effectiveness (Vieluf et al., 2012).

There is broad recognition that supporting teachers' professional learning and development is central to achieving improved outcomes for young people and this has resulted in the reconceptualisation of 'teachers as learners' and their career-long professional development. This has led to a re-examination of approaches to teachers' professional education and the sites of professional learning. There has been much research into the nature, type and impact of teachers' professional learning (for example, Timperley, et al., 2007) and from this some key principles have been distilled. Two key factors are the importance of teachers' working and learning together in collaborative ways and the centrality of the classroom as the focus for teachers' learning. Approaches that reflect these include 'clinical approaches' to initial preparation, and a range of approaches to teacher continuing learning, including learning rounds, collaborative professional enquiries, 'Lesson Studies' and teacher learning communities or professional learning communities. Below we look at learning communities and consider the ways in which they promote a climate of leadership for learning in schools.

Thinking point

As a beginning teacher you may already have some experienced some of the approaches to teachers' professional learning mentioned above. From your experience what has seemed to be most effective and why?

One of most effective approaches to teachers' professional learning that has been adopted in many schools is the establishment of professional learning communities (PLCs) or teacher learning communities (TLCs). As Stoll et al. (2006) acknowledge in their review of professional learning communities there is no universal definition of a professional learning community. They found, however, that there appears to be:

> a broad international consensus that it suggests a group of people sharing and critically interrogating their practice in an ongoing, reflective, collaborative, inclusive, learning-orientated, growth promoting way; operating as a collective enterprise. (Stoll et al., 2006: 222)

Many of the principles and practices associated with professional learning communities have been influenced by Richard DuFour's work (2004). In setting up a PLC DuFour advised that teachers should 'focus on learning rather than teaching, work collaboratively, and hold yourself accountable for results'. For him, PLCs should focus on 3 'big ideas': ensuring that pupils learn; a culture of collaboration; a focus on results (DuFour, 2004). The OECD TALIS study, *Teaching Practices and Pedagogical Innovation*, identified 5 essential elements or condition for professional learning communities:

- cooperation;
- shared vision;
- focus on learning;
- reflective inquiry;
- deprivatisation of practice.

The 'deprivatisation of practice' is an important element in changing cultures and climates for learning. While primary teachers routinely work together with stage partners, the TALIS study suggests that collaboration needs to go beyond this:

> A critical appraisal and ideas for improvement from colleagues are not part of everyday teaching in schools. *De-privatization of practice* has the goal to end this isolation of teachers. It implies talking about practice and sharing ideas and problems, but it also involves opening up one's own practice to other adults through programmes of peer coaching, teamed teaching and structured classroom observations. Teachers observe each other, give feedback, and act as mentor, advisor or specialist. (Vieluf et al., 2012: 35)

As we noted above, leadership for learning is part of a wider shift in how schools are organised and led and the ways in which positive cultures and climates for learning are fostered. This shift towards more distributed and democratic forms of leadership in schools, where teachers are empowered to lead within and beyond their classrooms is seen as central to improved learning for young people. Research undertaken to inform discussions at the first International Summit on the Teaching

Profession in 2011 looked at the successful features of high performing systems, as measured by PISA scores. It found that:

> in many high-performing education systems teachers do not only have a central role to play in improving educational outcomes, they are also at the centre of the improvement efforts themselves. In these systems it is not that top-down reforms are ordering teachers to change, but that teachers embrace and lead reform, taking responsibility as professionals. (Asia Society, 2011: 5)

This emphasis on teachers' improvement reflects a concern globally with the question of teacher quality but also recognises that teacher learning needs to model the pedagogical approaches that are routinely part of their classroom practice. As national curricula change to become more inquiry-led, interdisciplinary, personalised and collaborative, then teachers' learning needs to embrace similar approaches to enable them to design and lead learning for themselves, their pupils and their teaching peers. PLCs and TLCs give teachers both the legitimacy and space to develop this.

One of the distinguishing features of PLCs or TLCs is that they are teacher-driven rather than overseen by school leaders. While the latter may participate and contribute it is the teacher-led dimension of such learning communities that enables then to be generative and organic. Coordination and leadership of such communities generally rotates around the members and through this members can gain experience in coordinating and leading professional learning for themselves and their peers.

View from practice

Leading a professional learning community

Sam is in the third year of her teaching career. Having successfully completed her newly qualified (NQT) year, she is keen to consolidate her professional experiences and practice.

She is undecided about the possible future directions in teaching that she may take but is enjoying working in a long-established school with a good reputation in the local community. A new head teacher was appointed just before Sam arrived and the new senior management team (SMT) have been working to try to promote learning for teachers as well as pupils. Sam has recently resumed studies with a local university and is engaged in a postgraduate programme of study on effective classroom learning.

One of the initiatives that the new headteacher and SMT have introduced is teacher learning communities (TLC). Last year Sam participated in a TLC that chose to focus on assessment. This year the TLC has chosen to focus on literacy across the curriculum. Sam is delighted with this choice as she feels she is developing expertise in this area. She focused on this for her final year dissertation and it is one of the first modules she will undertake in her postgraduate programme.

The first meeting of the TLC is imminent and Sam knows that role of TLC leader will be discussed. She would like to take on this role as she feels she has the developing expertise and commitment to take forward the agreed focus of literacy of across the curriculum. She has some doubts, however, about whether she could volunteer for this role.

She is concerned that some of the staff might consider that she is too young and lacks professional experience. She knows, however, that already she has a wealth of learning, gained from her own reading, research and practice that could really make contribution to the work of the TLC. Although she feels she knows most of the staff, she has only worked directly and collaboratively with her stage partners. Working with other staff would require her to extend and develop her skills in working across the school. Leading the TLC seems like a great opportunity but Sam is not sure.

What would you advise Sam to do?

PLCs and TLCs are one current manifestation of how teachers are able to influence, contribute to and lead learning within their schools. There are many ways in which such 'teacher leadership' is evident in schools. While specific schemes such as the Advanced Skills Teacher in England and the Chartered Teacher Initiative in Scotland were designed to enable accomplished teachers to lead learning, increasingly classroom teachers have greater opportunities to contribute to specialist projects or short-life working groups within their own school, cluster or federation and in many cases, within the wider education system. This recognises the expertise that teachers gain as they advance in their teaching career and that is developed through their ongoing professional learning (Forde and McMahon, 2011).

Thinking point

- To what extent should teachers be involved in leading the learning of their peers?
- What are some of the benefits of this? Are there any disadvantages?

Summary: Learning for all

Leadership for learning is occupying a favoured place in the policy discourses and there is a danger that such an idea lacks real substance in shaping teaching practices and as a consequence improving the learning experiences of pupils in classrooms. In this chapter we have related this broad idea of 'leadership for learning' to the evolving role of the primary teacher. The changing expectations mean that a primary teacher must demonstrate:

- leadership *for* learning through her/his role in contributing to the development and realisation of the vision and values of the school;
- leadership *of* learning by focusing on the visible learning of pupils in constructing learning experiences for pupils and reflecting on the impact these have on pupil achievement;
- leadership *by* learning through working collaboratively to develop and share their pedagogic expertise in order to improve the quality of the pupil learning experiences and ensure achievement.

The focus on attainment – by politicians, policy makers, the wider media and parents – as the means of judging success in education is of limited value and tends to overlook significant groups of pupils. Instead underpinning this idea of 'leadership for, of and by learning' is an inclusive vision (Head, 2011) where the focus has to be on the quality of learning experiences and outcomes achieved by all pupils.

There is now a greater appreciation that learning is not confined to the classroom, the importance of the culture of the school in shaping the opportunities for learning is also recognised and again this has had implications for the role of the teacher. Primary teachers now contribute to the development of the wider context of the school and leading learning support assistants in the classroom. In addition, there is greater appreciation that wider factors such as care, welfare, health can impact significantly on pupil learning and so teachers are increasingly expected to act as a 'leader of learning' in interprofessional settings working with other professionals from social work, health or youth justice, for example to find solutions to enable individual pupils learn and achieve (McCulloch, 2011). This wider role demands high levels of expertise in teaching and learning on the part of teachers working with other professional groups: in these various contexts teachers then are leaders working to ensure the learning of all pupils.

   Reflective questions

- As a teacher your 'leadership for learning' has to be underpinned by a vision and set of values. What is your pedagogic vision and why is this vision important?
- Shapiro and Stefkovich (2011) argue that professionals should have and be able to articulate personal and professional codes based on sets of values.

What would you see as your core values as an educator and give some instances of the way in which these values shape your decisions and actions in the classroom.

- In the discussion of 'leadership *of* learning' we have argued that teaching is a complex process where teachers need to draw from a variety of strategies to enable pupils to learn. Reflect on your practice and list the different approaches you adopt to support the learning of different groups of pupils. Consider ways of trialling other approaches to address the learning needs of specific groups and individuals.
- As a 'leader *of* learning' Hattie argues that a teacher should evaluate their practice in terms of the effect their teaching has on pupil learning. In what ways do you reflect and evaluate your teaching? How could you draw systematically on pupil voice and their achievements to help you look critically at your pedagogic practice?
- What have been the most significant professional learning opportunities you have had? What made these effective learning opportunities? How might you seek similar experiences to further your development as a teacher?
- What opportunities have you had to work collaboratively? What skills do you think you need to develop to lead and engage fully in collaborative learning with colleagues?

Further reading

Crowther, F. (2009) *Developing Teacher Leaders*. 2nd edn. Thousand Oaks, CA: Corwin Press.

Durant, J. and Holden, G. (2006) *Teachers Leading Change: Doing Research for School Improvement*. London: Paul Chapman Publishing.

Forde, C. (2011) 'Being a teacher leader', in M. McMahon, C. Forde and M. Martin (eds), *Contemporary Issues in Learning and Teaching*. London: SAGE. pp. 153–64.

Katzenmeyer, M. and Moller, G. (2009) *Awakening the Sleeping Giant: Helping Teachers Develop as Leaders*. 3rd edn. Thousand Oaks, CA: Corwin Press.

Martin, M. (2011) 'Professional learning communities', in M.McMahon, C. Forde and M. Martin (eds), *Contemporary Issues in Learning and* Teaching. London: SAGE. pp. 142–52.

REFERENCES

Adams, K. (2008) 'What's in a name? Seeking professional status through degree studies within the Scottish early years context', *European Early Childhood Education Research Journal*, 16(2), 196–209.

Adams, F.R. (1999) '5–14: Origins, development and implementation', in T.G.K. Bryce, and W.M. Humes, (eds), *Scottish Education: Post-Devolution*. 2nd edn. Edinburgh: Edinburgh University Press. pp. 369–79.

Addison, B.V. (2012) 'Academic care, classroom pedagogy and the house group teacher: 'making hope practical' in uncertain times', *Pastoral Care in Education*, 30(4), 303–15.

Adey, P. and Shayer, M. (1994) *Really Raising Standards: Cognitive Intervention and Academic Achievement*. London: Routledge.

Alasuutari, M. and Karila, K. (2010) 'Framing the picture of the child', *Children and Society*, 24(2), 100–111.

Alexander, R., Rose, J. and Woodhead, C. (1992) *Curriculum Organisation and Classroom Practice in Primary Schools: A discussion paper*. London: Department of Education and Science.

Allen, J.P., Porter, M.R., McFarland, F.C., McElhaney, K.B. and Marsh, P.A. (2007) 'The relation of attachment security to adolescents' paternal and peer relationships, depression, and externalizing behavior', *Child Development*, 78(4), 1222–39.

Allen, J., Potter, J., Sharp, J. and Turvey, K. (2011) *Primary ICT Knowledge, Understanding and Practice*. 5th edn. Exeter: Learning Matters Ltd.

Anderson, L.W. and Krathwohl, D.R. (eds) (2001) *A Taxonomy for Learning, Teaching and Assessing*. New York: Longman.

Angelides, P., Constantinou, C. and Leigh, J. (2009) 'The role of paraprofessionals in developing inclusive education in Cyprus', *European Journal of Special Needs Education*, 24(1), 75–89.

Argyris, C. and Schön, D.A. (1995) *Organisational Learning: Theory, Method and Practice*. Reading, MA: Addison Wesley.

Arizpe, E., Farrell, M. and McAdam, J. (2013) 'Opening the classroom door to children's literature: A review of research', in K. Hall, T. Cremin, B. Comber, and L. Moll (eds), *International Handbook of Research in Children's Literacy, Learning and Culture*. London: Wiley Blackwell. pp. 241–57.

Armstrong, F. and Barton, L. (2007) 'Policy, experience and change and the challenge of inclusive education: The case of England', in L. Barton and F. Armstrong (eds), *Policy, Experience and Change: Cross-cultural Reflections on Inclusive Education*. London: Springer. pp. 5–18.

Arshad, R. (2012a) 'Shaping practice: The impact of personal values and experiences', in R. Arshad, T. Wrigley and L. Pratt (eds), *Social Justice Re-examined: Dilemmas and Solutions for the Classroom Teacher*. Stoke on Trent: Trentham. pp. 3–17.

Arshad, R. (2012b) 'The twenty first century teacher needs to engage with race and racism', in R. Arshad, T. Wrigley and L. Pratt (eds), *Social Justice Re-examined: Dilemmas and Solutions for the Classroom Teacher*. Stoke on Trent: Trentham. pp. 193–207.

Ashton, R. (2008) 'Improving the transfer to secondary school: How every child's voice can matter', *Support for Learning*, 23(4), 176–82.

Asia Society (2011) *Improving Teacher Quality Around the World: The International Summit on the Teaching Profession, Summit Report*. http://asiasociety.org/education/learning-world/worlds-education-leaders-support-teachers (accessed 15 August 2013).

Assessment Reform Group (ARG) (2002) *Assessment for Learning: 10 Principles*. www.assessment-reform-group.org.uk. (accessed 17 December 2012).

Ayers, H., Clarke, D. and Murray, A. (2000) *Perspectives on Behaviour: A Practical Guide to Effective Interventions for Teachers*. London: David Fulton.

Bailey, S. (2007) *So, What's all the Fuss about Nurture Groups?* Paper presented at the British Educational Research Association Annual Conference, Institute of Education, University of London, 5–8 September 2007. http://www.leeds.ac.uk/educol/documents/166003.htm (accessed 13 February 2013).

Ball, C. (1994) *Start Right: The Importance of Early Learning*. London: Royal Society of Arts.

Bandura, A. (1977) 'Self-efficacy: toward a unifying theory of behavioral change', *Psychological Review*, 84(2), 191–215.

Bandura, A. (1994) 'Self-efficacy', in V.S. Ramachaudran (ed.), *Encyclopedia of human behavior* (Vol. 4, pp. 71–81). New York: Academic Press. http://www.uky.edu/~eushe2/Bandura/BanEncy.html (accessed 13 May 2013).

Banks, J.A. (2008) *An Introduction to Multicultural Education*. London: Pearson.

Banks, J.A. (ed.) (2009) *The Routledge International Companion to Multicultural Education*. Oxon: Routledge. pp. 121–133.

Barber, M. and Mourshed, M. (2007) *How the World's Best-performing School Systems Come Out on Top*. http://www.mckinsey.com/clientservice/social_sector/our_practices/education/knowledge_highlights/best_performing_school.aspx (accessed 15 August 2013).

Barnes, D. (2008) 'Exploratory talk for learning', in N. Mercer, and S. Hodgkinson (eds), *Exploring Talk in School*. London: SAGE. pp. 1–15.

Barrow, A. (2005) 'The changing educational scene', in C. Bold (ed.), *Supporting Learning and Teaching*. Abingdon: David Fulton. pp. 15–34.

Bartolo, P. and Smyth, G. (2009) 'Teacher education for diversity', in A. Swennen and M. van der Klink (eds), *Becoming a Teacher Educator*. Dordrecht: Springer. pp. 117–32.

Bass, B.M. and Riggio, R.E. (2006) *Transformational Leadership*. 2nd edn. Mahwah, NJ: Lawrence Erlbaum Associates.

Baumfield, V.M. (2006) 'Tools for pedagogical enquiry: The impact of teaching thinking skills on teachers', *Oxford Review of Education*, 32(2), 185–96.

Baumfield, V.M., Wall, E. and Hall, K. (2008) *Action Research in the Classroom*. London: SAGE.

Baumfield, V.M., Hall, E. and Wall, K. (2013) *Action Research in Education*. London: SAGE.

Beane, J. (1991) 'The middle school: The natural home of integrated curriculum', *Educational Leadership*, 49(2), 9–13.

Bedford, D., Jackson, C. and Wilson, E. (2008) 'New partnerships for learning: Teachers' perspectives on their developing professional with teaching assistants in England', *Journal of In-service Education*, 34(1), 7–25.

Bell, J. (2010) *Doing your Research Project: A Guide for First-time Researchers in Education, Health and Social Science*. 5th edn. Maidenhead: Open University Press.

Bennett, J. and Tayler, C.P. (2006) *Starting Strong II: Early Childhood Education and Care*. Paris: OECD.

Bergman, J. and Sams, A. (2012) *Flip your Classroom: Reach Every Student in Every Class Every Day*. Washington, DC: International Society for Technology in Education.

Black, P. and Wiliam, D. (1998a) *Inside the Black Box: Raising Standards through Classroom Assessment*. London: GL Assessment.

Black, P. and Wiliam, D. (1998b) 'Assessment and classroom learning', *Assessment in Education: Principles Policy and Practice*, 5(1), 7–73.

Black, P. and Wiliam, D. (2009) 'Developing the theory of formative assessment', *Educational Assessment, Evaluation and Accountability*, 21(1), 5–31.

Blackburn, S. (2002) *Being Good: A Short Introduction to Ethics*. 2nd edn. Oxford: Oxford University Press.

Blair, E. and Francis, L. (2011) 'Was it right to abandon the creative curriculum?' *Practical Research for Education*, 44(1), 26–32.

Blatchford, P., Bassett, P., Brown, P. and Webster, R. (2009) 'The effect of support staff on pupil engagement and individual attention', *British Educational Research Journal*, 35(5), 661–6.

Blatchford, P., Kutnick, P., Baines, E. and Galton, M. (2003) 'Toward a social pedagogy of classroom group work', *International Journal of Educational Research*, 39(1–2), 153–172.

Blatchford, P., Russell, A., Bassett, P., Brown, P. and Martin, C. (2007) 'The role and effects of teaching assistants in English primary schools (Years 4 to 6) 2000–2003. Results from the Class Size and Pupil–Adult Ratios (CSPAR) KS2 Project', *British Educational Research Journal*, 33(1), 5–26.

Boden, M.A. (2004) *The Creative Mind: Myths and Mechanisms*. 2nd edn. London: Routledge.

Bohm, S. and Land, C. (2009) 'No measure for culture? Value in the new economy', *Capital & Class*, 33(1), 75–98.

Booth, E. (online) *The Habits of Mind of Creative Engagement*. http://ericbooth.net/the-habits-of-mind-of-creative-engagement/ (accessed 24 June 2013).

Borland, J.H. (1989) *Planning and Implementing Programs for the Gifted*. New York, NY: Teachers College Press.

Bothelo, M.J. and Rudman, M.K. (2009) *Critical multicultural analysis of children's literature: mirrors, windows and doors*. London: Routledge.

Bowers, K.S., Regehr, G., Balthazard, C. and Parker, K. (1990) 'Intuition in the context of discovery', *Cognitive Psychology,* 22(1), 72–110.

Bowlby, J. (1969) *Attachment and Loss, Vol. 1: Attachment*. New York: Basic Books.

Boxall, M. (2010) *Nurture Groups in School: Principles and Practice*. 2nd edn. London: SAGE Publications.

Bradshaw, J. and Richardson, D. (2009) 'An index of child well-being in Europe', *Child Indicators Research*, 2(3), 319–51.

Brand, B.R. and Triplett, C.F. (2012) 'Interdisciplinary curriculum: an abandoned concept?' *Teachers and Teaching: Theory and Practice*, 18(3), 381–93.

Braund, M. (2007) "Bridging work' and its role in improving progression and continuity: an example from science education', *British Educational Research Journal* 33(6), 905–26.

Brehony, K.J. (2005) 'Primary schooling under New Labour: The irresolvable contradiction of excellence and enjoyment', *Oxford Review of Education*, 31(1), 29–46.

Brewin, M. and Statham, J. (2011) 'Supporting the transition from primary school to secondary school for children who are Looked After', *Educational Psychology in Practice: Theory, research and practice in educational psychology* 27(4), 365–81.

British Educational Research Association (BERA) (2011) *Ethical Guidelines for Educational Research*. http://www.bera.ac.uk/ (accessed 20 July 2013).

Bronfenbrenner, U. (1979) *The Ecology of Human Development*. Cambridge, MA: Harvard University Press.

Bronfenbrenner, U. (1994) 'Ecological models of human development', in *International Encyclopaedia of Education*. 2nd ed. Oxford: Elsevier.

Brown, F. (2008) 'The playwork principles: A critique', in F. Brown and C. Taylor (eds), *Foundations of Playwork*. Maidenhead: McGraw Hill/Open University Press. pp. 123–7.

Bruner, J. (1960) *The Process of Education*. Cambridge, MA: Harvard University Press.

Bruner, J. (1961) 'The act of discovery', *Harvard Educational Review*, 31(1), 21–32.

Bruner, J. (1996) *The Culture of Education*. Cambridge, MA: Harvard University Press.

Bruner, J. (1999) 'Folk pedagogies', in J. Leach and B. Moon (eds), *Learners and Pedagogy*. London: Paul Chapman Publishing. pp. 4–20.

Buchanan, M. and Hyde, B. (2008) 'Learning beyond the surface: Engaging the cognitive, affective and spiritual dimensions within the curriculum', *International Journal of Children's Spirituality*, 13(4), 309–20.

Burgess, H. and Mayes, A.S. (2007) 'Supporting the professional development of teaching assistants: Classroom teachers' perspectives on their mentoring role', *The Curriculum Journal*, 18(3), 389–407.

Calder, I. and Grieve, A. (2004) 'Working with other adults: What teachers need to know', *Educational Studies*, 30(2), 113–26.

Calman, L.J. and Tarr-Whelan, L. (2005) *Early Childhood Education for All: A Wise Investment*. http://web.mit.edu/workplacecenter/docs/Full%20Report.pdf (accessed 22 August 2012).

Campaign for Learning (online) *Learning to Learn Homepage*. http://www.campaign-for-learning.org.uk/cfl/learninginschools/l2l/index.asp (accessed 12 August 2013).

Campbell, A. (2007) *Practitioner Research*. London: TLRP. http://www.tlrp.org/capacity/rm/wt/campbell (accessed 20 July 2013).

Campbell, A. and Groundwater-Smith, S. (eds) (2007) *An Ethical Approach to Practitioner Research: Dealing with Issues and Dilemmas in Action Research*. London: Routledge.

Campbell, A., McNamara, O. and Gilroy, P. (2004) *Practitioner Research and Professional Development in Education*. London: Paul Chapman.

Capel, S., Zwozdiak-Myers, P. and Lawrence, J. (2007) 'The transfer of pupils from primary to secondary school A case study of a foundation subject: physical education.' *Research in Education 77*. Manchester: Manchester University Press.

Carr, W. and Kemmis, S. (1986) *Becoming Critical: Education, Knowledge and Action Research*. Lewes: Falmer Press.

Causton-Theoharis, J. and Malmgren, K. (2005) 'Building bridges: Strategies to help paraprofessionals promote peer interaction', *Teaching Exceptional Children*, 37(6), 18–24.

Chedzoy, S.M. and Burden, R.L. (2005) *Making the Move: Assessing Student Attitudes to Primary-secondary School Transfer. Research in Education 74*. Manchester: Manchester University Press.

Chen, W. and Looi, C.K. (2011) 'Active classroom participation in a Group Scribbles primary science classroom', *British Journal of Educational Technology*, 42(4), 676–86.

Child Poverty Action Group (CPAG) (2012) *Child Poverty Facts and Figures*. http://www.cpag.org.uk/child-poverty-facts-and-figures (accessed 13 May 2013).

Children's Workforce Development Council (CWDC) (2007) *Every Child Matters: Change for Children*. http://media.education.gov.uk/assets/files/pdf/m/multi-agency%20working%20factsheet.pdf (accessed 22 August 2012).

Children's Workforce Development Council (CWDC) (2012) *EYPS Standards Review*. http://www.iqf.org.uk/early-years/graduate-leaders-in-early-years/eyps-standards (accessed 22 August 2012).

Cho, S. (2013) *Critical Pedagogy and Social Change*. London: Routledge.

Clandinin, D. J. and Connelly, F. M. (2000) *Narrative Inquiry: Experience and Story in Qualitative Research*. San Francisco: Jossey-Bass.

Claxton, G. (2006) *Expanding the Capacity to Learn: A New End for Education?* Keynote address BERA conference, Warwick University, September 2006.

Claxton, G. and Lucas, B. (2007) *The Creative Thinking Plan*. London: BBC Books.

Cline, T., de Abreu, G., Fihosy, C., Gray, H., Lambert, H. and Neale, J. (2002) *Minority Ethnic Pupils in White Schools*. Research Report RR365. London: DfES.

Cochran-Smith, M. and Lytle, S. (1999) 'Relationship of knowledge and practice: Teacher learning in communities', in A. Iran-Nejad and C. Pearson (eds), *Review of Research in Education, 24*. Washington DC: American Educational Research Association. pp. 249–306.

Cochran-Smith, M. and Lytle, S. (2009) *Inquiry as Stance*. New York: Teachers College Press.

Cohen, L. and Uhry, J. (2007) 'Young children's discourse strategies during block play: A Bakhtinian approach', *Journal of Research in Childhood Education*, 21(3), 302–16.

Compton, W. (2005) *An Introduction to Positive Psychology*. Belmont: Wadsworth Publishing.

Craft, A. (2003) 'The limits to creativity in education: dilemmas for the educator', *British Journal of Educational Studies*, 51(2), 113–27.

Cropley, A.J. (1992) *More Ways than One: Fostering Creativity*. Norwood, NJ: Ablex.

Cross, M. (2011) *Children with Social, Emotional and Behavioural Difficulties and Communication Problems: There is Always a Reason*. 2nd edn. London: Jessica Kingsley.

Csikszentmihalyi, M. (1997) *Finding Flow: The Psychology of Engagement with Everyday Life*. New York: Basic Books.

Cummins, J. (2001) 'Empowering minority students: a framework for intervention', *Harvard Educational Review*, 71(4), 649–75.

Cunningham, H. (1995) *Children and Childhood in Western Society Since 1500*. London: Longman.

Curtis, W. and Pettigrew, A. (2009*) Learning in Contemporary Culture,* Exeter: Learning Matters Ltd.

Dalai Lama (1999) *Ancient Wisdom, Modern World: Ethics for the New Millennium.* London: Abacus.

Damasio, A. (1994) *Descartes' Error: Emotion, Reason and the Human Brain.* New York: Harper Collins.

Dana, N.F. and Yendol-Silva, D. (2009) *The Reflective Educator's Guide to Classroom Research: Learning to Teach and Teaching to Learn Through Practitioner Inquiry.* London: SAGE.

Darling-Hammond, L. and Bransford, J. (eds) (2005) *Preparing Teachers for a Changing World: What Teachers Should Learn and Be Able to Do.* San Francisco: John Wiley and Sons Inc.

Davies, B. (2011) *Leading the Strategically Focused School: Success and Sustainability.* London: SAGE.

Davies, D. and McMahon, K. (2004) 'A smooth trajectory: developing continuity and progression between primary and secondary science education through a jointly-planned projectiles project', *International Journal of Science Education,* 26(8), 1009–21.

Day, C., Kington, A., Stobart, G. and Sammons, P. (2006) 'The personal and professional selves of teachers: stable and unstable identities', *British Educational Research Journal,* 32(4), 601–16.

De Lièvre, B., Depover, C. and Dillenbourg, P. (2006) 'The relationship between tutoring mode and learners' use of help tools in distance education', *Instructional Science,* 34(2), 97–29.

De Souza, M. (2009) 'Spirituality and well-being', *International Journal of Children's Spirituality,* 14(3), 181–4.

Department for Children, Education, Lifelong Learning and Skills (DfCELLS) (2008) *Foundation Phase: Framework for Children's Learning for 3 to 7–year-olds in Wales.* Cardiff: DfCELLS.

Department for Children, Schools and Families (DfCSF) (2007) *New Arrivals Excellence Programme Guidance: Primary and Secondary National Strategies.* Norwich: DCSF.

Department for Education (DfE) (2011a) *Remit for Review of the National Curriculum in England.* http://www.education.gov.uk/schools/teachingandlearning/curriculum/ nationalcurriculum2014/nationalcurriculum/b0073043/remit-for-review-of-the-national-curriculum-in-england (accessed 20 July 2013).

Department for Education (DfE) (2012a) *Statistical First Release: School Pupils and their Characteristics – January 2012.* London: DfE.

Department for Education (DfE) (2012b) *Provision for Children under Five years of Age in England – January 2012.* London: DfE.

Department for Education (DfE) (2013a) *Teachers' Standards.* https://www.gov.uk/government/ uploads/system/uploads/attachment_data/file/208682/Teachers_Standards_2013.pdf (accessed 20 July 2013).

Department for Education (DfE) (2013b) *Digital Technology in Schools.* http://www.education. gov.uk/a00201823/digital-technology-in-schools (accessed 25 July 2013).

Department for Education (DfE) (2013c) *The National Curriculum in England Framework Document.* London: DfE.

Department for Education and Employment (DfEE) (1998) *National Childcare Strategy: Meeting the Childcare Challenge a Framework and Consultation Document.* London: The Stationery Office.

Department for Education and Skills (DfES) (2001) *SEN Code of Practice on the Identification and Assessment of Pupils with Special Educational Needs.* Nottingham: DfES.

Department for Education and Skills (DfES) (2003) *Aiming High: Raising the Achievement of Minority Ethnic Pupils: Consultation Document* (London, DfES/0183).

Department for Education and Skills (DfES) (2004a) *Aiming High: Understanding the Educational Needs of Minority Ethnic Pupils in Mainly White Schools: A Guide to Good Practice*. Nottingham: DfES.

Department for Education and Skills (DfES) and Health Development Agency (HAD) (2004b) *Promoting Emotional Health and Wellbeing Through the National Healthy Schools Standard*. http://www.nice.org.uk/niceMedia/documents/promoting_health_wellbeing.pdf (accessed 18 July 2012).

Department for Education and Skills (DfES) (2005a) *Aiming High: Meeting the Needs of Newly Arrived Learners of English as an Additional Language*. London: DfES/1381.

Department for Education and Skills (DfES) (2005b) *Every Child Matters: Children's Workforce Strategy*. Nottingham: DfES.

Department of Education (Northern Ireland) (DfE(NI)) (2004) *Review of Pre-school Education in Northern Ireland*. Bangor, Co. Down: DfE.

Department of Education and Science (DES) (1967) *Children and their Primary Schools (The Plowden Report)*. London: Central Advisory Council for Education (CACE) – HMSO.

Department of Education and Science (DES) (1987) *The National Curriculum 5–16: A Consultation Document*. London: DES/Welsh Office.

Department of Education and Science (DES) (1990) *Starting with Quality; Report of the Committee of Inquiry into the Quality of Educational Provision for Under Fives*. Rumbold Report. London: HMSO.

Department of Health, Social Services and Public Safety (DHSSPS – Northern Ireland) (2011) *Understanding the Needs of Children in Northern Ireland*. http://www.welbni.org/uploads/file/pdf/unocini_guidance_043651.pdf (accessed 22 August 2012).

Dewulf, S. and Baillie, C. (1999) *How to Foster Creativity*. DfEE: London.

Diamond, J.B. and Spillane, J. (2004) 'High-Stakes Accountability in Urban Elementary Schools: Challenging or Reducing Inequality?' *Teachers College Record*, 106(6): 1145–76.

Dillon, P. (2006) 'Creativity, integrativism and a pedagogy of connection', *International Journal of Thinking Skills and Creativity*, 1(2), 69–83.

Dillon, P. (2008) 'A pedagogy of connection and boundary crossings: methodological and epistemological transactions in working across and between disciplines', *Innovations in Education and Teaching International*, 45(3), 255–62.

Donaldson, G. (2011) *Teaching Scotland's Future*. Edinburgh: Scottish Government.

Doran, G.T. (1981) 'There's a S.M.A.R.T. way to write management's goals and objectives', *Management Review*, 70(11), 35–6.

DuFour, R. (2004) 'Schools as learning communities', *Educational Leadership*, 61(8): 6–11.

Dunne, J. (2008) 'Education and childhood', *Yearbook of the National Society for the Study of Education*, 107(1), 258–73.

Dunnell, K. (2008) *Office for National Statistics: Population Trends*. London: Palgrave Macmillan.

Dweck, C.S. (1999) *Self Theories: Their Role in Motivation, Personality and Development*. Philadelphia: Psychology Press.

Early Years Foundation Stage (EYFS) (2007) *Parents as Partners*. http://www.peal.org.uk/pdf/The%20EYFS%20Parents%20as%20Partners2.pdf (accessed 22 August 2012).

Education Scotland (online-a) *Promoting Diversity and Equality: Developing Responsible Citizens for 21st Century Scotland*. http://www.educationscotland.gov.uk/resources/p/genericresource_tcm4747991.asp (accessed 13 June 2013).

Education Scotland (online-b) *Curriculum for Excellence: Health and Wellbeing Experiences and Outcomes.* http://www.educationscotland.gov.uk/Images/health_wellbeing_experiences_outcomes_tcm4–540031.pdf (accessed 18 July 2012).

Education Scotland (online-c) *The Purpose of the Curriculum.* http://www.education scotland. gov.uk/thecurriculum/whatiscurriculumforexcellence/thepurposeofthe curriculum/index. asp (accessed 14 August 2013).

Education Scotland (online-d) *Interdisciplinary Learning.* http://www.educationscotland.gov. uk/learningteachingandassessment/learningacrossthecurriculum/interdisciplinarylearning/ index.asp (accessed 24 June 2013).

Education Scotland (online-e) *The Role of the Key Adult.* http://www.educationscotland.gov.uk/ supportinglearners/whatissupport/universalsupport/roleofkeyadult.asp (accessed 10 August 2013).

Ee Loh, C. (2009) 'Reading the world: reconceptualising reading multicultural literature in the English language arts classroom in a global world', *Changing English: Studies in Culture and Education,* 16(3), 287–99.

Einstein, A. (1931) *Cosmic Religion: With Other Opinions and Aphorisms.* New York: Covici-Friede.

Elton-Chalcraft, S., Hansen, A. and Twisleton, S. (eds) (2008) *Doing Classroom Research: A Step-by-step Guide for Student Teachers.* Maidenhead: Open University Press.

Erikson, E.H. (1959) *Identity and the Life Cycle.* New York: International Universities Press.

Evangelou, M., Taggart, B., Sylva, K., Melhuish, E., Sammons, P. and Siraj-Blatchford, I. (2008) *What Makes a Successful Transition from Primary to Secondary School?* Effective Pre-school, Primary and Secondary Education 3–14 Project (EPPSE 3–14) London: Institute of Education, University of London.

Fazey, D.M.A. and Fazey, J.A. (2001) 'The potential for autonomy in learning: Perceptions of competence, motivation and locus of control in first-year undergraduate students', *Studies in Higher Education,* 26(3), 345–61.

Fletcher, S. *Introduction Teacher Research.* http://www.teacherresearch.net/ (accessed 20 July 2013).

Florian, L. and Black-Hawkins, K. (2011) 'Exploring inclusive pedagogy', *British Educational Research Journal,* 37(5), 813–28.

Fogarty, R. (2009) *How to Integrate the Curricula.* 3rd edn. Thousand Oaks, CA: Corwin.

Forde, C. and McMahon, M. (2011) *Accomplished Teaching, Accomplished Teachers in Scotland: A Report Submitted to the Committee Reviewing Teacher Employment in Scotland.* Glasgow: University of Glasgow. http://eprints.gla.ac.uk/62070/ (accessed 15 August 2013).

Forde, C., McMahon, M., MacPhee, A. and Patrick, F. (2006) *Professional Development, Reflection and Enquiry.* London: Paul Chapman.

Fox, R. (2001) 'Constructivism examined', *Oxford Review of Education,* 27(1): 23–35.

Friend, M. and Cook, L. (2007) *Interactions: Collaboration Skills for School Professionals.* 5th edn. Boston: Allyn & Bacon.

Friendly, M. and Beach, J. (2004) *Early Childhood Education and Care in Canada, 2004.* Toronto: Childcare Resource and Research Unit, University of Toronto.

Funder, D.C. and Block, J. (1989) 'The role of ego-control, ego-resiliency, and IQ in delay of gratification in adolescence', *Journal of Personality and Social Psychology,* 57(6), 1041–50.

Gagné, R.M. (1985) *The Conditions of Learning.* 4th edn. New York: Holt, Rinehart and Winston.

Gammage, P. (2008) *The Social Agenda and Early Childhood Care and Education: Can we Really Help Create a Better World?* Online outreach paper 4. The Hague: Bernard van Leer

Foundation. http://www.bernardvanleer.org/The_social_agenda_and_early_childhood_care_and_education_Can_we_really_help_create_a_better_world (accessed 22 August 2012).

Gardner, H. (1993) *Frames of Mind: Theory of Multiple Intelligences*. London: Fontana Press.

Gardner, H. (2000) *Intelligence Reframed: Multiple Intelligences for the 21st Century*. New York, NY: Basic Books.

Gardner, H. (2006) 'Replies to my critics', in J. Schaler (ed.) *Howard Gardner under Fire: The Rebel Psychologist Faces his Critics*. Chicago: Open Court. pp. 277–344.

Gardner, H. (2007) *Five Minds for the Future*. Cambridge, MA: Harvard Business School Press.

Gardner, H. (2011) *Truth, Beauty Goodness Reframed: Educating for the Virtues in the Age of Truthiness and Twitter*. New York: Basic Books.

General Teaching Council for Northern Ireland (GTCNI) (2004) *Code of Values and Professional Practice*. http://www.gtcni.org.uk/uploads/docs/GTC_code.pdf (accessed 20 July 2013).

General Teaching Council for Northern Ireland (GTCNI) (2007) *Teaching: The Reflective Profession*. http://www.gtcni.org.uk/uploads/docs/GTCNI_Comp_Bmrk%20%20Aug%2007.pdf (accessed 10 August 2013).

General Teaching Council of Scotland (GTCS) (2006) *A Standard for Initial Teacher Education*. Edinburgh: GTCS.

General Teaching Council of Scotland (GTCS) (2012) *The Standards for Registration: Mandatory Requirements for Registration with the General Teaching Council of Scotland*. http://www.gtcs.org.uk/web/FILES/the-standards/standards-for-registration-1212.pdf (accessed 13 May 2013).

General Teaching Council for Wales (GTCW) (2010) *Code of Professional Conduct and Practice for Registered Teachers* http://www.gtcw.org.uk/gtcw/images/stories/downloads/professional_standards/GTCW_Professional_Code.pdf (accessed 20 July 2013).

Gesell, A. (1925) *The Mental Growth of the Pre-school Child*. http://www.unz.org/Pub/GesellArnold-1925?View=FindIt (accessed 14 February 2010).

Giangreco, M.F., Yuan, S., McKenzie, B., Cameron, P. and Fialka, J. (2005) '"Be careful what you wish for…": Five reasons to be concerned about the assignment of individual para-professionals', *Teaching Exceptional Children*, 37(5), 28–34.

Gillies, D. (2008) 'The politics of Scottish Education', in T.G.K. Bryce and W.M. Humes *Scottish Education: Beyond Devolution*. 3rd edn. Edinburgh: Edinburgh University Press. pp. 80–9.

Gillies, R.M. (2007) *Cooperative Learning: Integrating Theory and Practice*. London: SAGE.

Gillies, R.M. and Ashman, A.F. (2003) 'An historical review of the use of groups to promote socialization and learning', in R.M. Gillies, and A.F. Ashman (eds), *Co-operative Learning: The Social and Intellectual Outcomes of Learning in Groups*. London: Routledge Falmer. pp. 1–18.

Gillies, R.M. and Boyle, M. (2005) 'Teachers' scaffolding behaviours during cooperative learning', *Asia-Pacific Journal of Teacher Education*, 33(3), 243–59.

Gillies, R.M. and Boyle, M. (2008) 'Teachers' discourse during cooperative learning and their perceptions of this pedagogical practice', *Teaching and Teacher Education*, 24(5), 1333–48.

Gonzalez, N., Moll, L.C. and Amanti, C. (2005) *Funds of Knowledge: Theorizing Practices in Households, Communities and Classrooms*. London: Lawrence Erlbaum Associates.

Gopalakrishnan, A. and Ulanoff, S. (2003) *Making Connections to Cultural Identity: Using Multicultural Children's Literature and Storytelling to Explore Personal Narrative*. Paper presented at the Hawaii International Conference on Education Honolulu.

Gorwood, B. (1991) 'Primary-Secondary Transfer after the National Curriculum', *School Organisation* 11(3), 283–90.

Gough, N. (1998) 'Reflections and diffractions: functions of fiction in curriculum inquiry' in W. Pinar (ed.) *Curriculum: Toward New Identities.* New York: Garland Publishing. pp. 94–127.

Graham, C. and Hill, M. (2003) *Negotiating the Transition to Secondary School.* Spotlight 89. Glasgow: SCRE Centre, University of Glasgow.

Gray, C. (online) *Social Stories.* http://thegraycenter.org/social-stories (accessed 13 June 2013).

Greene, T.R. and Noice, H. (1988) 'Influence of positive affect on creative thinking and problem solving in children', *Psychological Reports,* 63(3), 895–8.

Guildford, J.P. (1950) 'Creativity', *American Psychologist,* 5, 444–4.

Haldane, J. *On the Very Idea of Spiritual Values* in D. Carr and J. Haldane (eds) (2003) *Spirituality, Philosophy and Education.* London: RoutledgeFalmer.

Hanke, V. (2011) 'Learning about literacy: Children's versions of the literacy hour', *Journal of Research in Reading,* 23(3), 287–97.

Hardy, A. (1979) *Spiritual Nature of Man: Study of Contemporary Religious Experience.* Oxford: Oxford University Press.

Hargreaves, D. (ed.) (2005) *About Learning: Report of the Learning Working Group.* London: Demos.

Harris, V. (2008) 'A cross-curricular approach to 'learning to learn' languages: government policy and school practice', *The Curriculum Journal,* 19(4), 255–68.

Hartman, H. (2002) *Scaffolding and Co-operative Learning: Human Learning and Instruction.* New York: City College of the City University of New York Press.

Hattie, J. (2009) *Visible Learning: A Synthesis of over 800 Meta-analyses Relating to Achievement.* Abingdon: Routledge.

Hattie, J. (2012) *Visible Learning for Teachers: Maximizing Impact on Learning.* Abingdon: Routledge.

Hauge, J.M. and Barkie, A.M. (2006) 'Develop collaborative special educator-paraprofessional teams: One para's view', *Intervention in School and Clinic,* 42(1), 51–3.

Hauser, M. (2008) *Moral Minds: How Nature Designed our Universal Sense of Right and Wrong.* London: Abacus.

Hay, D. with Nye, R. (2006) *The Spirit of the Child: Revised Edition.* London: Jessica Kingsle.

Hayes, D. (2010) 'The seductive charms of a cross-curricular approach', *Education 3–13,* 38(4), 381–7.

Hayward, L.., Menter, I., Baumfield, V., Daugherty, R., Akhtar, N., Doyle, L., Elliot, D., Hulme, M., Hutchinson, C., MacBride, G., McCulloch, M., Patrick, F., Spencer, E., Wardle, G., Blee, H., and Arthur, E. (2012) *Assessment at Transition.* Project Report. Glasgow: University of Glasgow.

Head, G. (2007) *Better Learning, Better Behaviour.* Edinburgh: Dunedin Academic Press.

Head, G. (2011) 'Inclusion and pedagogy', in M. McMahon, C. Forde, and M. Martin (eds), *Contemporary Issues in Learning and Teaching.* London: SAGE. pp. 60–71.

Head, G. and O'Neill, W. (1999) 'Introducing Feuerstein's Instrumental Enrichment in a school for children with social, emotional and behavioural difficulties', *Support for Learning,* 14(3), 122–8.

Heckman, J. and Masterov, D. (2007) 'The productivity argument for investing in young children', *Review of Agricultural Economics,* 29(3), 446–93.

Her Majesty's Inspectorate of Education (HMIe) (2009) *Count us In: Meeting the Needs of Children and Young People Newly Arrived in Scotland.* Livingston: HMIe.

Herrnstein, R.J. and Murray, C. (1994) *The Bell Curve*. New York: The Free Press.

Hickman, L. (1990) *John Dewey's Pragmatic Technology*. Bloomington, IN: Indiana University Press.

Higgins, S., Wall, K., Baumfield, V.M., Hall, E., Leat, D., Moseley, D. and Woolner, P. (2007) *Learning to Learn in Schools: Phase 3 Evaluation, Final Report*. London: Campaign for Learning.

HMSO (2002) *Education Act*. http://www.legislation.gov.uk/ukpga/2002/32/section/78 (accessed 20 July 2013).

Hodson, D. and Hodson, J. (1998) 'From constructivism to social constructivism : A Vygotskian perspective on teaching and learning science', *School Science Review*, 79(289), 33–41.

Hofkins, D. and Northen, S. (eds) (2009) *Introducing the Cambridge Primary Review*. http://www.primaryreview.org.uk/downloads/CPR_revised_booklet.pdf (accessed 20 July 2013).

Howe, M.J.A. (1999) *Genius Explained*. Cambridge, UK: Cambridge University Press.

Howes, A., Farrell, P., Kaplan, I. and Moss, S. (2003) *The Impact of Paid Adult Support on the Participation and Learning of Pupils in Mainstream Schools*. London: EPPI-Centre, Institute of Education.

Hyde, B. (2008) *Children and Spirituality*. London: Jessica Kingsley.

Hymer, B. and Harbron, N. (1998) 'Early transfer: a good move?' *Educating Able Children*, Spring, 38–48.

James, A. and James, A. (2004) *Constructing Childhood. Theory, Policy and Social Practice*. London: Palgrave.

James, A., Jenks, C. and Prout, A. (1998) *Theorising Childhood*. Cambridge: Polity Press.

James, M., Black, P., McCormick, R., Pedder, D. and Wiliam, D. (2006) 'Learning how to learn in classrooms, schools and networks: Aims, design and analysis', *Research Papers in Education*, 21(2), 101–18.

James, M.E. (2013) *Educational Assessment, Evaluation and Research: The Selected Works of Mary E. James*. London: Routledge.

Jarvis, M. (2005) *The Psychology of Effective Learning and Teaching*. Cheltenham: Nelson Thornes.

Jenks, C. (2005) *Childhood*. 2nd edn. London: Routledge.

Jindal-Snape, D. and Miller, D.J. (2008) 'A challenge of living? Understanding the psycho-social processes of the child during primary-secondary transition through resilience and self-esteem theories', *Educational Psychology Review*, 20, 217–36.

John, P.D. (1991) 'A qualitative study of British student teachers' lesson planning perspectives', *Journal of Education for Teaching*, 17, 301–20.

John, P.D. (1992) *Lesson Planning for Teachers*. London: Cassell.

John, P.D. (2006) 'Lesson planning and the student teacher: Re-thinking the dominant model', *Journal of Curriculum Studies*, 38, 483–98.

Johnson, D.W. (2003) *Reaching Out: Interpersonal Effectiveness and Self Actualisation*. Boston: Allyn & Bacon.

Johnson, D.W. and Johnson, R.T. (2004) *Assessing Students in Groups: Promoting Group Responsibility and Individual Accountability*. Thousand Oaks, CA: Corwin Press.

Jordan, A., Carlile, O. and Stack, A. (2008) *Approaches to Learning*. Maidenhead: Open University Press.

Joubert, M.M. (2001) 'The art of creative teaching: NACCCE and beyond', in A. Craft, B. Jeffrey and M. Leibling (eds), *Creativity in Education*. London: Continuum. pp. 17–34.

Kagan, S. (1994) *Kagan Cooperative learning (Second Edition)*. San Clemente, CA: Kagan Publishing.

Kelly, A.V. (2009) *The Curriculum Theory and Practice*, 6th edn. London: SAGE.

Kennedy, A. (2005) 'Models of continuing professional development: A framework for analysis', *Journal of In-service Education*, 31(2), 235–50.

Kockelmans, J.J. (1979) *Interdisciplinarity and Higher Education*. University Park, PA: Pennsylvania State University Press.

Kohn, A. (2006) *Beyond Discipline: From Compliance to Community*. 2nd edn. Ohio: Merrill Prentice Hall.

Kornfeld, J. and Prothro, L. (2005) 'Envisioning possibility: Schooling and students agency in children's and young adult literature', *Children's Literature and Education*, 36(3), 217–39.

Kumpulainen, K. and Wray, D. (eds) (2002) *Classroom Interaction and Social Learning: From Theory to Practice*. London: RoutledgeFalmer.

Lambeir, B. (2005) 'Education as liberation: the politics and techniques of lifelong learning', *Educational Philosophy and Theory*, 37(3), 349–55.

Lancy, D.F. (2008) *The Anthropology of Childhood: Cherubs, Chattels, Changelings*. Cambridge: Cambridge University Press.

Lauder, H., Brown, P., Dillabough, J. and Halsey, A.H. (2006) *Education, Globalization and Social Change*. Oxford: Oxford University Press.

Laurillard, D.M. (1993). *Rethinking University Teaching: A Framework for the Effective Use of Educational Technology*. London: Routledge.

Layard, R. and Dunn, J. (2009) *A Good Childhood: Searching for Values in a Competitive Age*. The Children's Society: London.

Leithwood, K., Jantzi, D. and Steinbach, R. (1999) *Changing Leadership for Changing Times*. London: Taylor and Francis.

Lingard, B., Hayes, D., Mills, M. and Christie, P. (2003) *Leading Learning*. Maidenhead: Open University Press.

Lucas, B. and Claxton, G. (2010) *New Kinds of Smart*. Berkshire, England: McGraw-Hill.

Lucey, H. and Reay, D. (2002) 'Carrying the beacon of excellence: social class differentiation and anxiety at a time of transition', *Journal of Education Policy*, 17(3), 321–36.

Lyngsnes, K.M. (2012) 'Embarking on the teaching journey: Pre-service teachers reflecting upon themselves as future teachers', *World Journal of Education*, 2(2), 2–9.

MacBeath, J. and Dempster, N. (2009) (eds) *Connecting Leadership and Learning: Principles for Practice*. London: Routledge.

MacGilchrist, B., Myers, K. and Reed, J. (2004) *The Intelligent School*. 2nd edn. London: SAGE.

MacPherson, W. (1999) *The Stephen Lawrence Inquiry*. London: Stationery Office.

McAdam, J. and Arizpe, E. (2011) 'Journeys into culturally responsive teaching', *Journal of Teacher Education and Teachers' Work*, 2 (1). http://www.strath.ac.uk/media/faculties/hass/education/JTETW_Issue2.pdf (accessed: 13 June 2013).

McCullagh, J. and Jarman, R. (2009) 'Climate change? A comparison of language and literacy practices relating to the teaching of science across the Key Stage 2/3 interface in two school clusters', *Literacy*, 43(3), 143–51.

McCulloch, M. (2011) 'Interprofessional approaches to practice', in M. McMahon, C. Forde and M. Martin (eds), *Contemporary Issues in Learning and Teaching*. London: SAGE. pp. 165–78.

McLean, A. (2004) *The Motivated School*. London: Paul Chapman Publishing.

Maisuria, A. (2005) 'The turbulent times of creativity in the National Curriculum', *Policy Futures in Education*, 3(2), 141–52.

Malm, B. (2009) 'Towards a new professionalism: enhancing personal and professional development in teacher education', *Journal of Education for Teaching*, 35(1), 77–91.

Margaryan, A. (2006) *Work-based Learning: A Blend of Pedagogy and Technology*. Dissertation (published). The Netherlands: University of Twente, Enschede.

Markstrom, A.M. and Hallden, G. (2009) 'Children's strategies for agency in preschool', *Children and Society*, 23(2), 112–22.

Marshall, T.H. (1950). *Citizenship and Social Class, and Other Essays*. Cambridge: Cambridge University Press.

Marshall, B. and Drummond, M.J. (2006) 'How teachers engage with Assessment for Learning: lessons from the classroom', *Research Papers in Education*, 21(2), 133–49.

Martin, M. (2007) *Building a Learning Community in the Classroom*. Edinburgh: Dunedin Academic Press Ltd.

Maylor, U. and Read, B. (2007) *Diversity and Citizenship in the Curriculum: Research Review*. Research Report RP819. London: DfES.

Meek, M. (1988) *How Texts Teach what Readers Learn*. Stroud: Thimble Press.

Menmuir, J. and Hughes, A. (2004) 'Early education and childcare: The developing professional', *European Early Childhood Education Research Journal*, 12(2), 33–41.

Mercer, N. (2000) *Words and Minds: How we use Language to Think Together*. London: Routledge.

Mercer, N. and Hodgkinson, S. (eds) (2008) *Exploring Talk in School*. London: SAGE.

Milkie, M.A. and Warner, C.H. (2011) 'Classroom learning environments and the mental health of first grade children', *Journal of Health and Social Behavior*, 52(4), 4–22.

Miller, J. (2009) *Never too Young: How Young Children Can Take Responsibility and Make Decisions*. London: Save the Children.

Mistry, M., Burton, N. and Brundrett, M. (2004) 'Managing LSAs: An evaluation of the use of learning support assistants in an urban primary school', *School Leadership and Management*, 24(2), 125–37.

Mitchell, L. (2012) 'Individual teachers making a difference in the classroom and school', in R. Arshad, T. Wrigley and L. Pratt (eds), *Social Justice Re-examined: Dilemmas and Solutions for the Classroom Teacher*. Stoke on Trent: Trentham. pp. 19–31.

Montgomery, D. (1990) *Gifted and Talented Children: Double Exceptionality*. London: NACE/David Fulton Publishers.

Mooney G. and McCafferty T. (2005) '"Only looking after the weans?" The Scottish nursery nurses' strike, 2004', *Critical Social Policy*, 25, 223–39.

Moran, A. and Abbott, L. (2002) 'Developing inclusive schools: The pivotal role of teaching assistants in promoting inclusion in special and mainstream schools in Northern Ireland', *European Journal of Special Needs Education*, 17(2), 161–73.

Morrison, K. (1994) *Implementing cross-curricular themes*. London: David Fulton Publishers.

Moseley, D., Baumfield, V., Elliot, J., Gregson, M., Higgins, S., Miller, J. and Newton, D.P. (2005) *Frameworks for Thinking: A Handbook for Teaching and Learning*. Cambridge: Cambridge University Press.

Mowat, J.G. (2010) 'Towards the development of self-regulation in pupils experiencing social and emotional behavioural difficulties (SEBD)', *Emotional and Behavioural Difficulties*, 15(3), 189–206.

Muijs, D. and Reynolds, D. (2003) 'The effectiveness of the use of learning support assistants in improving the mathematics achievement of low achieving pupils in primary school', *Educational Research*, 45(3), 219–30.

Munday, I. (2013) *Creativity: Performativity's Poison or its Antidote?* Philosophy of Education Society of Great Britain Annual Conference, New College, Oxford 22–4 March 2013. http://www.philosophyofeducation.org/uploads/2013%20Conference/Papers/Munday.pdf (accessed 20 July 2013).

Murphy, D. (2007) *Professional School Leadership: Dealing with Dilemmas*. Edinburgh: Dunedin Academic Press.

Murphy, J. (2005) *Connecting Teacher Leadership and School Improvement*. Thousand Oaks, CA: Corwin Press.

NAPTA News (2005) *The OFSTED View of Teaching Assistants*. http://www.napta.org.uk/resources/news/news_2005–04.pdf (accessed 13 June 2013).

Nash, P. and Henderson, L. (2010) 'Work in progress: Facilitating transition for vulnerable learners moving to secondary school', *The Psychology of Education Review*, 342, 39–42.

National Advisory Committee on Creative and Cultural Education (NACCCE) (1999) *All Our Futures*. London: Department of Education and Employment.

National Commission on Education (NCE) (1993) *Learning to Succeed: A Radical Look at Education: Today and a Strategy for the Future*. Report of the Paul Hamlyn Foundation. National Commission on Education. London: Heinemann.

New, R.S. and Cochran, M. (2007) *Early Childhood Education: An International Encyclopaedia*. Westport: Greenwood Press.

Newman, T. and Blackburn, S. (2002) *Transitions in the Lives of Children and Young People: Resilience Factors*. Edinburgh: Scottish Executive.

Nieto, S. (2009) 'Foreword', in M. J. Botelho and M. K. Rudman (eds), *Critical Multicultural Analysis of Children's Literature: Mirrors, Windows and Doors*. London: Routledge. pp. ix–xi.

Northern Ireland Assembly (2006) *Our Children and Young People – Our Pledge. A Ten Year Strategy for Children and Young People in Northern Ireland 2006–2016*. Belfast: Office of the First Minister and Deputy First Minister.

Nutbrown, C. (2012) *Nutbrown Review on Early Education and Childcare   Qualifications*. http://www.education.gov.uk/nutbrownreview (accessed 20 August 2012).

Ofsted (2011) *ICT in Schools 2008–11*. Manchester: Crown Publishers.

Ofsted (2012) *Subsidiary Guidance Supporting the Inspection of Maintained Schools and Academies from January 2012*. http://www.ofsted.gov.uk/resources/subsidiary-guidance-supporting-inspection-of-maintained-schools-and-academies-january-2012 (accessed 20 July 2013).

Organization for Economic and Co-operative Development (OECD) (2000) *Early Childhood Education and Care Policy in the United Kingdom*. http://www.oecd.org/dataoecd/52/32/2535034.pdf (accessed 22 August 2012).

Organization for Economic and Co-operative Development (OECD) (2006) *Starting Strong II: Early Childhood Education and Care*. http://www.oecd.org/dataoecd/14/32/37425999.pdf (accessed 22 January 2011).

Organisation for Economic Development and Cooperation (OECD) (2010) *The High Cost of Low Educational Performance: The Long-run Economic Impact of Improving PISA Outcomes*. Paris: OECD.

Osborn, M., McNess, E. and Pollard, A. (2006) 'Identity and transfer: a new focus for home-school knowledge exchange', *Educational Review*, 58(4), 415–33.

Palmer, S. (2006) *Toxic Childhood*. London: Orion.

Palmer, S. (2007) *Toxic Childhood: How the Modern World is Damaging our Children and What we can Do About it*. Orion: New Edition.

Parker, J., Heywood, D. and Jolley, N. (2012) 'Developing pre-service primary teachers' perceptions of cross-curricular teaching through reflection on learning', *Teachers and Teaching: Theory and Practice*, 18(6), 693–716.

Pedder, D. and James, M. (2012) 'Professional learning as a condition for assessment for learning', in J. Gardner (ed.), *Assessment and Learning*. 2nd edn. London: SAGE. pp. 33–48.

Perry, B.D. (2008) 'Foreword', in C.A. Malchiodi (ed.), *Creative Interventions with Traumatised Children*. New York: The Guilford Press. pp. ix–xi.

Perry, B. and Dockett, S. (2011) '"How 'bout we have a celebration!" Advice from children on starting school', *European Early Childhood Education Research Journal*, 19(3), 373–86.

Perumal, J. (2008) 'Student resistance and teacher authority: the demands and dynamics of collaborative learning', *Journal of Curriculum Studies*, 40(3), 381–98.

Peterson, C. and Seligman, M. (2004) *Character Strengths and Virtues: A Handbook and Classification*. Oxford University Press: Oxford.

Pfeffer, N. and Coote, A. (1996) *Is Quality Good for You? A Critical Review of Quality Assurance in Welfare Services*. London: Institute for Public Policy Research.

Pollard, A. (2008) *Reflective Teaching*. 3rd edn. London: Continuum.

Pons, F., de Rosnay, M. and Cuisinier, F. (2011) 'Cognition and emotion' in S. Järvelä (ed.), *Social and Emotional Aspects of Learning*. Oxford: Elsevier. pp. 70–6.

Pope, R. (2009) *Creativity Theory, History, Practice*. London, Routledge.

Porter, L. (2000) *Behaviour in Schools. Theory and Practice for Teachers*. Buckingham: Open University Press.

Poster, M. (1993) *The Mode of Information: Poststructuralism and the Social Context*. Chicago, IL: University of Chicago Press.

Price, H. (No date) *ICT in the Early Years*. http://ictearlyyears.e2bn.org/ (accessed 8 July 2013).

Qualifications and Curriculum Authority (QCA) (2004) *Creativity: Find it, Promote it*. London: QCA. http://dera.ioe.ac.uk/18087/1/1847211003.pdf (accessed 28 June 2013).

Qualifications and Curriculum Development Agency (QCDA) (2010) *Introducing the New Primary Curriculum: Guidance for Primary Schools*. Coventry: Qualifications and Curriculum Development Agency.

Quality Assurance Agency Scotland (QAAS) (2007) *Scottish Subject Benchmark Statement: The Standard for Childhood Practice*. Glasgow: QAA Scotland.

Richardson, R. (2004) 'Curriculum, ethos and leadership: confronting Islamophobia in UK education', in B. van Driel (ed.) *Confronting Islamophobia in Educational Practice*. Stoke on Trent: Trentham Books. pp. 19–34.

Roberts, P. (2006) *Nurturing Creativity in Young People: A Report to Government to Inform Future Policy*. London: DCMS/DES.

Robinson, E. (1977) *The Original Vision: A Study of the Religious Experience of Childhood*. Religious Experience Research Centre.

Robinson, K. (2001) *Out of our Minds: Learning to be Creative*. Capstone Publishing: Chichester.

Rose, J. (2009) *Independent Review of the Primary Curriculum: Final Report*. London: DCSF.

Rubie-Davies, C.M., Blatchford, P., Webster, R., Koutsoubou, M. and Bassett, P. (2010) 'Enhancing learning? A comparison of teacher and teaching assistant interactions with pupils', *School Effectiveness and School Improvement*, 21(4), 429–49.

Schön, D.A. (1983) *The Reflective Practitioner: How Professionals Think in Action*. New York: Basic Books.

Schul, J.E. (2011) 'Revisiting an old friend: The practice and promise of cooperative learning for the twenty-first century', *Social Studies*, 102(2), 88–93.

Schutz, P.A., Quijada, P.D., de Vries, S. and Lynde, M. (2011) 'Emotion in educational contexts', in S. Järvelä (ed.) *Social and Emotional Aspects of Learning*. Oxford: Elsevier, 64–9.

Scottish Education Department (SED) (1965) *Primary Education in Scotland (The Primary Memorandum)*. Edinburgh: HMSO.

Scottish Education Department (SED) (1987) *Curriculum and Assessment in Scotland: A Policy for the 90s (Consultative Paper)*. Edinburgh: HMSO.

Scottish Executive (SE) (2004) *A Curriculum for Excellence: The Curriculum Review Group*. Edinburgh: Scottish Executive.

Scottish Executive (SE) (2004b) *Ambitious Excellent Schools: A Curriculum for Excellence, The Report of the Curriculum Reform Group*. Edinburgh, Scottish Executive.

Scottish Government (SG) (2008a) *Curriculum for Excellence: Building the Curriculum 3 – A Framework for Learning and Teaching*. Edinburgh: Scottish Government.

Scottish Government (SG) (2008b) *The Early Years Framework*. Edinburgh: Scottish Government.

Scottish Government (SG) (2008c) *Getting it Right for Every Child*. Edinburgh: The Scottish Government.

Scottish Government (SG) (2009a) *Statistical Bulletin: Pupils in Scotland 2008*. (Edn/B1/2009/1). http://www.scotland.gov.uk/Resource/Doc/301281/0093985.pdf (accessed 13 June 2013).

Scottish Government (SG) (2009b) *Statistical Bulletin: Teachers in Scotland 2008*. (Edn/B1/2009/2). http://www.scotland.gov.uk/Resource/Doc/270926/0080623.pdf (accessed: 13 June 2013).

Scottish Government (SG) (2009c) *Building Curriculum for Excellence through Positive Relationships and Behaviour*. Edinburgh: Scottish Government.

Scottish Government (SG) (2009d) *Curriculum for Excellence: Technologies Principles and Practice*. Edinburgh: LTS (Learning and Teaching Scotland now known as Education Scotland).

Scottish Government (SG) (2012a) *Nursery Education*. http://www.scotland.gov.uk/News/Releases/2012/03/nurseryed10032012 (accessed 20 August 2012).

Scottish Government (SG) (2012b) *A Guide to Getting it Right for Every Child*. http://www.scotland.gov.uk/Resource/0039/00394308.pdf (accessed 18 July 2012).

Scottish Office Education Department (SOED) (1991) *Curriculum and Assessment in Scotland: A Policy for the 90s Working Paper 13, Report of the Review and Development Group on Environmental Studies 5–14*. Edinburgh: HMSO.

Scottish Office Education Department (SOED) (1993) *The Structure and Balance of the Curriculum 5–14*. Edinburgh: SOED.

Second Vatican Council (1965) *Nostra Aetate* – Declaration on the Relation of the Church to Non-Christian Religions. Available at http://www.vatican.va/archive/hist_councils/ii_vatican_council/documents/vat-ii_decl_19651028_nostra-aetate_en.html (accessed 30 January 2014)

Semrud-Clikeman, M. (2007) *Social Competence in Children*. New York: Springer.

Sergiovanni, T. (1994) *Building Community in Schools*. San Francisco: Jossey-Bass.

Shaffer, D.R. (2009) *Social and Personality Development*. 6th edn. Wadsworth: Cengage Learning.

Shapiro, J.P. and Stefkovich, J.A. (2011) *Ethical Leadership and Decision Making in Education: Applying Theoretical Perspectives in Complex Dilemmas*. 3rd edn. New York: Routledge.

Shayer, M. and Adey, P. (2002) *Learning Intelligence: Cognitive Acceleration across the Curriculum from 5 to 15 years*. Buckingham: Open University Press.

Shelter (2006) *Chance of a Lifetime: The Impact of Bad Housing on Children's Lives*. http://england.shelter.org.uk/__data/assets/pdf_file/0004/66442/Lifechancereport.pdf (accessed 13 May 2013).

Siraj-Blatchford, I. and Woodhead, M. (2009) *Effective Early Childhood Programmes. Early Childhood in Focus*. Milton Keynes: Open University.

Sleeter, C.E. and Grant, C.A. (2002) *Making Choices for Multicultural Education: Five Approaches to Race, Class and Gender*. New Jersey, Prentice-Hall.

Sliwka, A. and Spencer, E. (2005) *Scotland: Developing a Coherent Assessment System in Formative Assessment: Improving Learning in Secondary Classrooms*. Paris: OECD.

Smidt, S. (2005) *Observing, Assessing and Planning for Children in the Early Years*. Abingdon: Routledge.

Smith, C. and Sutherland, M.J. (2006) 'Setting or mixed ability?: Pupils' views of the organisational arrangement in their school', *Journal of Research in Special Educational Needs*, 6(2), 69–75.

Smith, I. (2003) *Changing our Minds About Intelligence*. Cheltenham: Hawker Brownlow Education.

Smyth, G., Corrigan, A., McAdam, J. and Mohamed, K. (2011) *Diverse Teaching in Scotland's Diverse Future: These Students all Seem the Same*. Paper presented at Scottish Educational Research Association (SERA) conference on 24th November 2011.

Spitzberg, B.H. (2003) 'Methods of interpersonal skill assessment', in J.O. Greene and B.R. Burleson (eds), *Handbook of Communication and Social Interaction Skills*. Mahwah, NJ: Erlbaum. pp. 93–34.

Stenhouse, L. (1985) *Research as a Basis for Teaching*. London: Heinemann.

Stoll, L., Bolam, R., McMahon, A., Wallace, M and Thomas, S. (2006) 'Professional learning communities: A review of the literature', *Journal of Educational Change*, 7(4): 221–58.

Sugrue, C. (1997) 'Student teachers' lay theories and teaching identities: their implications for professional development', *European Journal of Teacher Education*, 20(3), 213–25.

Sylva, K., Melhuish, E., Sammons, P. and Siraj-Blatchford, I. (2004) *Effective Pre-school Education*. London: DfES. http://eprints.ioe.ac.uk/5309/1/sylva2004EPPEfinal.pdf (accessed, 22 August 2012).

Takala, M. (2007) 'The work of classroom assistants in special and mainstream education in Finland', *British Journal of Special Education*, 34(1), 50–7.

The Children's Society (2012) *The Good Childhood Report 2012: A Review of our Children's Well-being*. http://www.childrenssociety.org.uk/sites/default/files/tcs/good_childhood_report_2012_final_0.pdf (accessed 13 May 2013).

Thurston, A., Topping, K., Tolmiec, A., Christie, D., Karagiannidou, E. and Murray, P. (2010) 'Cooperative learning in science: Follow-up from primary to high school', *International Journal of Science Education*, 32(4), 501–22.

Timperley, H., Parr, J.M. and Bertanees, C. (2009) 'Promoting professional inquiry for improved outcomes for students in New Zealand', *Professional Development in Education*, 35(2), 227–45.

Timperley, H., Wilson, A. Barrar, H. and Fung, I. (2007) *Teacher Professional Learning and Development: Best Evidence Synthesis Iteration (BES)*. Wellington, New Zealand: Ministry of Education. http://educationcounts.edcentre.govt.nz/goto/BES (accessed 15 August 2013).

Tomlinson, S. (2009) 'Multicultural education in the United Kingdom', in J.A. Banks (ed.), *The Routledge International Companion to Multicultural Education*. Abingdon: Routledge. pp. 121–33.

Topping, K. (2011) 'Primary-secondary transition: Differences between teachers' and children's perceptions', *Improving Schools*, 14(3), 268–85.

Torres-Guzmán, M. (2013) Private conversation with Professor Guzmán at Teacher's College, University of Columbia, New York.

Trawick-Smith, J.W. (2013) *Early Childhood Development: A Multicultural Perspective*. 6th edn. Upper Saddle River, NJ: Pearson/Merrill Prentice Hall.

Troyna B. and Williams, J. (1986) *Racism, Education and the State: The Radicalisation of Educational Policy.* London: Croom Helm.

Tyler, R.W. (1949) *Basic Principles of Curriculum and Instruction.* Chicago, IL: University of Chicago Press.

UNICEF (online) *The United Nations Convention on the Rights of the Child* http://www.unicef. org.uk/UNICEFs-Work/Our-mission/UN-Convention/ (accessed 13 June 2013).

Van Manen, M. (1991) *The Tact of Teaching: The Meaning of Pedagogical Thoughtfulness.* Albany: NY SUNY Press.

Vieluf, S., Kaplan, D., Klieme, E. and Bayer, S. (2012) *Teaching Practices and Pedagogical Innovation: Evidence from TALIS.* Paris: OECD Publishing. http://dx.doi.org/10.1787/9789264123540–en (15 August 2013).

Vogler, P., Crivello, G. and Woodhead, M. (2008) *Early Childhood Transitions Research: A Review of Concepts, Theory and Practice.* Working Paper no. 48. The Hague, The Netherlands: Bernard van Leer Foundation.

Vygotsky, L.S. (1978) *Mind in Society: The Development of Higher Psychological Processes.* Cambridge, MA: Harvard University Press.

Vygotsky, L.S. (1986) *Thought and Language.* Cambridge: Massachusetts Institute of Technology.

Waks, L.J. (2006) 'How globalization can cause fundamental curriculum change: an American perspective', in H. Lauder, P. Brown, J. Dillabough and A.H. Halsey (eds), *Education, Globalisation and Social Change.* Oxford: Oxford University Press. pp. 835–49.

Wall, K. and Higgins, S. (2006) 'Facilitating metacognitive talk: A research and learning tool', *International Journal of Research Methods in Education*, 26(1), 39–53.

Wardle, G. (2011) 'Children's social relationships', in M. McMahon, C. Forde and M. Martin (eds), *Contemporary Issues in Learning and Teaching.* London: SAGE Publications. pp. 102–11.

Watkins, C., Carnell, E., Lodge, C., Wagner, P. and Walley, C. (2001) *Effective Learning.* Research Matters No. 13. London: Institute of Education.

Watkins, C., Carnell, E. and Lodge, C. (2006) *Effective Learning in the Classroom.* London: Paul Chapman Publishing.

Watson, D., Emery, C. and Bayliss, P. with Boushel, M. and McInnes, K. (2012) *Children's Social and Emotional Wellbeing in School: A Critical Perspective.* Bristol: The Policy Press.

Wegerif, R. (2007) *Dialogic Education and Technology.* New York: Springer.

Welsh Assembly Government (2010) *Thinking Positively: Emotional Health and Well-being in Schools and Early Years Settings.* http://wales.gov.uk/topics/education-andskills/publications/guidance/thinkingpositively/?lang=en (accessed 18 July 2012).

West, P., Sweeting, H. and Young, R. (2010) 'Transition matters: Pupils' experiences of the primary-secondary school transition in the West of Scotland and consequences for well-being and attainment', *Research Papers in Education*, 25(1), 21–50.

Whitty, G. (2010) 'Revisiting school knowledge: Some sociological perspectives on new school curricula', *European Journal of Education*, 45(1), 28–45.

Wildenger, L. and McIntyre, L. (2011) 'Family concerns and involvement during kindergarten transition', *Journal of Child and Family Studies*, 20(4), 387–96.

Wilson, P. (2011) *Investigating the Drop in Attainment during the Transition Phase with a Particular Focus on Child Poverty.* Cardiff: Welsh Assembly Government Social Research.

Winstanley, C. (2010) *The Ingredients of Challenge.* London: Trentham Books.

Wiske, M.S. (1998) (ed.) *Teaching for Understanding: Linking Research and Practice.* San Francisco, CA: Jossey-Bass.

Wood, D., Bruner, J.S. and Ross, G. (1976) 'The role of tutoring in problem solving', *Journal of Child Psychology and Psychiatry*, 17, 89–100.

Woolfolk, A. (2007) *Educational Psychology*. 10th edn. Boston, MA: Allyn & Bacon.

Wright, A. (2000) *Spirituality and Education*. London: RoutledgeFalmer.

Younger, M., Brindley, S., Pedder, D. and Hagger, H. (2004) 'Starting points: Student teachers' reasons for becoming teachers and their preconceptions of what this will mean', *European Journal of Teacher Education*, 27(3), 245–64.

Zahn-Waxler, C. and Radke-Yarrow, M. (1990) 'The origins of empathic concern', *Motivation and Emotion*, 14(2), 107–30.

Zazkis, R., Liljedahl, P. and Sinclair, N. (2009) 'Lesson plays: Planning teaching versus teaching planning', *For the Learning of Mathematics*, 29, 40–7.

Zeedyk, M., Gallacher, J., Henderson, M., Hope, G., Husband, B. and Linsday, K. (2003) *Negotiating the Transition from Primary to Secondary School*. London: SAGE.

Ziegler, A. and Stoeger, H. (2012) 'Shortcomings of the IQ-based construct of underachievement', *Roeper Review*, 34(2), 123–32.

INDEX

Added to a page number 'f' denotes a figure and 't' denotes a table.